A LOCAL HISTORY
OF GLOBAL CAPITAL

HISTORIES OF ECONOMIC LIFE

*Jeremy Adelman, Sunil Amrith, and
Emma Rothschild, Series Editors*

A Local History
of Global Capital

JUTE AND PEASANT LIFE
IN THE BENGAL DELTA

TARIQ OMAR ALI

PRINCETON UNIVERSITY PRESS

PRINCETON & OXFORD

Copyright © 2018 by Princeton University Press

Requests for permission to reproduce material from this work
should be sent to Permissions, Princeton University Press

Published by Princeton University Press,
41 William Street, Princeton, New Jersey 08540

In the United Kingdom: Princeton University Press,
6 Oxford Street, Woodstock, Oxfordshire OX20 1TR

press.princeton.edu

Jacket image: Munem Wasif / Agence VU

All Rights Reserved

ISBN 978-0-691-17023-7
Library of Congress Control Number 2017963398

British Library Cataloging-in-Publication Data is available

This book has been composed in Arno Pro

Printed on acid-free paper. ∞

Printed in the United States of America

10 9 8 7 6 5 4 3 2 1

To Mama and Baba

CONTENTS

ACKNOWLEDGMENTS

THIS BOOK has been possible due to the support, assistance, and friendships of numerous people in universities, archives, libraries, and cities in the United States, the UK, India, and Bangladesh.

First and foremost, I must acknowledge my debt and gratitude to archivists and librarians in Bangladesh, India, and the UK, without whose labors it would not be possible to write any book in South Asian history. In Dhaka, the staff at the National Archives Bangladesh were extremely accommodating and welcoming, going above and beyond their professional obligations to help me locate materials and photocopy files. In India, I owe an immense debt to librarians at the National Library of India in Kolkata and archivists at the National Archives of India in New Delhi. I spent many months in the UK, researching at the Dundee University Archives in Dundee, Scotland, and the India Office Records at the British Library in London: in both places, I was in awe of the professionalism and care with which written records of the past are preserved and made publicly accessible. I would also like to thank librarians at Widener Library at Harvard University, where I began work on this book, and University Library at the University of Illinois, where I completed it.

The History Department of the University of Illinois has provided an enriching and supportive scholarly home for the past six years. Numerous colleagues have read various chapters and provided generous feedback, companionship, and camaraderie. I want to particularly thank Antoinette Burton and Mark Steinberg who have been exceptional mentors over these years. I am also especially grateful to the numerous people who have made Champaign, Illinois, home for me over the past few years, especially Ikuko Asaka, Jayadev Athreya, Andrew Bauer, Jim Brennan, Utathya Chattopadhyay, Kim Curtis, Ken Cuno, Behrooz Ghamari, Radhika Govindarajan, Marc Hertzman, Rana Hogarth, Brian Jefferson, Diane Koenker, Craig Koslowsky, Rini Bhattacharya Mehta, Bob Morrissey,

Mauro Nobili, Dana Rabin, John Randolph, David Roediger, Carol Symes, and Rod Wilson.

I have received generous funding from the Campus Research Board and the Unit for Criticism and Interpretive Theory at the University of Illinois, which has enabled me to conduct archival research in London and Dhaka. I want to particularly thank Susan Koshy at the Unit for Criticism and Interpretive Theory for organizing a manuscript workshop for an early draft. Douglas Haynes, Ericka Beckman, Antoinette Burton, and Mark Steinberg read a very rough draft of the manuscript for the workshop and provided detailed and thoughtful feedback and advice. I have incorporated much of their advice into substantially revising that draft into the present book, though, of course, all shortcomings are my own.

I have presented portions of this book at Brac University, Tufts University, University of Iowa, MIT, and Dhaka University. The incisive comments and criticism at each of these locations have informed and shaped this book. I hope I have been able to do justice to the thoughtful feedback I have received from so many people who have been so generous in engaging with the arguments presented in this book.

It has been a privilege to publish this book with Princeton University Press. I want to especially thank Amanda Peery for providing incisive feedback on the individual chapters, which led to substantive revisions and to "eagle-eye" Karen Carroll who spotted numerous errors and typos. Special thanks to David Campbell, Ali Parrington, and Brigitta van Rheinberg for making the publishing process so smooth and painless. The two anonymous readers at Princeton University Press provided comments and suggestions that have greatly helped in revising the manuscript.

I began this work at Harvard University under the supervision of Sugata Bose. I benefited and continue to benefit from his knowledge and guidance, his willingness to let me pursue my own paths of inquiry, and his warmth and generosity, not only in Cambridge, Massachusetts, but also in his family home in Calcutta. Emma Rothschild was another guide, who read and commented extensively on the text. I particularly benefited from her seminar on Histories of Economic Life, and I feel privileged that the book is now appearing in a series titled Histories of Economic Life. Walter Johnson and Sven Beckert were inspirational, and it was their influence that has informed much of my thinking on commodities, capital, markets, labor, and ecology. I was particularly fortunate to be surrounded by a community of fellow graduate students who provided camaraderie, inspiration, and intellectual engagement. I want to particularly thank Sana Aiyar, Misha Akulov, Antara Dutta, Jesse Howell, Kuba Kabala, Stefan Link, Hassan Malik, Johan Mathew, Sreemati Mitter, Ricardo Salazar, Julia Stephens, Gitanjali Surendran, Heidi and Michael Tworek, and Jeremy Yellen. My brother Zain Ali arrived at Harvard as a graduate student during my final year of writing up my research, and provided welcome distraction from the travails of writing.

My archival travels were enriched by numerous friendships. In London, I lived at various times with Salman Azim, Burt Caesar, and Syed Anwarul Hafiz. Mishu Ahasan, Zirwat Choudhuri, Rohit De, Fanar Haddad, and Mahfuz Sadique provided distraction and entertainment in this great city. In New Delhi, Ania Loomba and Suvir Kaul allowed me to stay in their beautiful home, and Rohit De, Pallavi Raghavan, and Julia Stephens were compatriots in the reading room of the National Archives. In Calcutta, Subir and Supriya Datta opened their lovely home to me, where the talented Ishwarda cooked delicious meals and their cats provided further entertainment and company. I was fortunate to be able to explore this city—one of my favorite in the world—with wonderful people: Momo Ghosh, Durba Mitra, Poulomi Roychowdhuri, and Gitanjali Surendran.

It was while conducting research at the British Library in London that I met Simin Patel, who has been a source of love and support as I finished writing this book. Simin has been patient and generous in reading portions of the book, hearing me out as I tried to formulate my thoughts into coherent chapters, and bearing with me as I devoted my energies to finishing this book.

Dhaka is my home, where I am surrounded by family and childhood friends. I want to thank my closest childhood friends in Dhaka who provided brilliant company while I conducted research: Imran Ahmed, Sumagna Karim, Shazia Omar, Nausher Rahman, Shadab Sajid, and Radwan Siddique. Yasir Karim, who tragically passed away before this book came out, was a constant companion—more often than not, I would go directly to Yasir's house from the National Archives, and spend the evening with him, his siblings, and his parents.

I am especially grateful to my maternal grandfather, S. A. Azim: his wide-ranging intellectual curiousity and tireless energy have been constant inspirations throughout my life.

I wish to acknowledge a very special debt to relatives and family friends in my father's village home: Bhatshala in Brahmanbaria, Bangladesh. This book has its origins in childhood visits to Bhatshala and tales of village life and family history recounted by my father.

The greatest debt is to my parents, Firdous Azim and Bashirul Haq. My gratitude cannot be expressed in words. Their unstinting and unconditional love and support has sustained me throughout my life and continues to sustain me. I dedicate this book to Mama and Baba as a small token of my gratitude.

MAPS

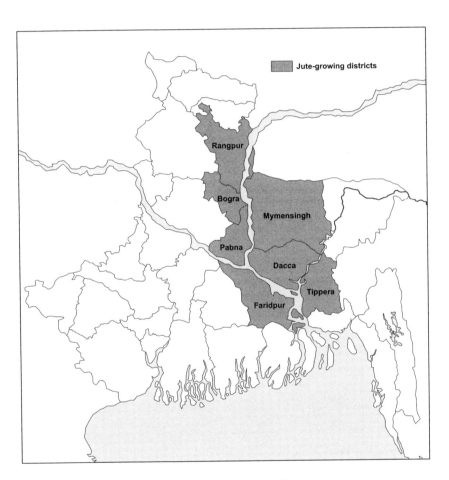

Jute-growing districts

MAP 1. Jute-growing districts of Bengal

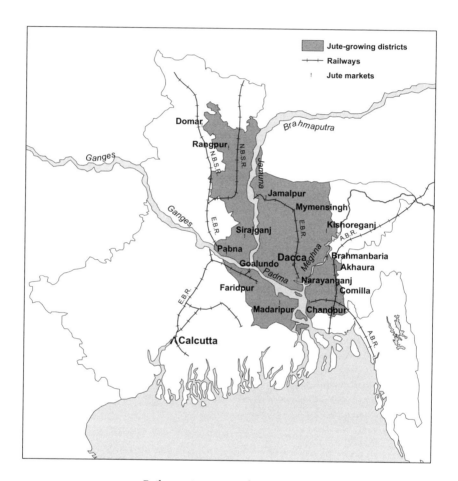

MAP 2. Railways, riverways, and jute markets, ca. 1900

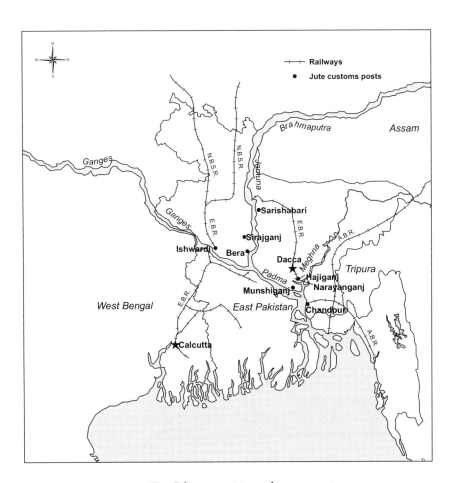

MAP 3. East Pakistan: partition and customs posts

A LOCAL HISTORY
OF GLOBAL CAPITAL

Introduction

FROM THE mid-nineteenth to the mid-twentieth century, jute fabrics—gunnies, hessians, burlap—were the premier packaging material in world trade. Before the advent of artificial fibers and the shipping container, jute sacks packed the world's grains, cotton, sugar, coffee, guano, cement, and bacon, as these commodities made their journey from farms to centers of consumption.[1] While the fabric circulated globally, the plant was cultivated in a small corner of the world: the Bengal delta, an alluvial tract formed out of the silt deposits of the Ganges, Brahmaputra, and Meghna river systems.[2] Peasant smallholders cultivated jute on small lots of land, using a combination of household and hired labor, and stored and borrowed capital. Peasant-produced fiber journeyed westward from the peasant homestead, along the delta's waterways and railways, through river ports and railway towns, to Calcutta. From Calcutta, part of the crop went north, to the jute mills along the banks of the Hooghly, and the remainder was exported overseas, to jute mills in Britain, Continental Europe, and North America. The mills spun and wove fibers into fabrics that were dispatched to the world's farms, plantations, mines, and quarries. From there, wrapped around a multitude of primary products, jute sacks traveled the globe. Jute connected the Bengal delta's peasant smallholder to global circuits of commodities and capital, to the rhythms and vicissitudes of global commodity prices.

Jute emerged as a global commodity in the mid-nineteenth century, when the Crimean War (1853–56) interrupted Britain's supply of Russian flax and hemp, and manufacturers in Dundee, Scotland, switched en masse to jute. Over the following decades, jute sacks cornered the global packaging market. In addition to Dundee, jute manufacturing industries emerged in Continental Europe, the United States, and, most importantly, in the vicinity of Calcutta, to the north and south of the city and along the banks of the Hooghly: by the turn of the century, jute mills along the Hooghly housed half the world's jute manufacturing capacity.[3] The Bengal delta's peasant smallholders responded readily to rising global demand for fiber: jute acreage increased from about fifty thousand acres prior to the Crimean War to just under four million acres, close to 20 percent of the delta's farmland, in 1906.[4] Calcutta's jute exports increased from eighteen tons of raw fiber in 1829 to thirteen million tons of fabric and fiber in 1910.[5] In the half century since the Crimean War, jute transformed from a little-traded and little-known commodity into a major commodity of empire, the second most widely consumed fiber in the world after cotton.

Jute entangled the delta's peasant households in a dense web of commodity exchanges, as cultivators traded fiber for food, clothing, intoxicants, illumination, construction materials, and household utensils. Market entanglements transformed peasant households' material and bodily practices of work, subsistence, consumption, leisure, domesticity, and sociality. Market entanglements also created new forms of vulnerability. Peasant households' well-being was dependent on prices in distant European metropolises. A sudden collapse in prices—a recurrent feature in the boom-and-bust global economy—caused severe hardship. Depending on their abilities and means, peasant households responded to price shocks by scaling back consumption, taking emergency loans, or selling assets. If they did not have the means, they starved. Market entanglements entailed consumerism, risk, and vulnerability and, in turn, informed new ideas and discourses of markets and prices, property and credit, class and community, morality, ethics and justice, piety and religiosity, and governance and statecraft.

This book examines the history of jute in the Bengal delta over the hundred years spanning the mid-nineteenth to the mid-twentieth century, beginning with the emergence of jute as a global commodity and concluding in the early years of the postcolonial period, after South Asia's partition had carved the delta's jute tracts out of the colonial province of Bengal and incorporated them into the postcolonial nation-state of Pakistan. This hundred-year span covers two distinct periods with respect to the jute-cultivating peasantry's quality of life. The period between the Crimean War and World War I was an era of relative prosperity, when favorable markets enabled new forms of consumption: of machine-made textiles, corrugated iron roofs, kerosene lamps, children's toys, English-language education, and lawsuits. World War I brought this period of prosperity to an abrupt end, as jute prices collapsed, devastating floods caused crop failures, and waterborne epidemics ravaged peasant households. World War I began a thorough and rapid process of immiseration in the agrarian delta, as fragmented smallholdings, a rising debt burden, unfavorable commodity markets, and deteriorating ecology drove

peasant households into penury. The scale and scope of immiseration intensified during the depression decade of the 1930s—a prolonged period of
extremely low prices for peasant-produced commodities. Following World
War I, the focus of peasant economic life shifted from the pleasures and possibilities of consumption toward a struggle to ensure the viability of market-
entangled livelihoods.

Further, by tracing the history of jute over a hundred years, I demonstrate
that the local history of capital in the Bengal delta was continuous and ongoing. Each time cultivators sowed land with jute, brought fiber to sale, or used
earnings from fiber to purchase consumer goods, they reiterated, reimagined,
and renewed their connections to global circuits of commodities and capital.
Instead of a singular moment of a transition to capitalism, with a less capitalist
before and a more capitalist after, this book posits local histories of global
capital that are continuous and repetitive, where material lives and structures
of meaning were continually constructed and reconstructed through ongoing
engagements with global flows of commodities and capital.

The first section of this introduction contextualizes jute cultivation within
the global rise of peasant commodity production during the nineteenth and
twentieth centuries, as peasant communities in colonized Asia and Africa
began to specialize in producing plant-based raw materials for European
industry and calories for European industrial workers. The second section
discusses and elaborates the analytical categories through which this book
narrates the history of jute cultivators in the Bengal delta as a local history
of global capital. The third section introduces readers to the main protagonists of the book: the Bengal delta's jute-cultivating peasantry. I conclude
the introduction with a description of the book's narrative trajectory and a
chapter outline.

The Global Countryside

During the late nineteenth and early twentieth centuries, under the twinned
impetus of European empire and European capital, peasant households in
colonized Asia and Africa devoted ever-increasing proportions of land and
labor to producing cotton, jute, hemp, cocoa, sugar, rice, palm oil, peanuts,
and rubber to feed and fuel European industry. The enormous expansion in
jute production (an eightyfold increase in acreage between 1850 and 1910)
was mirrored in agrarian localities across the colonized tropics: Ghanaian
cocoa production increased from 95 *pounds* to 100,000 *tons* between 1890

and 1920; Senegalese peanut production increased from 5 metric tons in 1850 to 95,000 metric tons in 1898; in the Philippines, peasant production of *abaca*, or Manila hemp, increased from 18,000 tons to more than 160,000 tons between the 1850s and the 1920s; in colonial Malaya, peasant households planted 918,000 acres of rubber trees between 1910 and 1922; Burmese peasants increased their rice lands from 700,000 to 5 million acres and increased rice exports from 162,000 tons to 2 million tons between 1855 and 1905; and India's exports of raw cotton rose from about 76,500 tons during the 1830s to 310,500 tons during the 1880s.[6] This enormous expansion of peasant commodity production knitted disparate agrarian localities in the colonized tropics into what Sven Beckert has called the "global countryside," a vast hinterland devoted to the production of calories and raw materials for imperial metropolises in Europe and North America.[7]

This emerging global countryside was constituted by the technologies of commodification, whereby small lots of peasant-produced jute fibers, cotton bolls, cocoa beans, and rubber sap were transformed into exchange values in European markets. The power of global capital found its most succinct expression in imperial marketplaces, where peasant labor, agrarian ecologies, and plant biologies were transformed into lists and tables of quantities, qualities, and prices available to the speculations of global capital—"cocoa: common to good, at 46s. 6d. to 75s 6d.; fine and very fine, 80s to 95s per cwt."[8] The transformation of peasant produce into abstraction was made possible by railways, steamships, and the telegraph. Commodity production was accompanied by railways linking peasant farms to colonial port cities and, thence, to the global marketplace. Railways and steamships not only made the journey of peasant produce to imperial markets faster, cheaper, and safer, but also made it possible to bulk, assort, and pack small lots of peasant produce into the standardized units of international shipping, to transform, for example, the one or two hundred pounds of cotton bolls produced by a sharecropper in Berar into standardized and quality-graded four-hundred-pound bales.[9] The telegraph enabled the abstract form of the commodity to circulate faster, more frequently, and independent of its material and physical form. Through the global telegraph system, merchants, financiers, and industrialists across the world transmitted information ceaselessly, as orders to buy and sell and information on availability and demand, weather conditions, crop forecasts, and worker strikes pinged back and forth across the world. The telegraph subjected peasant labor to the continuous speculations of capital, from before the plant was sown to after it was harvested.

The Bengal delta's jute cultivators, in common with other peasant inhabitants of the global countryside, lived under the shadow and at the mercy of global capital. Global capital imposed conditions, promised opportunities, and created risks and vulnerabilities for the commodity-producing peasantry. First, global markets demanded that peasant households respond to capitalist speculations by reapportioning labor and land between the production of household subsistence and exchange values—to scale up or scale back production according to the diktats of global prices. Second, market entanglements created new forms of vulnerability, as peasant households' well-being depended on the fluctuations of prices in distant markets. Third, commodity production was accompanied by its corollary, commodity consumption. Peasant households across the colonized tropics consumed from similar bundles of goods: clothing, accessories, foods, intoxicants, construction materials, household utensils, indoor illumination, and so on. However, though global capital imposed similar conditions, it did not produce uniformity and homogeneity. Instead, peasant households responded to the challenges and opportunities of global commodity markets with initiative and creativity, and constructed agrarian localities that were diverse and distinct. Local histories were shaped as much by the particularities and specificities of peasant communities as they were by global capital's attempt to conjure an abstract universality.

Sven Beckert masterfully demonstrates the formation of the global countryside through a single commodity—cotton. Beckert shows that the cotton manufacturers in Manchester responded to the cotton famine caused by the American Civil War by lobbying British imperial institutions to promote peasant cotton cultivation in its far-flung empire, particularly in India. The British Empire's apparatuses of "war capitalism" went to work, transforming the social relations of land, labor, and debt to force peasants into producing cotton. These efforts consisted mostly of introducing railways, telegraphs, and cotton gins and of reforming property and contract laws that would enable colonial capital to finance and speculate on peasant produce. These efforts were successful: exports of peasant-produced raw cotton from India and Egypt rose sharply, and commercial cultivation soon spread to west and east Africa, central Asia, and Latin America. Beckert describes the rise of peasant-produced cotton as a "reconstruction" of global capitalism, as the old world of slaves and cotton planters in the American South was replaced by a new global structure based on the coercion of peasant labor through imperial state power and debt bondage.[10]

Whereas Beckert emphasizes the power of European empires and capitalists, this book focuses on the initiative and creativity of peasant households. Sugata Bose has argued that jute represented the "second phase" in the commercialization of agriculture in Bengal, as the statist and capitalist coercion that characterized an earlier period of indigo cultivation gave way to market forces and pressures.[11] Similarly, in Dutch Java, the colonial state relaxed its brutal system of forced cultivation, known as the "Cultivation System," after the sugar crisis of 1884. Historians of peasant production of cocoa in Ghana, peanuts in Senegal, rice in Burma, rubber in Borneo, and Manila hemp in the Philippines have emphasized peasant initiative over colonial coercion.[12] For instance, peanut cultivation in Senegal was driven not by colonial coercion but by the expansion of a Sufi brotherhood, the Murudiyya. During the late nineteenth century, the Mouride brotherhood founded new villages, which established themselves financially and commercially through the cultivation and sale of peanuts.[13]

Peasant households demonstrated considerable creativity in adapting the rhythms of work and leisure, ecologies of soil and water, and seasons of rain and sunshine to the biological requirements of plants. In most agrarian localities, including the Bengal delta's jute tracts, peasant households devised ecological and labor strategies in order to produce a combination of exchange values for global markets and household subsistence out of their smallholdings. Consider, for example, peasant rubber cultivation in Southeast Asia. The colonial state provided the impetus to peasant rubber production through the sale and distribution of saplings to peasant households. Peasant households planted saplings into dense copses, carefully distributed throughout the smallholding so as to align the labor of tapping rubber with the labor of tending and harvesting other crops.[14] To ascribe the making of the global countryside purely to the power of European empire and capital is to erase peasant creativity in responding to the diktats of global capitalist speculation.

Commodity production provided peasant households access to new and novel consumer products: umbrellas, clothing, corrugated iron sheets, soaps, tea, coffee, tobacco, kerosene oil, metal and porcelain utensils, toys, and confections. Historians of peasant commodity producers have not written at length on the practices of peasant consumption, though their narratives hint at its significance. For instance, a critical factor in the rise of rice production in Burma, Michael Adas argues, was Britain's nonenforcement of precolonial sumptuary laws that regulated the types and sizes of homes, clothing, jewelry, and domestic implements upon its conquest of the Irrawaddy delta.[15] Amadou

Bamba, the founder of the Mouride brotherhood which was critical to the expansion of peanut cultivation in Senegal, wrote treatises praising God for creating tea and coffee, stimulants that had only recently become available to the rural Senegalese consumer.[16]

C. A. Bayly has argued that the nineteenth-century "making of the modern world" consisted of simultaneous processes of economic specialization and cultural homogenization. Bayly demonstrates that communities began specializing in the production of particular commodities for export and, at the same time, adopted uniform types of dress, diet, time keeping, naming practices, sports, and language that were considered modern by their contemporaries. Though elite male city dwellers were the exemplars of modern uniformity, Bayly suggests that subaltern communities could also access modernity through consumption. The nineteenth century, he argues, was "a modern age because poorer and subordinated people around the world thought that they could improve their status and life-chances by adopting badges of this mythical modernity, whether these were fob watches, umbrellas, or new religious texts."[17] Expanding on Bayly's insight, this book argues that consumer goods constituted the raw materials through which peasant men and women fashioned new and distinctive material lives.

Through consumption, peasant households transformed their bodies, dwellings, and diets and fashioned new practices of domesticity, sociality, and religiosity. However, their bodily and social practices did not conform to European or urban ideals of the modern: most peasant men did not adopt trousers and buttoned shirts; peasant homes did not change into multiroom dwellings with specialized spaces for entertaining, eating, and sleeping; and peasant families did not dine at raised tables, seated upright on chairs, using forks, knives, and spoons to convey food to their mouths. The distinctiveness of peasant bodies, dwellings, and diets probably explains why peasant men and women are represented as the quintessential nonmodern. Anticolonial nationalists depicted peasant men and women as the "timeless essence of the nation," Marxists scholars have characterized peasant modes of production as "semi-feudal" or "proto-capitalist," and subalternist history has placed "peasant consciousness" in an autonomous domain outside the reach of modern forms of rationality. However, as I demonstrate in this book, Bengal's jute cultivators fashioned new material and intellectual lives through their very *modern* entanglements with global commodity markets.

These entanglements also created an experience of simultaneity across the global countryside. As telegraphs disseminated prices instantaneously, peasant producers across the colonized tropics confronted the possibilities of hunger and starvation simultaneously. Commodity-producing peasant households in the colonized tropics were among the most precarious subjects of the global marketplace, utterly powerless to shape and influence the prices on which their well-being and indeed survival depended. Depressions of the nineteenth century were accompanied by devastating famines in the commodity-producing colonies, particularly the cotton tracts of India and Egypt; the Great Depression of the 1930s impoverished swaths of agrarian Asia and Africa, resulting in mass sales of peasant assets; and the price shocks of World War II resulted in severe famines in Bengal's jute tracts and the rice tracts of Southeast Asia.

The simultaneity of global prices resulted in concurrent peasant political movements across the global countryside, as peasant commodity producers attempted to protest, resist, and disrupt unremunerative and unviable commodity markets. These movements, however, differed considerably in form and content. The extreme and prolonged price slump of the 1930s was accompanied by peasant protests across the global countryside: in Borneo, peasants dreamed that their rubber trees were eating subsistence rice, triggering a mass felling of standing rubber trees; in Sarawak, rubber cultivators perceived the collapse in prices as a breaking of faith on the part of the English rajah, prompting mass rebellions against the rajah; in Burma, rice cultivators professed their loyalty to Saya San, a Buddhist monk who had been proclaimed the Galon Raja, and attacked Indian merchants and moneylenders; in Bengal, peasant men organized raids of moneylenders' homes and destroyed their records of outstanding debts; in Ghana, cocoa farmers organized "cocoa holdups" and focused on the ability of tribal chiefs to organize and enforce an embargo on cocoa sales.[18] Capitalist speculations produced simultaneity in global commodity prices and concurrence in peasant political movements across the global countryside, but it did not determine the form and content of peasant political action. Even as global capital conjured a universal world of abstract commodities out of peasant land and labor, peasant communities fashioned distinctive and particular agrarian ecologies, material and intellectual lives, and political programs. Local histories of global capital, such as the one narrated in this book, focus on the heterogeneity and particularity produced out of global capital's universalizing drive.

Local Histories of Global Capital

This book narrates the history of jute in the Bengal delta as a local history of global capital at three levels. First, fibers entangled peasant households in a dense web of commodity exchanges, as they exchanged jute for food, clothing, intoxicants, illumination, construction materials, and a host of other commodities required and desired by the households. These new forms of production and consumption constituted the market-entangled *economic lives* of jute cultivators. Second, global commodities flowed out of and into peasant households through a network of railways, river steamers, docks, stations, warehouses, and telegraph lines. These *spaces of capital* physically connected the peasant homestead to the circuits of global commodities, via small market towns within the hinterland and the colonial metropolis of Calcutta. Third, *peasant politics* was informed, shaped, and produced through the enactments of market-entangled economic lives against these spaces of capital. This book demonstrates that both spectacular episodes of peasant collective action and everyday peasant politics of elections and voting were informed by commodity markets as well as by the spatial relations of the countryside, towns, and cities.

The history of economic life narrated in this book is a critique of economic histories based on abstract categories, whether on Marxist concepts of peasant modes of production or liberal economic theories of market responsiveness. Instead of the abstract category of labor, I examine how jute production transformed the rhythms of work and leisure and the agrarian ecology of soil and water in the Bengal delta (chapter 1). In devoting ever-increasing quantities of land and labor to jute, the Bengal delta's peasant households altered agrarian space and time. They rearranged the distribution of plants over the delta's unique ecology of soil and water or, as a colonial official described it, the delta's landscape of "new mud, old mud, and marsh."[19] They reorganized rhythms of work and leisure through aligning the arduous tasks of sowing, thinning, reaping, rotting, stripping, and drying jute with the delta's seasons of rains, floods, and sunshine, and the growth cycles of plants.

Jute cultivators fashioned economic and material lives through the consumption of new and novel goods: corrugated iron roofs, metal utensils, kerosene oil and lamps, German-made toys, luxury fishes and fruits, English-language education, and colonial legal services (chapter 2). After World War I and the onset of rapid immiseration, however, consumption became an unviable strategy for peasant self-fashioning. During this period of adverse market conditions, the delta's peasantry formulated religious discourses that promoted hard work, austerity, abstinence, and patriarchal authority as Islamic virtues that would restore the viability and even prosperity of market-entangled peasant households (chapter 5). My analysis of self-fashioning through market entanglements draws on Dipesh Chakrabarty's concept of History 2. Chakrabarty proposes a distinction between analytical and Marxist histories of capital (History 1) and hermeneutic and Heideggerian histories of the life-worlds of individuals and communities (History 2). Marxist histories of capital, History 1, examine the ways in which capital obliterates local specificities that provided resistance to the circulation, reproduction, and augmentation of capital. On the other hand, History 2 focuses on the multiple histories of life-worlds of individuals and communities that were not subsumed by capital, but exist alongside and occasionally interrupt and subvert the history of capital. As Chakrabarty formulates the difference: "the first [Marxist] tradition tends to evacuate the local by assimilating it to some abstract universal . . . the hermeneutic tradition, on the other hand, finds thought intimately tied to places and to particular forms of life."[20] Peasant self-fashioning through global market entanglements is an attempt to craft a "habitation of modernity," to create meaningful and authentic lives within the context of commodity production for global markets.

Peasant efforts to fashion lives out of market entanglements took place against a backdrop of shifting spatial relations traced out by the circulation of commodities into and out of peasant homes. David Harvey argues that the circulation and reproduction of capital—whether capital embodied as commodities or abstract and disembodied capital—entails "fixing capital into the land" in the form of farms, plantations, mines, factories, railways, steamers, telegraph lines, seaports, warehouses, and so forth.[21] Virtually the entirety of Bengal's jute was destined for Calcutta's seaport and mills, and the majority of peasant-consumed commodities were also imported from Calcutta. Thus the built-up capital through which jute circulated constituted the delta as Calcutta's hinterland and, conversely, Calcutta as the delta's metropolis.[22] The most significant spaces of capital in the Bengal delta were the intermediary spaces between the hinterland and the metropolis, the riverside and railway towns where peasant-produced jute and peasant-consumed goods were bulked, stored, and assorted on journeys in and out of peasant homes. These towns constituted the *mofussil*—an in-between space between the metropolis and the hinterland.[23] The mofussil was the most significant spatial formation of capital for jute-cultivating peasants, as peasant men visited mofussil towns to buy and sell commodities, contest lawsuits, and enroll sons in government schools (chapter 3). During the early twentieth century, these towns emerged as vibrant and autonomous centers of cultural and intellectual production and political action. This book examines the burgeoning mofussil print industry and the constitution of a mofussil Muslim intelligentsia with roots in the countryside during the post–World War I years (chapter 5). The partition of Bengal severed the delta's jute tracts from its metropolis in Calcutta and incorporated it into the new nation-state of Pakistan—creating an East Pakistan that was a hinterland without a metropolis. The postcolonial Pakistani state sought to rearrange the spatial relations of hinterland, mofussil, and metropolis by asserting the state's sovereignty over fiber (chapter 7).

Jute cultivators' political actions were produced out of their attempt to fashion meaningful lives out of their market entanglements against the backdrop of these shifting spatial relationships. Jute cultivators' resistance to the Swadeshi movement in 1905–6 is an instance of how market entanglements and spatial relations informed peasant politics (chapter 2). The Swadeshi movement was the first anticolonial nationalist movement that attempted to mobilize rural jute cultivators. Swadeshi activists imposed a consumer boycott of imported commodities, particularly Manchester cloth, but also European-made toys and confections. Market-entangled peasant households endeavored to protect rural and mofussil marketplaces as spaces of pleasurable consumption from metropolitan Swadeshi activists' attempts to forcibly prevent the sale of imported consumer goods. Peasant resistance to Swadeshi activists manifested spatially as peasant households in the *hinterland* resisted attempts by *metropolitan* nationalists to mobilize supporters in mofussil towns (chapter 3). After World War I, peasant politics focused on restoring the viability of market-entangled lives in the context of rapid peasant immiseration. Peasant rebellions against state authority during the Khilafat movement of 1920–22 were informed by the unviability of market-entangled lives during those years. Further, numerous episodes of Hindu-Muslim violence during the 1920s, 1930s, and 1940s were informed by processes of immiseration—by agrarian Islamic discourses and by the shifting relations of hinterland, mofussil, and metropolis (chapters 5 and 6).

Peasant politics did not consist solely of spectacular episodes of collective action, but also of more mundane acts of campaigning and voting. After World War I, colonial reforms carved the delta's jute tracts into territorial constituencies that formed the basis for municipal or village-level local government or elected representatives to the provincial legislature in Calcutta.

Chapter 6 examines jute cultivators' support for the peasant populist Krishak Praja Party during the 1937 elections as an ultimately unsuccessful attempt to restore the viability of market-entangled lives during the depression decade. Chapter 7 investigates jute cultivators' overwhelming support for the Muslim League and the Pakistan cause in the 1946 elections, arguing that it should be understood in terms of a post-famine politics of immiseration. The idea of Pakistan as peasant utopia, the book argues, was grounded in agrarian Islamic discourses that emerged in the context of agrarian immiseration. Remarkably, jute cultivators' utopian action consisted not of revolutionary violence but of votes for a political platform.[24]

The local history of jute cultivators is thus a history of how global market entanglements transformed peasant households' material, intellectual, and political lives: rhythms of work and leisure; agrarian ecology; practices and ideas of domesticity, sociality, and religiosity; and political actions and pro-cesses. Analogous yet distinct transformations took place across the dispa-rate localities that constituted the global countryside, as peasant commodity producers restructured their lives around particular plants, purchased new kinds of consumer goods, and created meaning and significance out of their market-entangled lives. However, for many of these peasant communities, these commodities of empire did not threaten to disrupt their lives quite so thoroughly at the moment they took up their production. Peasant households combined commodity production with subsistence cultivation, distributing commercial and food crops on their lands so as to minimize disruptions to existing rhythms of work and leisure. Jute, as I indicate below, appealed to the Bengal delta's peasant smallholders precisely because it slotted relatively easily into their farmlands and work schedules. I will now introduce the major protagonists of this local history of global capital: the Bengal delta's peasant smallholders during the mid-nineteenth century, on the eve of jute's conquest of their land, labor, and lives.

The Bengal Delta's Peasant Households

The majority of the Bengal delta's peasants were Muslim, and a significant minority belonged to low-caste Hindu communities, especially the Namasu-dras.[25] Most peasant households were family units that shared a hearth and jointly labored to produce plants for subsistence and sale on a small plot of arable land. The majority of households consisted of a male patriarch, his wife or wives, elderly parents, sons, sons' wives, grandchildren, and unmarried, young daughters. Daughters would move to their husband's home upon marriage and sons' households would separate from the patriarch's—with arable lands divided equally among sons—upon or sometimes before the patriarch's death.

The peasant homestead consisted of several one-room dwellings facing an internal courtyard. One of the huts served as a kitchen, another as a granary and a cowshed, and the others were multipurpose spaces for sleeping, dining, socializing, and storage. The homestead was built on raised land, to protect dwellings and belongings from the annual monsoon floods. The earth excavated to raise the homestead land created a small tank or pond that provided the household with drinking, bathing, cleaning, and cooking water. The homestead was surrounded by a dense thicket of trees and plants that shielded the dwellings and courtyard from prying eyes and from the heat. Peasant homes were not clustered together into dense settlements, but separated from each other by farmlands. From afar, peasant homesteads appeared as isolated thickets of greenery surrounded by an expanse of farmland.[26]

In the mid-nineteenth century, peasants' holdings of arable land varied between small farms of one or two acres to large farms of around twenty acres, with the median holding of close to five acres. However, average holdings shrank during the nineteenth century, as the delta's population increased and lands were subdivided among sons. Substantial peasant households with very large holdings were present only in northern Bengal, notably in Rangpur district. These substantial peasant households, known as *jotedar*s, cultivated their land through sharecroppers and wage laborers. However, in the rest of the delta, there was very little variation in peasant smallholders' landholdings.[27] Unlike substantial jotedars, most of the delta's peasantry used primarily household labor to cultivate their lands, hiring extra wageworkers during busier times in the crop calendar, during sowing, transplanting, or harvesting. The peasant households owned, maintained, and replaced their own capital equipment, iron hoes and scythes, wooden plows, and plow oxen—far and away the most important form of capital. For their right to occupy and cultivate their arable land, peasant households paid a tax to the state or to intermediary rent collectors, known as *zamindar*s.

The delta's peasantry located their origins in acts of labor that resulted in ecological transformation—in the clearing of jungles, draining of swamps, and leveling the soil to prepare land for paddy cultivation. The moment of origin varies in different regions of the delta: some peasant households claim to have settled their land as far back as the thirteenth century and others as recently as the nineteenth century. These peasant origin narratives are supported by the historical scholarship which describes the Bengal delta as an "agrarian frontier" that was gradually settled by peasant smallholders starting from the second millennium CE to the beginning of the twentieth century, when the delta's agrarian limits were finally reached.[28] The eastward shift of the Ganges river system, which culminated in the shift of the Ganges's main tributary to the river Padma during the sixteenth century, provided an impetus to peasant migration and settlement into eastern Bengal. Notably, this coincided with the establishment of Mughal rule in Bengal. The Mughal administration provided incentives for peasant households to clear land for cultivation. The East India Company and British Raj continued many of these incentives during the eighteenth and nineteenth centuries.

Peasant origin stories, Andrew Sartori has argued, are also stories of property: the peasant labor of transforming swamp and jungle into paddy land constituted a claim to property ownership.[29] The labor of ecological transformation inducted peasant households into Mughal property regimes and the Mughal Empire's revenue-collection mechanisms, which were inherited and transformed by the East India Company after the Battle of Buxar in 1764. The Mughal Empire distinguished two kinds of rights to land: the right to live and labor on land and the right to collect revenue from the land. The former belonged to peasants who cleared the land and the latter to the empire's military and bureaucratic elite—zamindars and *jagirdars* who had provided a service to the empire or were expected to provide military assistance when required. The East India Company collapsed this distinction between the right to occupy land and the right to collect revenue from land in the Permanent Settlement Act of 1793. The Permanent Settlement Act fixed the dues of a zamindar in perpetuity and placed no limits on the zamindar's power to extract revenue or evict peasant households from their lands.[30] *Zamindari* power in the delta was, however, limited. Iftekhar Iqbal has shown that recently settled lands were generally outside the ambit of the zamindari system and Jon Wilson has demonstrated that peasants who found a particular zamindar's revenue demands too onerous during the eighteenth century found it easy to relocate in the delta's expanding agrarian frontier.[31]

Peasant origin narratives are also stories of securing subsistence. Rice was the first plant cultivated on newly settled land, and rice provided for the simple subsistence and reproduction of the peasant household. The bulk of peasant land and labor was devoted to paddy, and the delta produced two major rice crops—a spring or *aus* paddy and an autumn or *aman* paddy. The significance of rice cultivation to procure subsistence in peasant origin narratives should not, however, obscure the importance of commercial cash crops to the peasant economy. The Bengal delta, along with the rest of South Asia, experienced intensive commercialization during the seventeenth and eighteenth centuries, through South Asia's burgeoning trade with European trading companies and its growing consumption of silver mined in the New World. Rice was not only subsistence food, but also a major commercial crop. The eighteenth century witnessed a sharp increase in the delta's rice trade, and the creation of networks of indigenous merchants and colonial capital that were involved in purchasing and trading peasant-produced rice.[32] Bengal rice was exported to the burgeoning British "factory towns" of Calcutta, Madras, and Bombay, to the sugar islands of the Indian Ocean, and to Europe. Rice was not the only important cash crop produced by the delta's peasantry. The "up-country" produce trade that enriched private European traders after the East India Company's conquest of Bengal included a long list of peasant-produced plant commodities in addition to rice: notably, tobacco, cotton, *ganja*, betel nuts, mustard, sesame, ginger, turmeric, and chilies. Many of these commercial crops were winter or *rabi* crops—oilseeds, vegetables, and spices. Indigo was also cultivated in the delta from the early nineteenth century. However, more than any other peasant-produced plant commodity, indigo relied on the coercive powers of planters and zamindars, and the dye was thus limited to those parts of the delta where zamindars were able to effectively exert authority over their tenants. Thus the delta's peasant households were connected to local, regional, and oceanic networks of commodities, cash, and credit even prior to the rise of jute.

The "rise of Islam" in the Bengal delta, Richard Eaton has demonstrated, was associated with the settlement of the agrarian frontier. Mughal incentives for land clearance encouraged conversions to Islam by offering tax exemptions to land adjoining mosques. The delta's particular practice of Islam, however, arrived not with conquerors coming overland from the west, but with Sufi saints from Arabia arriving across the sea from the Bay of Bengal.[33] These Sufi saints inspired Islamic practices that were syncretic, combining Islamic rituals and beliefs with the devotional practices of Vaishnavism and the continued worship of local deities.[34] During the first half of the nineteenth century, new Islamic movements emerged in Bengal that sought to purify Islam of un-Islamic, syncretic practices and to insist on a rigid monotheism. The most popular of these movements was the Faraizi movement, founded by Haji Shariatullah (1781–1840) in Faridpur in 1819. Shariatullah went to Mecca for

Haj at the age of eighteen and returned to Faridpur after spending twenty years studying Islam in Mecca. Shariatullah urged peasant Muslims to stop worshipping non-Muslim deities and Sufi saints and to discontinue "impure" ceremonies associated with birth, marriage, and death. Under the leadership of Shariatullah's son, Dudu Miyan (1819–1862), the Faraizi movement spread throughout the delta and established practices of dress, speech, and domesticity that became emblematic of the Bengali Muslim peasantry during the nineteenth century.[35]

In the mid-nineteenth century, when jute entered the Bengal delta's agrarian economy, peasant households were bringing more of the delta's land under the plow; were combining subsistence rice cultivation with the production of a variety of cash crops; were integrated into regional and oceanic networks of trade and credit; were subsumed under imperial property regimes; enjoyed a degree of autonomy from intermediary revenue collectors like zamindars; and were undergoing a popular Muslim reform movement. Jute cultivation expanded rapidly during the late nineteenth century because the fiber did not disrupt peasant methods of production and labor, networks of credit and trade, the delta's ecology of soil and water, and discourses and practices of Islam. Jute, however, would prove to be transformative. Fiber and the connections to global capital forged by fiber transformed local histories of peasant economic and political life in the Bengal delta.

Chapter Outline

The first half of the book relates the broad transformations brought about by jute cultivation during the late nineteenth century, between the Crimean War and World War I. This was a period of relative prosperity, where favorable commodity markets, the size of peasant smallholdings, and the agrarian ecology enabled the jute cultivators to fashion new forms of self-presentation and sociality out of the proceeds of jute sales. The first three chapters describe how the rise of jute cultivation in the late nineteenth century transformed peasant production, consumption, and politics. World War I interrupted this prosperity, as unfavorable commodity markets, fragmenting smallholdings, deteriorating ecological conditions, and rising levels of indebtedness drove the bulk of the jute-cultivating peasantry into utter penury. Chapter 4 discusses these processes of immiseration and provides an interregnum between the nineteenth-century period of relative prosperity and the twentieth-century period of absolute poverty. The second half of the book examines how the increasing unviability of market-entangled lives gave rise to new forms of self-fashioning and new kinds of political action. In the final three chapters, I discuss the emergence of new discourses of agrarian Islam which promoted hard work, abstinence, and patriarchal control as Muslim virtues that would restore the viability of market-entangled peasant lives; the increasing incidences of Hindu-Muslim violence in the Bengal delta; and jute cultivators' enthusiastic participation in electoral politics—particularly in their support for the peasant populist Krishak Praja Party in the 1937 elections and the utopian Pakistan program of the Muslim League in 1946. The book concludes with an examination of the postcolonial Pakistani state's attempts to harness jute as a source of national income. Jute cultivators experienced the postcolonial state's intrusions into their agrarian life as violence and harassment, leading to their rapid disillusionment with Pakistan.

Chapter 1 describes how the rise in jute cultivation between the Crimean War and World War I, when acreage increased from fifty thousand to close to four million acres, entailed a thorough reorganization of peasant life: of the rhythms of work and leisure and of abundance and scarcity. Peasant decisions to grow more jute were, correspondingly, decisions to grow less rice. By the 1900s, jute acreage in the Bengal delta was roughly equal to the acreage of spring or aus paddy and about one-third of winter or aman paddy. The simultaneous production of two major crops—fiber and grain—entailed a considerably greater amount of peasant labor. Reduced rice production created new vulnerabilities to hunger, as was cruelly revealed at the start of World War I, when jute prices plummeted, causing hunger throughout the jute tracts.

Chapter 2 examines jute cultivators' consumption of colonial legal services, clothing, ornaments, metal utensils, corrugated iron roofing, kerosene oil and lamps, and luxury fruits and fishes. I argue that jute-cultivating households fashioned distinctively rural, Muslim, and Bengali forms of modernity in dress, domesticity, and sociality through the consumption of these goods and services. The chapter also shows the defense by peasant households of their consumption practices during the Swadeshi movement, when metropolitan and mofussil nationalist activists attempted to forcibly impose a consumer boycott in rural marketplaces in the delta. I argue that clashes between peasants and nationalists were not simply due to financial motives, but were driven by psychic desires and by the possibilities of peasant self-fashioning through consumption during the boom in jute prices.

The Swadeshi movement and peasant resistance to the Swadeshi boycott were enacted in the spaces of capital carved out by circulations of jute. From their headquarters in Calcutta, metropolitan Swadeshi activists undertook whistlestop tours of the jute-growing districts by train and river steamers, stopping to address mass meetings in the small towns located on rail and steamer routes. They thus followed in reverse the same routes through which jute traveled from peasant farms and homes to Calcutta. Chapter 3 examines how the circulation of peasant-produced jute and peasant-consumed commodities constituted the agrarian delta as Calcutta's hinterland and Calcutta as the delta's metropolis. The chapter focuses on intermediary towns between the hinterland and the metropolis—mofussil towns. These small towns accommodated the warehouses, docks, railway sidings, and presses of jute merchants and the courthouses, revenue offices, police stations, agricultural extension services, and other paraphernalia of the colonial state. Mofussil towns, the chapter demonstrates, were at the center of clashes between the hinterland peasantry and metropolitan nationalists.

Chapter 4 describes the processes of immiseration that began during World War I, intensified during the depression decade of the 1930s, and culminated in the Great Bengal Famine of 1943–44. During these decades, market shocks, fragmenting peasant landholdings, ecological disasters, and rising indebtedness reduced the majority of jute cultivators to destitution. However, the era of peasant immiseration was also a period of peasant differentiation. A small minority of jute cultivators who had invested profits from the earlier boom years into diversifying their livelihoods not only survived but even prospered. The most common forms of diversification were moneylending and the acquisition of intermediary rent-collection rights, known as talukdaris and jagirdaris. Some families diversified by establishing business enterprises in mofussil towns, and an even smaller minority through educated sons who gained professional employment, also in mofussil towns or even in metropolitan Calcutta.

The arrival of Muslim men with origins in the countryside into mofussil towns during this era of immiseration changed the spatial relations of town and countryside in the Bengal delta. During the Swadeshi movement, mofussil towns appeared as islands of Hindu metropolitan culture surrounded by a Muslim rural hinterland. After World War I, the town became much more closely integrated into the surrounding countryside. One of the ways in which town and country became integrated, chapter 5 demonstrates, was through the mofussil print industry. Newly arrived Muslim men from the countryside constituted themselves as a mofussil Muslim intelligentsia by authoring and patronizing the publication of pamphlets, poems, and newspapers. Agrarian immiseration was the burning issue of the day for this intelligentsia and their writings on peasant poverty circulated between the towns and the countryside. These writings, I explain in chapter 5, constituted a discourse of agrarian Islam that urged comprehensive reforms of everyday peasant life—of work, commerce, consumption, attire and hairstyle, patriarchal control over wives and children, and neighborly relations. These reforms would bring Muslim peasants this-worldly salvation, that is, an escape from poverty and, perhaps, even prosperity.

Chapter 6 explores peasant participation in the limited forms of representative and electoral politics introduced by the colonial state after World War I. The chapter shows how colonial reforms created new kinds of spaces in the delta's jute tracts—superimposing spatially demarcated electoral constituencies and local government bodies over existing spaces of hinterland, mofussil, and metropolis. Chapter 6 explores the ways in which elections to local government bodies were informed by discourses of agrarian Islam and shifts in the relationship between mofussil towns and the agrarian hinterland during the era of immiseration. In the 1937 elections, the first held after the reforms of 1935 expanded the franchise and redrew the territorial boundaries of constituencies, jute cultivators voted for the peasant populist Krishak Praja Party (KPP). The KPP's electoral victory, the chapter argues, was rooted in the discourses of agrarian Islam. The chapter also examines the KPP's inability to raise jute prices, despite numerous and varied efforts to intervene in produce and futures markets. The KPP's failure to assert control over jute prices foreshadowed the devastating famine of 1943–44, when rice prices rose faster and higher than jute prices causing mass hunger and starvation for marginal peasant households.

Famine spelled the end of peasant populism and gave rise to the utopian politics of Pakistan. For jute cultivators, Pakistan implied a society free of hunger and want, a place of justice, ethical behavior, and moral reciprocity. Chapter 7 examines the Muslim League's 1946 electoral campaign, when it swept the rural Muslim vote in the delta's jute tracts on the promise of Pakistan. However, while jute cultivators envisioned Pakistan as a post-famine utopia, Muslim elites envisioned Pakistan as a modern nation-state, endowed with the appropriate paraphernalia and pageantry. Partition and the severance of the jute tracts from their metropolis in Calcutta frustrated elite aspirations. Chapter 7 demonstrates the Pakistani state's efforts to transform jute from a commodity of empire into a national producer of revenue and resources for the postcolonial state. The Pakistani state was confounded by smuggling: the illicit trade of fiber across freshly drawn partition lines that evaded the state's mechanisms to monitor, police, and tax commodity flows across its borders. In its desire to extract revenue from fiber, the Pakistani state undertook increasingly draconian measures against jute smuggling—including shoot-to-kill orders on their borders. Statist violence turned, in Ahmed Kamal's phrase, "the state against the nation" and thus destroyed jute cultivators' visions of Pakistan as a peasant utopia.[36]

Jute thus transformed the Bengal delta and its peasant inhabitants. The production and sale of jute entangled peasant households and the region in global circuits of commodities and capital that, in turn, transformed material and intellectual lives, the spaces of mofussil towns, ideas and practices of religiosity, and the form and content of political action. While the local history of global capital narrated in the following chapters is particular to the Bengal delta and jute, analogous yet distinct transformations took place across the global countryside, in the cocoa and peanut tracts of West Africa, the rubber and rice farms of Southeast Asia, and among cotton and sugar cultivators of northern and central South Asia. In each of these localities, the production and circulation of commodities resulted in new forms of peasant labor, urban spaces, and political commitments and engagements and peasant commodity producers fashioned distinctive and particular material and intellectual lives out of their entanglements with global commodity markets. Even as global capital sought to conjure a universal world of fungible labor and commodities, expressed in lists and tables of exchangeable commodities in metropolitan markets, peasant commodity producers created particular, distinctive, and incommensurable local histories of global capital. The following chapter commences the delta's history of global capital in the mid-nineteenth century, at the moment when the Bengal delta's peasant households began devoting an ever-increasing proportion of their land and labor to producing fiber.

1

Cultivating Jute

PEASANT CHOICE, LABOR, AND HUNGER

BETWEEN THE CRIMEAN WAR (1853–56) and World War I (1914–18), jute cultivation in Bengal expanded exponentially. In 1850 approximately 50,000 acres of Bengal's land was sown with jute; in 1906 jute cultivation reached its historic high of close to four million acres.[1] From an insignificant commodity of international trade, jute became Bengal's leading export. In 1829, the first year that jute exports were enumerated by customs authorities in Calcutta, Bengal exported just eighteen tons of raw fiber valued at about 62 pounds sterling.[2] In 1910 Bengal exported thirteen million tons of raw jute valued at 13 million Indian rupees and another 17 million rupees of jute manufactures.[3] The enormous increase in jute cultivation was concentrated in a relatively small part of the province: the active delta of the Brahmaputra, Ganges, and Meghna river systems of eastern and northern Bengal, comprising the districts of Rangpur, Pabna, Bogra, Faridpur, Dacca, Mymensingh, and Tipperah (see map 1). This region of silt and alluvium, annual floods, and shifting soil, mud, and water produced between 70 and 80 percent of the world's jute.[4] When jute cultivation reached its historical high during the 1900s, more than 20 percent of these districts' cultivated lands were sown with fiber.[5]

   The enormous increase in jute production took place without colonial coercion, or even incentives and subsidies. The colonial government of Bengal was, in fact, taken by surprise by the new commodity. In 1873, after jute was already established as Bengal's leading commercial crop, Bengal's lieutenant governor expressed embarrassed and profound ignorance regarding fiber: "Gentlemen who have come from home with a practical interest in such questions [about jute] have lately asked His Honor to answer some of them, and he has been unable to answer them. . . . Mr. Campbell does not know to what language the word jute belongs, nor what it really means."[6] Unlike other contemporary commodities of empire, jute cultivation was not accompanied by enslavement, genocide, the violent enforcement of rigged contracts, massive irrigation projects, large-scale ecological engineering schemes, or the distribution of subsidized credit, seeds, and production technologies. The expansion of jute cultivation took place entirely through peasant choice, through the autonomous and independent decisions of tens of thousands of peasant households in the Bengal delta to devote increasing quantities of land and labor to fiber.

Economic historians of the delta have established that peasant decisions to grow jute were driven by markets, prices, and profits. Sugata Bose describes the expansion of jute as the "second phase" in the commercialization of agriculture, as the statist and capitalist coercion that characterized indigo cultivation in the early nineteenth century gave way to market forces and pressures during the late nineteenth century.[7] Omkar Goswami has shown, through careful statistical analysis of admittedly flawed colonial agricultural data that year-to-year variations in jute acreage corresponded to fluctuations in the price of fiber, at least prior to the Great Depression of 1930.[8] The close correspondence between acreage and price is revealed in the expansion of fiber over time: jute acreage increased in bursts, with spikes in global prices followed by periods of rapid expansion. Between the Crimean War and World War I, there were three booms in jute cultivation: between the mid-1860s and 1873, from the mid-1880s to 1890, and, finally, between 1905 and the beginning of World War I in 1914. These periods of rapid expansion closely corresponded with booms and busts in global capital.

The first jute boom took place during the late 1860s and the early 1870s, as jute prices increased sharply driven by the enormous increase in demand from Dundee manufacturers. Calcutta's fiber exports increased from 2.3 million tons in 1866 to 7 million tons in 1873. In several jute-growing districts in the delta— for instance, Pabna, Mymensingh, Dacca, and Faridpur—commercial jute cultivation began in the early to mid-1860s.[9] When prices reached a record high in 1872, cultivators responded by "[taking] up whatever land was ready at hand" and extended acreage by 30 percent from the previous year, to 760,000 acres. This was a fifteenfold increase from the estimated 50,000 acres sown with jute in 1850.[10] In a pattern that was repeated over the coming decades, prices collapsed in August and September 1872, just as cultivators were preparing to harvest their record crop. The Long Depression had set in, and prices would remain depressed for the remainder of the decade. Jute cultivators abandoned their crops, allowing the plants to rot in the fields, and sharply reduced jute acreage the following year.

Jute acreage recovered to 1872 levels only at the end of the decade, reaching an estimated 795,000 acres in 1880. Cultivation then began to expand rapidly, as prices doubled from an average of 2 rupees and 11 annas per *maund* in 1882 to 4 rupees and 15 annas in 1890. Jute acreage expanded sharply at the end of the decade, from 1.45 million in 1888 to 2 million acres in 1890. When prices collapsed again in 1890, falling by 35 percent, cultivators responded as they had done in 1872—allowing standing crops to rot and sharply reducing acreage the following year, by 12.5 percent to 1.75 million acres.[11]

Jute acreage averaged at just above 2 million acres between 1890 and 1905, when increases in prices led cultivators to amp up jute production. Calcutta prices rose sharply in 1905, a 28 percent increase followed by a 29 percent increase the following year. Increased acreage followed on the heels of high prices, rising by 11 percent in 1906 and then 13 percent in 1907. The 3.9 million acres sown with jute in 1907 was a historic high (see table 1.1). When prices fell again in 1907, cultivators reduced acreage. The increase in prices after 1911, and the record prices of 1913—10 rupees and 8 annas a maund—spurred

TABLE 1.1. Variations in Acreage and Price of Jute in Bengal, 1904–1915

	Acreage*		Price**	
	Acres	Percentage change	Rupees per maund	Percentage change
1904	2,850,000		5.375	
1905	3,090,700	8.4%	6.875	27.9%
1906	3,434,000	11.1%	8.875	29.1%
1907	3,846,500	12.0%	6.625	-25.4%
1908	2,766,300	-28.1%	5.5625	-16.0%
1909	2,773,100	0.2%	5.625	1.1%
1910	2,841,600	2.5%	5.5	-2.2%
1911	2,737,600	-3.7%	6.5625	19.3%
1912	2,536,900	-7.3%	8.375	27.6%
1913	2,456,600	-3.2%	10.5	25.4%
1914	2,872,600	16.9%	6.25	-40.5%
1915	2,086,300	-27.4%	6.9375	11.0%

* The acreage is for the entire province of Bengal. The Bengal delta accounted for more than 80% of the province's acreage. These figures are from Department of Statistics, *Estimates of Area and Yield of Principal Crops in India, 1914–15*, Calcutta: Superintendent Government Printing Press, 1915, p. 11.
** This is the average price of fiber in markets across Bengal during a fiscal year, that is from July to July. The prices are compiled from Government of Bengal, *Reports on Trade Carried by Rail and River in Bengal during the Years 1904/5 to 1914/15*, Calcutta, 1905 to 1916.

an increase of 17 percent in acreage in 1914. However, just as cultivators were preparing to harvest their crop in August 1914, World War I commenced, global trade came to a temporary standstill, the German market disappeared, and prices plummeted. This time, jute cultivators did not allow their crops to rot in the field, as they had during previous price busts. Instead, they relied on women and children rather than wageworkers to harvest fiber and tried desperately to sell their produce at whatever prices were available. The price collapse of World War I began a rapid and thorough process of peasant immiseration in the Bengal delta.

These statistics of acreage and price do not, however, reveal the extent to which peasant households had to reorganize the distribution of plants over farmlands and rearrange rhythms of work and leisure in order to accommodate fiber. In and of themselves, statistics do not explain why cultivators could respond to price busts by allowing their crops to rot in 1873 and 1891 but not in 1914. This chapter goes beyond statistical analyses of market responsiveness to explore what decisions to grow more jute entailed in terms of agrarian space and time. Peasant decisions to grow more jute were, simultaneously, decisions to not grow rice. Jute competed for peasant land and labor with the delta's two major rice crops—winter or aman paddy and spring or aus paddy. Choices between commercial fiber and subsistence grain dominated peasant economic life and were the most consequential decisions made by peasant households during the agrarian year. This chapter examines how peasant households responded to global markets by adapting to rhythms of work, ecologies of smallholdings, seasons of rain, sunshine, and monsoons, and the growth cycles of plants to produce combinations of jute for global markets and rice for household subsistence.

Jute remained inextricably tied to the soil of the Bengal delta. Nineteenth-century attempts to transfer jute cultivation to other parts of the world failed. In 1873 the Queensland society in Australia requested and received jute seeds from Bengal, though little seems to have come out of it.[12] A more concerted attempt to introduce jute cultivation in Louisiana, in the Mississippi delta, during the same period also failed—though it caused consternation among colonial officials in Bengal.[13] A report by the US Department of Agriculture noted success in growing the plant in the Mississippi delta but concluded that unless the process of extracting the fiber from plants was mechanized, farmers would not take up large-scale cultivation.[14] In other words, white settler farmers in the United States and Australia were not willing to adapt rhythms of life and agrarian ecologies to the demands of jute—to exploit household labor or to risk hunger, as the Bengal peasantry did in growing jute.

The first section of this chapter explores how the competition between rice and jute for peasant land and labor was played out against the delta's ecology of soil and water and its calendar of rains, sunshine, and floods. The second section examines how the displacement of rice by jute introduced seasonal hunger into the peasant calendar, and how it spurred peasant indebtedness and reduced peasant households' ability to withstand market shocks. Hunger and market-based subsistence explain why peasant households were able to abandon standing jute crops in the 1870s and 1890s, but not in the 1900s. The chapter concludes by demonstrating how the market collapse of World War I triggered the mass immiseration of the delta's jute cultivators.

Fiber and Grain

The colonial official J. C. Jack wrote the following description of the Bengal delta's ecology of soil and water in his account of Faridpur district:

> The delta of the Ganges is a peculiar country, worth knowledge and worth description. It is made up of new mud, old mud and marsh; it contains rivers as large as any in the world, linked together by an amazing network of lesser rivers, streams and ditches; it mostly disappears under water for several months in the year; yet it grows abundant crops everywhere and supports a very considerable population in considerable idleness.[15]

This description of "new mud, old mud and marsh" is an apt typology of the delta's ecology though, of course, the "considerable population" that labored on this landscape was most certainly not living in "considerable idleness." Jack's distinction of "new mud" and "old mud" mapped onto the formal and less poetic categories of "low land" and "high land" widely used in official and merchant accounts of the delta's ecology.[16] New mud (low land) consisted of the newest alluvial deposits of the delta's river systems, loamy soil closer to riverbanks and the earliest to flood during the monsoons. High lands were older silt formations, firmer and more clayey soil and only a few feet above the lowlands that flooded later in the monsoons. Marshes consisted of the extensive lakes and swamps—*beels* and *haors*—scattered throughout the delta. Though categorized as wastelands, marshes were important sources of fish and fodder grass. This landscape of new mud and old mud was in constant flux, as the delta's shifting rivers produced "new mud" at an astonishing rate through the formation of river islands, or *chars*, and exposed riverbeds, or *diara* lands. The nineteenth century witnessed considerable augmentation of cultivable land, as peasant households cleared jungles and drained marshes, converting "wasteland" into arable farmland.

In the expanding agrarian frontier of the nineteenth century, land appeared unlimited. Peasant production was constrained by the households' ability to mobilize human and animal labor rather than the limitations of land. W. W. Hunter's statistical accounts of the jute-growing districts of the 1870s distinguished between small, medium, and large farms, with small farms generally less than five acres, medium farms ranging from five to fifteen acres, and large farms consisting of twenty acres or more. Significantly, however, Hunter provided another measure of landholdings more appropriate to the relatively sparsely cultivated delta: the number of pairs of plow oxen required to cultivate the peasant farm. Small farms could be cultivated with one pair of oxen, medium with two, while large farms required three or more. By the end of the nineteenth century, when the limits of the agrarian frontier were reached— that is, there was no more so-called wasteland to convert into arable farmland— land rather than labor became the major constraint to peasant production. In 1900 the majority of peasants cultivated no more than four acres.[17] Peasant holdings fragmented rapidly during the twentieth century: by 1930 the average landholding in the jute-cultivating districts varied between one and two acres.[18]

Peasant decision making consisted of choices regarding which plants to cultivate when on which portions of their arable lands. The major crops were autumn (aus) and winter (aman) rice, jute, and a winter (rabi) crop of oilseeds, pulses, or spices. Colonial statistics suggest that, during the early 1900s, peasants sowed about 44 percent of their land with aman, 14 percent with aus, 17 percent with jute, and 20 percent with rabi pulses, oilseeds, and spices.[19] This distribution of plants over peasant holdings was influenced by prevailing prices but was also constrained by soil, labor, seasons, and the growth cycles of plants.

Aus rice and jute were sown broadcast—scattered by hand—after spring rains in February and March. Lowlands were sown first, to give the plants a chance to survive early inundation with the onset of monsoon floods during June and July. Sowings on highlands began later, during April and May. Highlands were sown with *tossa* jute—*Corchorus olitorius*—whose lustrous fibers commanded a higher price. The deep roots of the tossa jute plant were unsuited for lowlands, which were sown with lower-quality white jute— *Corchorus capsularis*. In Mymensingh, jute was called aus or aman depending on whether it was planted on high or low land.[20] Aus paddy was almost exclusively sown on highlands, especially as jute came to dominate lowlands. The preference of lowlands for jute was also related to work: jute fields had to be plowed more heavily and frequently than rice fields and the more clayey and harder mud of the highlands required heavier plowing.

Aus paddy and jute germinated during the hot summer months of April and May. Jute fields were periodically thinned out as they gained in height, creating a gap of a few inches between each plant. The arrival of the monsoons was a critical period: if the monsoon rains came too early and heavy, floodwaters would overtop jute and aus plants; a delayed monsoon would stunt the plants and reduce yields. If rains and floods were timely, jute and aus would have a growth spurt, sometimes growing several inches in a day to outpace rising floodwaters. The plants were ready for harvest during the floods. Jute plants would have grown to twelve feet or higher, the bottom third or even half submerged with the rest of the plant forming a wall of lush green rising up from the inundated fields. Peasant workers waded into flooded fields, dipped their sickles underwater, and cut the plants a few inches above the roots. Harvested stalks were then steeped in water for one or two weeks, a process known as retting, that would rot the stems and allow fibers to be stripped from the stalk. Once retted and stripped, fibers were dried in the sun: packing and transporting still wet jute would damage the fibers. The end of the monsoon was perfectly suited for the jute harvest, as receding floods left behind plentiful standing water for retting and the post-monsoon sun shown bright and fierce to dry the fibers.

The considerable labor in preparing fibers was accompanied by the onerous tasks of preparing aman seedbeds and transplanting seedlings. Aman seedlings were transplanted in September and October, soon after the jute had been harvested. The paddy could be transplanted onto lands just cleared of jute, but this resulted in much reduced aman yields as jute was an exhaustive plant for the soil. As jute cultivation expanded, however, more and more cultivators double-cropped with jute and aman on lowlands. Aman was harvested during the winter, in December and January.

The winter witnessed the sowing of the delta's third and least important rice crop, *boro* paddy. During the dry winter, the delta's water levels dropped and marshes, streambeds, and riverbanks became available for rice cultivation. Boro rice was transplanted onto such lands during December and January and reaped during April and May, before monsoon floods once again inundated marshes and streambeds. Boro's acreage was limited by the availability of watered lands during the dry winter months. More significant winter crops included pulses like *moong* and *masoor dal*, spices such as chilies, ginger, and turmeric, and oilseeds, like mustard and sesame. These winter crops were collectively known as rabi crops. These plants were generally sown on highlands during the winter and harvested in the early spring. Rabi crops were concentrated on highlands partly because these plants were better suited to the more clayey soil but also because the lowlands were occupied by other plants: the aman was yet to be harvested when early rabi sowings began and rabi harvest coincided with the early preparation of lowlands for the following spring's jute sowing.

From the mid-1860s to the early 1870s, global jute prices rose steadily, culminating in a sharp and sudden rise in prices in 1872, before commodity markets went bust with the onset of the Long Depression in 1873. Peasant households responded to these prices by producing ever-increasing quantities of jute. The decision to devote more land and labor to fiber did not, however, lead to a diminution in rice production. In fact, peasant households extended both rice and jute cultivation between the 1850s and the 1870s. Mymensingh's jute acreage had increased to 84,000 acres by the mid-1870s while, simultaneously, increasing its rice exports "by about twenty percent."[21] Similarly, Tipperah experienced a "great extension of rice cultivation" while its jute acreage extended to 87,000 acres. With the exception of the densely populated Dacca district, the jute-growing districts were also substantial rice-exporting districts for much of the nineteenth century.

The delta's peasantry was able to extend both rice and jute production because of the expanding agrarian frontier, as more land was being brought under the plow. Colonial officials argued that lands newly formed by the delta's shifting rivers motivated jute cultivation. The collector of Brahmanbaria wrote: "the large *churs* thrown up by the Meghna . . . opened his [the cultivators'] eyes, and the plant [jute] now forms the staple produce of the country next to paddy."[22] Moreover, in Mymensingh, the shifting channels of the Brahmaputra had created considerable new lands attractive to jute cultivation: "The cultivation is largely carried on throughout nearly the whole District, but particularly in the rich alluvial tracts formed by the Brahmaputra in the south-eastern tract between Ghafargaon and Bhairab Bazar in the north of Dacca District. The river has here silted up a great deal of late years, and the alluvial accretions thus formed, are found to be exceedingly favourable to the growth of jute."[23] Jute cultivation also expanded onto lands freed from indigo production, following the anti-indigo revolt in 1859, when peasant households in indigo-growing regions in parts of the delta successfully resisted indigo planters' attempts to force indigo cultivation. The rising profitability of fiber may even have been one of the motivating factors behind cultivators' refusal to sow indigo during the 1850s.[24] The Jute Commission of 1873 noted: "In Mymensingh and Rungpore the cultivation [of jute] has been gradually spreading for the last twenty five years or thereabouts, but the extension has been notable there since the culti- vation of indigo was abandoned."[25] Jute cultivation also extended through the reduction of fallows, which led to a decrease in the availability of fodder for dairy cows and an increase in prices of milk and dairy products. The collector of Tipperah stated: "The two most important articles which appear during the last ten years to have been growing permanently dearer are milk and fish. The increased price of the former is owing to the absorption of pasture lands; and that of the latter to the improved condition of the people, and the larger demand for fish which has arisen in consequence."[26]

In 1872, after half a decade of steady increase dating back to 1866, jute prices rose steeply—by over 30 percent from the previous year. Motivated by the spike in prices, cultivators took up "whatever land was ready at hand," that is, land formerly devoted to aus and aman paddy. Writing in the aftermath of the jute boom, the jute commissioner Hemm Chunder Kerr estimated that two- thirds of the total land devoted to fiber consisted of former rice lands, another quarter consisted of "newly-reclaimed land not formerly under cultivation," and only one-sixteenth of land alienated from declining indigo production.[27] However, even this sudden diversion of land and labor from grain to fiber did not compromise peasant households' food security. As Kerr proceeds to note: "up to this time [1873], the alienation [of rice land] has not so reduced the supply of food as to be injuriously felt."[28]

Jute production resumed its upward trajectory during the 1880s and 1890s, as commodity prices continued to rise, though it was interrupted by another global depression in 1893. The extension of jute acreage during the 1880s reg- istered on the senses of the delta's observers, particularly their sense of smell. The retting of jute stalks in standing water was a smelly process and the stink of rotting fibers particularly repulsed Nabakumar Sen, a lawyer returning to Agartala after a visit to the countryside on a case. He recounted his sufferings to Shambhucharan Mukherjee, who described it in an account of his time at the court of the maharaja of Tipperah:

> The air is filled with the stink of jute—it was impossible to breathe—not a square inch of pure air is to be had in the whole country. . . . It was worse than dung—the jute decomposition. Worse than the vilest animal excreta! he [Sen] exclaimed. My own language! thought I, as I remembered my experience . . . when walking from the boat to the mansion of the Mooker- jees, I was obliged to run for life from the stench.[29]

Beyond causing a stink, the expansion of jute cultivation during the 1880s and 1890s sharply reduced the production of rice. For the first time, parts of the Bengal delta had become reliant on imports of rice. As a colonial report from 1891 noted: "There can be no doubt that the over-production of jute in 1890–91, which led to a serious drop in the price of that commodity, also had the effect of restricting the area devoted to rice. Throughout North and East Bengal there has been a tendency of late years to sacrifice 'the staff of life' to more lucrative crops. Districts which used to feed themselves must now import: stocks are short, and normal prices of grain very high."[30]

The expansion of jute production during the 1890s was also accompanied by a sharp increase in peasant indebtedness. Jute was a more expensive crop to cultivate than rice and required more hired labor in thinning out the fields during April and May and during harvest. Further, while laborers working on the rice harvest were often paid in kind, jute workers had to be paid in cash. Jute production was financed by cash loans to be repaid in cash after the fibers were sold. The substitution of commercial grain with commercial fiber hence entailed increasing dependence on loans and was a critical element in the rise of debt and interest as the major mechanism of expropriating peasant surplus.[31]

Peasant indebtedness did not, however, reach alarming proportions during the 1890s, as they would during the expansion after 1905. Fiber had not yet compromised food security for most peasant households, and much of the debt incurred was to smoothen household subsistence during periods of seasonal scarcity. Even as the agrarian frontier reached its limits and peasant smallholdings fragmented, most jute cultivators were able to extend jute cultivation without compromising subsistence rice production. They did so by increasingly double-cropping jute and aman on lowlands, by transplanting aman seedlings onto farms just cleared of jute. Double-cropping entailed considerably harder work, particularly during September and October, when jute was harvested, aman seedbeds prepared, and aman seedlings transplanted on the same piece of land. This extra labor, however, produced diminished returns: jute plants depleted the soil of nutrients and aman yields were drastically reduced when planted onto lands just cleared of jute. The 1890s thus witnessed the beginnings of a long decline in the productivity of agrarian labor in the delta, which would only reverse with the arrival of green revolution technologies in the 1970s.

The enormous increase in acreage following the price spikes of 1905 registered visually in the agrarian landscape: for the first time in the delta's history, jute acreage exceeded that of aus paddy. This created a powerful visual image of the dominance of fiber over grain: an observer looking over the delta's agrarian landscape between March and August could *see* that jute covered more land then paddy. Gobinda Chandra Das's poem "Jute Song," published in 1914, opened with the lines: "Oh my tasty jute! / You have covered Bengal's crown, Bengal's fields / Where ever I go, I see you / In every village you have an office, in every neighborhood, a mart."[32] During this period, Bengali middle-class intellectuals began speaking of a war between fiber and grain. In 1911 Dwijdas Datta, a lecturer in agriculture at Shibpur engineering college wrote: "Jute is now in competition with paddy. Both are involved in a great war. Who can predict whether our own food-grain will win or whether the foreign-required fiber will win in this Kurukshetra [the great battle recounted in the Mahabharata] and whether we will have to learn to eat jute in order to survive."[33]

The expansion of jute during the 1900s spelled the final end to subsistence rice production in the Bengal delta. Jute cultivators now produced only a portion of the household's food requirements and depended on jute profits to purchase their remaining subsistence from markets. During the 1900s, Bengal became a regular importer of rice from Burma, and the newly created rice tracts of the Irrawaddy delta, Britain's most recent territorial acquisition in South Asia.[34] J. C. Jack described jute cultivators' market-based subsistence strategies in Faridpur in 1916:

> some of the cultivators have given up the growing of their whole food supply on a calculation that it would be more profitable to grow jute and buy grain. . . . Nowadays the cultivator tends to grow jute on all the land fit for the purpose and to grow rice and other food crops only on the remainder. If that remainder is insufficient to supply the family requirements in food, he prefers to buy rather than to reduce the amount of land under jute.[35]

With the end of subsistence rice production, seasonal hunger became a regular feature of the peasant calendar. The aus harvest in July and August was no longer sufficient to tide the household over until the aman harvest of December and January, nor would the aman harvest last until the following aus harvest. Each year, the weeks before a grain harvest were periods of possible hunger, when the cash earnings from jute were necessary to ensure simple survival. Seasonal hunger and debt were closely related, as cultivators became reliant on loans—for the most part from *mahajan*s or professional money-lenders—to finance subsistence purchases from markets. Peasant households' needs for subsistence-smoothing loans peaked during the monsoons, during June and July, before the aus and jute harvests, when grain stocks from the aman harvest and cash earnings from the previous year's jute sales were running low. Peasant households depended on high-interest loans to survive these recurrent periods of seasonal scarcity and to stave off hunger, thus driving up levels of peasant indebtedness to crisis levels.

Colonial officials attributed this spike to "extravagant" and "frivolous" consumption. As F. A. Sachse, the district magistrate of Mymensingh, wrote in 1913: "The *crores* of rupees paid for the raw article have had no visible effect on the manliness or contentedness of the agricultural classes or even on their material prosperity. They have no idea of saving, and in most cases their earnings from jute are frittered away on profitless extravagances long before the next crop is on the ground. By increasing their credit the inflated prices of jute have deepened rather than diminished their general indebtedness."[36] However, simple subsistence rather than "profitless extravagance" drove peasant indebtedness.

Hunger

At the beginning of the 1873 jute season, prices fell sharply. The Long Depression, which has been described as the "first truly international crisis," had set in, resulting in a collapse in global commodity prices that was rapidly communicated to rural jute markets.[37] The price of best-quality jute in Sirajganj markets fell from 5 rupees per maund to 3½ rupees per maund, and the price of low-quality jute in Narayanganj was as low as one rupee a maund.[38] As prices collapsed, cultivators simply allowed a portion of their crops to rot in the field. In Dacca and Mymensingh, the jute commissioners were "informed, everywhere, that quantities of jute grown last season had been left abandoned in the fields."[39] The collector of Tipperah reported that "the rayats left one-fourth of the crops rotting in the fields uncut."[40] Cultivators thus chose to absorb the sunk costs of production rather than incur the additional expenditure of harvesting and preparing nonrenumerative fibers. Even if they prepared jute, cultivators were able to hold on to their fibers in the hope that prices would rise. In January 1873, jute traders reported that "cultivators are now withholding their fibre from the export depots, in the hope that prices may again rally."[41] The delta's peasantry were able to allow crops to rot in the field and to hold fiber back from the market because they did not rely on earnings from jute to stave off hunger.

During the 1870s, seasonal hunger was not yet a feature of peasant life and the enormous expansion of jute had, thus far, been accompanied by an increase in rice cultivation and export. As their granaries held sufficient rice for subsistence, peasant households were not forced to sell jute to stave off hunger. Thus peasant households responded to price collapses by abandoning the standing jute crop and focusing their labor on other crops—notably, aman paddy and rabi crops. In the meantime, they restricted market-based consumption and took on some loans to tide them over difficulty.[42]

The expansion of jute cultivation during the 1880s did not compromise food security. When prices collapsed in 1891, in response to yet another global economic depression, jute cultivators responded in much the same way as they had done in 1872, by allowing a portion of their crop to rot in the fields rather than incurring the additional expenses of harvesting unremunerative fiber.[43] However, by this time, rice production had been reduced to the bare requirements of subsistence, allowing a very small margin in case of failed harvests. While peasant households were insulated from price shocks during years of normal harvests, they were vulnerable to ecological shocks and partial failures in rice production. In August and September 1893, large portions of Brahmanbaria subdivision in Tipperah flooded, when the Gumti—a tributary of the Meghna river system—breached its embankment. This flood was an early indicator of the increased vulnerability of cultivators to external shocks as a result of reduced food production. The floods affected the standing aman crop, destroying fields and severely reducing yields, which, according to government estimates, were about half of what might be expected in a good year. Even in the 1890s, after almost three decades of continually expanding jute cultivation, a portion of Brahmanbaria's aman crop was normally exported. However, the reduced yields of that year meant that rice had to be imported into the delta: in other words, cultivators had to purchase rice from marketplaces. In May of the following year, a serious shortage of grain was felt in the district, or to use the colonial government's euphemism for seasonal hunger, residents in Brahmanbaria experienced "distress."[44] This distress lasted from April until August, when peasant households could harvest aus paddy and jute. During those months, peasant households in Brahmanbaria "managed to subsist by mortgaging their lands, selling some property, or borrowing to get enough to carry them on till the aus paddy and jute are cut."[45]

Peasant households' ability to withstand price shocks was, however, compromised with the adoption of market-based subsistence strategies in the 1900s. The rapid increase in jute cultivation during this period coincided with a diminution in the size of peasant holdings. Peasant households were only able to increase jute production by sacrificing subsistence rice cultivation—a sensible and profitable strategy as long as the terms of trade between jute and rice were favorable to jute produers. However, cultivators' dependence on cash proceeds from jute sales to procure simple subsistence meant that they were no longer able to allow their standing crops to rot or even to hold on to fibers in hopes of better prices. They simply had to sell to stave off starvation. The vulnerabilities of market-dependent livelihoods were cruelly exposed in August 1914, when World War I erupted just as cultivators were preparing to harvest jute.

World War I led to a virtual cessation of all shipping and trade and markets for jute virtually disappeared. When selling resumed in September, prices were absurdly low—two rupees a maund for the best jute, compared to the ten to twelve rupees that ordinary jute sold for during 1913.[46] Fearful of panic spreading through the delta, the colonial government distributed pamphlets through the jute tracts urging cultivators to hold on to their crop, as markets would be restored and prices would rise again. The pamphlet issued on August 15, 1914, stated: "On account of the sudden outbreak of war in Europe buyers have stopped buying jute temporarilybut such a state of things will not last long. . . . If you can wait a little, there will not be any big loss, but if you sell in a hurry, the loss will be great."[47]

However, cultivators were unable to hold on for any length of time. L. Birley, the magistrate of Dacca, toured the jute-growing villages in the district during August and September 1914 to keep an eye on developments. He noticed that cultivators had decided to forego employed labor and exploit household labor: "I was informed by all classes that cultivators were stripping their jute for themselves instead of by hired labour; in many places I saw a man with one or two small boys stripping jute and I think that this statement is correct."[48] Unlike in 1872, cultivators did not—*could not*—abandon their crop in the fields and instead they intensified the exploitation of household labor. Their inability to hold on to the crop was related to hunger. As Birley stated: "the tour had left me with the impression that the raiyats had more staying power than we had credited them with at first, but that they were feeling anxious, and that if they could not sell their jute soon those who did not get a good crop of aus *dhan* would feel the pinch until the time of the harvesting of the winter rice."[49] The most desperate cultivators had already sold their jute at very low prices, but found that they could not buy rice with their returns from jute. Birley spoke to a group of "small cultivators who had sold all their jute at this price [Rs. 2 a maund] and were subsisting on loans of rice from friendly cultivators."[50]

The price collapse of World War I marked the end of a period of peasant prosperity in the Bengal delta and began a process of rapid, thorough, and utter peasant immiseration. After World War I the majority of the delta's jute-cultivating peasantry would be rendered destitute by a combination of unfavorable global markets, ecological shocks such as floods and epidemics, land fragmentation, and a crushing debt burden. Many impoverished cultivators during the 1920s traced the beginnings of their destitution to the market shock of World War I. Shah Abdul Hamid's *Krishak Bilap* or *Peasant Lament*, published in Kishoreganj in 1922, narrates one such case of peasant immiseration, and demonstrates how the market shock at the beginning of World War I provided a decisive push toward a downward spiral into poverty for Bengal's jute-cultivating peasantry.

In 1921, on his way from Kishoreganj to Mymensingh, Shah Abdul Hamid observed the following scene of a tearful farewell at a rural railway station.[51] An elderly man was standing in the entrance to a third-class carriage. His wife and children, with their belongings wrapped up in sheets, were inside the car, behind him. On the platform stood another teary-eyed family, congregated to say farewell. A man was holding on to the elderly man's legs, kneeling on the platform and wailing and weeping. As the train started, he refused to let go, and had to be dragged away. After the train departed, Hamid asked this man what happened. The man replied that that was his brother, who had lost all his possessions and was going away with his family to build a new life in the jungles of Assam. The man proceeded to narrate how his brother was reduced to such destitution:

> In the last German war, when the price of rice was 16 takas a maund and that of jute, one taka, my older brother fell into trouble. He had about fifteen or sixteen mouths to feed in his family and they had to buy rice from the market. Driven by hunger, he went to see a large moneylender—who has over a lakh takas outstanding in loans at any time—in a nearby bazaar. From the moneylender, my brother borrowed six and a half maunds of rice, valued at 100 rupees.[52]

Three years later, he had not repaid anything and the moneylender sent a message that he was on "his way, with papers, to the courthouse in Mymensingh." The brothers caught up with the moneylender at the railway station, with fifty rupees in cash. The debt was renegotiated and, under the new terms, he owed the moneylender three hundred rupees and had mortgaged his farm. Misfortune, however, piled on misfortune. His two oldest sons, who looked after the farm, died of smallpox within a few days of each other. He lost his crop to floods one year. For five years, his debt continued to pile up until finally the moneylender claimed his mortgage—taking away the unfortunate farmer's arable land and, finally, even the tin sheets out of which his house was built. In the end, losing everything, he left with his family for the Assam jungles.[53]

Conclusion

Peasant decisions to grow jute were driven by prices, and booms in jute prices were closely followed by rapid expansions in peasant land and labor devoted to fiber. However, these decisions had significant ramifications. First, they entailed peasant households working considerably harder: sowing both jute and aus with the spring rains, harvesting and preparing both plants in August and September, and preparing and transplanting seedlings while harvesting and preparing jute. Double-cropping jute and aman on the same soil resulted in a further intensification of peasant labor and also to far-diminished yields. Second, it involved considerable risks, particularly the risk of hunger. The decision to pare down rice production to bare subsistence requirements during the 1890s created vulnerabilities to ecological disasters, where shortfalls in rice production could cause starvation. And the fateful decision during the 1900s to adopt market-based subsistence strategies created new vulnerabilities to market shocks, as was tragically revealed at the beginning of World War I.

Why were peasant households willing to rearrange their lives—even risk hunger—for the sake of fiber? The following chapter examines peasant households' desire for cash profits from fiber in terms of consumerist desires, their desire to purchase the myriad consumer commodities that had become available in the delta's rural marketplaces during the nineteenth century. Together, these two chapters constitute an attempt to flesh out economistic images of peasants as profit-driven automatons responding to fluctuations in prices. This chapter has argued that peasant market-responsiveness should not be viewed solely in terms of the cold calculus of prices and profits, but in terms of corporeal peasant bodies laboring on soil and in water and the imperatives of subsistence and hunger. The next chapter will investigate the consumerist desires and fantasies of peasant households.

2

Consumption and Self-Fashioning

THE POLITICS OF PEASANT CONSUMERISM

COLONIAL OFFICIALS and urban Bengali *bhadralok* (salaried professionls) observers of the Bengal delta during the late nineteenth and early twentieth centuries commented extensively on the prosperity of jute cultivators. This prosperity manifested itself through the myriad market-purchased consumer goods on peasant bodies and within and atop peasant homes. Sambhucharan Mukherjee, editor of *Mukherjee's Magazine* and prominent member of the Calcutta intelligentsia, noted in 1887, while floating down the Meghna through Tipperah, "It is something that so many about here are well protected in this cold weather by the cheap cottons and woolens of Europe. The women have all more costly ornaments. . . . Silver clearly predominates. . . . It was all due to jute."[1] A colonial report from 1891 similarly commented: "Owing to improved facilities of export, and the growing value of jute, the standard of comfort in the cultivating class has distinctly advanced during the decade. The raiyat wears better clothes and shoes than his father, eats more abundantly, and sleeps on a more luxurious bed. His cottage is brightly and cheaply lit by a rude kerosene lamp. He kindles his fire with Swedish safety matches which have driven the English product from the market. When ill, he calls in a doctor, and uses quinine and other costly drugs."[2] By the 1900s the list of peasant-consumed articles had expanded to include corrugated iron roofing, English education for sons, and multiple marriages for men. Rising levels of indebtedness and increasing food insecurity, however, meant that consumption was no longer viewed solely as a sign of peasant prosperity but also peasant improvidence. As a colonial official noted in 1913:

The jute cultivator is notoriously improvident. The high prices he has been getting during the past ten years has turned his head altogether and upset his domestic economy. The large amount of cash that he handles has made him extravagant, and his style of living has risen in a remarkable degree. He eats much better, wears better clothes, and lives a cleaner and more sanitary life than before. His house has improved, corrugated-iron has taken the place of thatch, and the compounds and gardens are cleaner. He educates his children in many cases, sending them to English schools, which are fast springing up, and calls in doctors in case of illness. He indulges more frequently in litigation and marries more wives, paying a good deal more for each than before. But all this advance in the ways of living is much more than is warranted by his material prosperity. The money that he gets by the sale of his crop he squanders in a few months, and very often, I am inclined to think, almost universally, he runs into debt before he can sell his next harvest.[30]

The previous chapter examined how peasant decisions to grow jute transformed the delta's landscape of plants, soil, and water and its rhythms of work and leisure and hunger and subsistence. This chapter examines why peasant households chose to rearrange their spaces and lives so thoroughly, even risking hunger, for the sake of fiber. Peasant decisions to grow more jute were driven by their desire for the various goods and services that they could purchase with proceeds from sales of fiber. Instead of the cold calculus of prices and profits, we should examine jute cultivators' hot desires for consumer goods.

Kaminikumar Chakrabarty, an employee of a zamindari estate in Mymensingh, described cultivators' relationship with jute in an 1882 agricultural manual: "These days there is a lot of affection (*ador*) towards jute in this country. For this reason cultivators plant an excessive (*odhik*) quantity of jute. The romantic (*shuromik*) cultivators love (*bhalobasha*) jute so much that they sing songs like 'there is no crop like jute' while working the fields."[4] It is unusual to think of the cultivators' relationship to the plant as one of "love" and "affection," and the phrase seems particularly out of place in an otherwise dry and technical manual on best cultivation practices for various crops. It is hard to explain the peasant ditty "there is no crop like jute"—jute was an onerous plant to cultivate and, as Bengali poets liked to point out, fibers were inedible.[5] Peasants' love of jute was, in fact, the desire for the myriad goods and services purchased from jute earnings in the delta's marketplaces.

Peasant households exchanged fiber for cloth, gold and silver ornaments, umbrellas, copper and brass utensils, corrugated iron sheets, kerosene lamps and oil, Swedish safety matches, cigarettes, gourmet fish, seasonal fruit, confections and sweets in rural marketplaces. Through the consumption of these myriad goods, jute-cultivating households crafted new forms of dress, domesticity, and sociality. However, unlike urban, middle-class South Asians during the same period, peasant men and women did not experiment with Western forms of dress and domesticity. Men and women did not adopt new styles of clothing, peasant families did not move into multiroom dwellings with specialized spaces for sleeping, entertaining and dining, and they did not furnish their homes with chairs on which to sit upright and tables on which to serve meals. As a result, colonial and urban bhadralok observers did not recognize jute cultivators' dress and domesticity as modern and, instead, held paradoxical views of peasant bodies and homes as signifying both prosperity and backwardness. Though crafted out of global flows of commodities, peasant "habitations of modernity" remained firmly rooted in precolonial, agrarian, and Muslim forms of dress, domesticity, and dining.[6]

Consumption-driven peasant self-fashioning extended to property, to peasant households' claims to enhanced rights to the land they tilled. As Andrew Sartori has convincingly demonstrated, property was integral to Bengali Muslim peasant subjectivity.[7] The mechanics of claiming and obtaining property rights were a form of market-based consumption. Property rights were colonial products, created through state legislation, which could be purchased—occasionally through expensive litigation against zamindars—in the form of stamped paper in subdivisional courtrooms and revenue offices. This chapter revisits the antirent movement, whose beginnings coincided with the jute boom of the early 1870s, in terms of the peasant consumption of enhanced property rights. I reinterpret colonial and bhadralok complaints of peasant litigiousness—"he indulges more frequently in litigation"—in terms of the consumption of colonial legal services. The consumption of property rights was not solely about economic security against zamindari depredation, but was also critical to the project of fashioning the idealized image of a property-holding peasantry.

The importance that peasant households attached to consumption was revealed in their resistance to the Swadeshi program of economic boycott of 1905–6. The Swadeshi movement arrived in the Bengal delta in the form of the forcible prevention of the sale and purchase of imported commodities in rural bazaars and fairs by urban, middle-class Swadeshi activists. This nationalist program coincided with the boom in jute prices of 1905, a period of heightened consumption. Jute cultivators resisted Swadeshi activists, sometimes forcefully, leading to clashes between peasants and nationalists in bazaars and fairs in Tipperah, Jamalpur, and Dacca. Historians of the Swadeshi movement have described these clashes between mostly Muslim peasants and mostly Hindu Swadeshi activists as "communal"—that is, primarily informed by religious difference. Historians have also viewed peasant consumption purely in economic terms: imported commodities were cheaper than locally made products and Bengal's peasantry resisted the boycott as it raised their cost of living. I argue that peasant resistance to Swadeshi activists was neither communal nor economistic: they were vigorous attempts to protect rural markets and fairs as spaces of *pleasurable* and *enjoyable* consumption.

Before embarking on a discussion of jute cultivators' consumption-driven self-fashioning and the politics of peasant consumerism, it will be useful to describe spaces of consumption. Jute cultivators purchased these new goods and services primarily from three kinds of marketplaces: *hat*s or occasional markets held once or twice a week in villages, *mela*s or annual fairs commemorating religious festivals, and *ganje*s, riverine and railway market towns that served as wholesale centers.[8] Peasant homesteads were generally within walking distance of several hats, and many peasant men—never women—frequented multiple hats. Itinerant traders traveled from hat to hat selling regular household necessities: salt, spices, cloth, utensils, kerosene oil, mustard oil, fish, fruit, grain, and vegetables. Peasant men did not just visit hats to purchase such necessities, but also to socialize. As J. C. Jack wrote about the Faridpur cultivator, "he does not ordinarily go to buy anything, but to talk with friends and neighbours."[9]

Melas or annual fairs were far larger and more vibrant events. They usually accompanied religious festivals, such as the bathing festival in Nangalband near Narayanganj, the celebration of Janmasthami, the birth of Krishna, in Jamalpur, and the death anniversary or *urs* of Sufi pirs, such as the Nekmard fair in Dinajpur. While the hats dealt in daily household necessities, melas focused on durable goods and exotic items. For instance, at the Neckmard mela at Dinajpur, held annually in April, traders sold oxen from Purnea, ponies from the Bhutan hills, horses from Kabul, elephants from Assam, and even camels from the northwest: "people from all parts of Northern India frequent the fair. Mughuls and Afghans bring dried fruits, embroidered saddlery, daggers, swords, looking-glasses, and so on. Sikhs may be seen manufacturing combs out of ivory and sandal-wood. The hill tribes bring down blankets, woolen cloths, walnuts, musk, ponies, and yak tails. The Nepalis sell *kukris* (heavy bill-hooks, the national weapon of the Gurkhas) and *chirda* leaf. Quantities of real and imitation coral beads are exposed for sale by the bankers of Dinajpur."[10]

Market towns or ganjes were spaces for wholesale trade, where itinerant traders purchased cloth, kerosene oil, rice, and other consumer articles that they retailed in rural hats. Certain retail commodities were only available at the market towns, rather than in rural bazaars. The *Mymensingh District Gazetteer* noted in 1915: "shops in the more important marts . . . sell English glass, mirrors, crockery, writing materials, medicines, lamps, stores, matches, cigarettes."[11] Further, legal, educational, and medical services were only available in small towns, in the courts, lawyers' and doctors' practices, and English-language schools that proliferated in mofussil towns as the colonial state penetrated deeper into the delta.

The first section of this chapter examines the peasant consumption of property rights during the antirent movement of the 1870s. The creation and consumption of state-legislated property rights were integral to projects of peasant self-fashioning and the first jute boom created opportunities for jute cultivators to enjoy the enhanced property rights that had been created by the Rent Act of 1859. The second section explores the consumption of myriad consumer goods in hats, melas, and ganjes, demonstrating the ways in which peasant men and women crafted distinctively agrarian, Muslim, and Bengali practices of dress, domesticity, and dining through the exchange of jute for machine-made cloth, metals, kerosene oil, and so forth in global commodity markets. The third section of this chapter examines peasant resistance to the Swadeshi program of economic boycott, arguing that the peasant resistance to Swadeshi attacks on their consumption of imported goods from rural hats and melas demonstrates the importance peasant households attached to practices of pleasurable consumption. The final section examines the crisis of World War I on peasant consumerism through episodes of peasants looting hats in protest of high prices of essentials during 1917–18.

Property

Colonial officials viewed the rise in peasant litigation accompanying the first jute boom of the early 1870s as a sign of prosperity. The collector of Bogra noted in 1873: "perhaps the most tangible evidence of the easy circumstances of the people is to be found in the rapidly increasing number of petty complaints brought before the courts."[12] Litigiousness was perceived as a form of frivolous entertainment, through which peasants enlivened their dull, rural existence. According to the collector of Tipperah, "the absurd quarrels among the people, which result in the most wantonly false charges at the police station, show they must take a positive pleasure in the progress of the case, quite apart from any idea of getting justice or obtaining any solid advantage. . . . I can only suppose that the investigation of a case is a pleasurable break in the monotony of a dull life; but it is at least to be regretted that choice should be made of so extravagant a diversion."[13]

Rather than an "extravagant diversion," litigation was critical to peasant self-fashioning. During the antirent movement of the 1870s, it was a means to access enhanced property rights legislated by the colonial state in the Rent Act of 1859. Continuous peasant struggles to obtain more secure rights to the land they tilled during the nineteenth and twentieth centuries were an ongoing attempt by jute-cultivating households to attain an idealized peasant selfhood. The paradox of property in the Bengal delta was that, while zamindari rents were not particularly onerous, and zamindari power was limited in most of the delta, peasants' political energies were focused on property and the rights of tenancy.[14] This paradox suggests that the peasant struggle for property rights was not solely about protection from zamindari depredation but was instead driven by a different set of desires. Andrew Sartori has argued that a Lockean conception of property, based on the principle that labor constituted claims to property, underpinned discourses of peasant Muslim-ness. I follow Sartori in taking seriously the place of property in the Bengal peasantry's ideals of selfhood, that to obtain secure property rights was to pursue an idealized conception of rights to the land they tilled.

Sartori ascribes a "resonance" or a "concatenation" between the Lockean forms of property created by the colonial state and "agrarian political energies."[15] This resonance between the colonial state's legislation and peasant politics is best understood in terms of the peasant consumption of colonial legal services. Unlike many subaltern communities, the Bengal peasantry did not take issue with the colonial state's authority to create, distribute, and guarantee property rights. Instead, peasant political energy was directed toward obtaining property rights and toward legislative reforms of property law. Property deeds printed on paper stamped and sealed with the judicial authority of the colonial state were among the few written documents owned and closely guarded by largely illiterate peasant households. Property was conceived as a state-constituted product that peasant households consumed by purchasing judicial stamps or, if their claims to property were resisted by zamindars, through expensive litigation. These legal expenditures were financed by fiber.

Colonial historians have tended to examine the relationship between the colonial law and agrarian society as a supply-side phenomenon, in terms of colonial debates on property rights and the penetration of colonial laws and legal institutions into the agrarian countryside.[16] Prior to the rise of jute, the East India Company state was not interested in providing legally codified property rights to peasant producers. The Permanent Settlement of 1793 focused on relations between zamindars and the company, allowing zamindars absolute freedom in their dealings with peasant tenants. Further, the legal costs of initiating property-related lawsuits were prohibitively high. Hence, during the early colonial period, peasant households responded to zamindari depredation through extralegal measures, such as moving out of a particular zamindar's estate, and not by taking recourse to courts of law.[17]

During the second half of the nineteenth century, colonial property law was made more relevant and accessible to cultivators, as the colonial state introduced new ideas of property into their agrarian dominions in South Asia. The Rent Act of 1859 set limits to zamindari powers to enhance rents or evict peasant households. At the same time, the colonial state also reduced court fees and stamp duties and expanded courthouses in the delta's smaller mofussil towns. After 1864, provincial civil courts—rather than the local Revenue Department—were empowered to adjudicate rent suits.[18] The Rent Act of 1859, the expansion of courtrooms and judges in the countryside, and the lowered costs of litigation constituted a broad set of supply-side measures that made property law accessible—*consumable*—by the delta's peasantry. Equally significantly, these supply-side reforms had to be accompanied by the peasant households' ability to finance the consumption of property. The influx of cash into peasant households during the first jute boom of the 1870s created an effective demand for colonial property rights.

In May 1873 peasant smallholders in the Yusufshahi Pargana of Pabna district organized themselves into an "agrarian league" and refused to pay their zamindars' demand for enhanced rent. Yusufshahi Pargana probably had one of the highest densities of jute cultivation in all of Bengal. Yusufshahi was in the Sirajganj subdivision, close to the port city Sirajganj, at the time the "greatest jute mart in eastern Bengal." It was estimated that of the 192 square miles sown with jute in Pabna during 1872–73, 123 square miles was in Sirajganj subdivision.[19] Within two months, agrarian leagues had emerged throughout Pabna and, over the following years, across Bengal, as cultivators organized themselves into agrarian leagues and resisted landlords' attempts to increase rents.[20] The rent-disputes were brought to a close only in 1885, with the introduction of a new Tenancy Act by the colonial state, granting cultivators enhanced security of tenure and further protection against rent enhancements.

For the most part, cultivators conducted their antirent struggle through colonial legal institutions. The formation of an Agrarian League in Yusufshahi was preceded and probably inspired by the conclusion of a court case in Sirajganj, where a peasant household had successfully sued against the landlords' rent increases. The primary function of the Pabna Agrarian League was to raise subscriptions to support members in legal disputes. Each of the districts convulsed by the antirent movement witnessed steep increases in rent suits during the period.[21] These suits were conducted under Act X of the Rent Act of 1859, which had created the legal category of "occupancy ryots" who enjoyed greater security of tenure and protection against rent enhancements. Peasants brought lawsuits against landlords attempting to raise rents or, alternatively, zamindars instituted suits against peasants who refused to pay enhanced rents. The outcome of the rent disputes turned on whether the peasants in question were entitled to the legal status of occupancy ryot under Act X.

K. K. Sengupta, the historian of the Pabna disturbances, ascribes an important role in the movement to a group of "substantial ryots," and proceeds to define that group in terms of its ability to make "huge profits through the cultivation of jute."

> The leadership of the league, therefore, was provided by men of considerable means such as petty landlords . . . village headmen . . . and jotedars . . . This disgruntled section of the rural gentry found a large number of supporters amongst the occupancy ryots described by Sir Richard Temple, "as the most influential section of ryots." Some of the occupancy ryots made huge profits through the cultivation of jute, a cash crop which only the substantial ryots could afford to cultivate. . . . These substantial ryots were sufficiently well-to-do to offer an effectual resistance to the zemindars.[22]

The role of the substantial, "sufficiently well-to-do," jute cultivating peasantry across the jute tracts of eastern Bengal was underpinned by their ability to finance expensive and lengthy lawsuits. From the peasant perspective, litigation was successful. The costs of litigation drained zamindars' resources quicker than that of the peasantry. K. K. Sengupta argues that, "the landlords who had enough resources in 1875 to harass their tenants in the civil courts had become by 1878 quite impoverished." The agrarian leagues were effectively pooling jute cultivators' resources, and the peasants' stoppage of all rents to zamindars while cases were pending had the desired effect.[23]

The colonial government had a different interpretation of the place of jute in the rent disputes of the 1870s. They did not see fiber as the source of finance for peasant consumption of legal services, but as forming the basis of conflicts between zamindars and ryots. The official theory of the rent disputes was that landlords were attempting to raise rents to gain an increasing share of the rising prosperity of the cultivators. In the words of the commissioner of Chittagong Division, "the rise which has taken place during the last few years in the price of produce and in the value of land, combined with the absence of any well-defined rules to regulate the rate of rent has caused a feeling of uncertainty to rise, which has alienated the tenantry from their landlords and embittered relations."[24] Act X of 1859 specified that increases to rents had to be passed through the civil courts of the government and peasants were aware of this stipulation. Hence, all attempts to raise rents made their way into the courtroom. However, while Act X allowed for rates to be enhanced because of the rising value of the produce, it was vague about the extent to which rents could be enhanced. Hence, the cases lingered in the courts. In the meantime, peasants organized to stop all payments of rent and an uneasy tension prevailed between landlords and tenants. This chain of events is neatly captured by the lieutenant governor of Bengal's three-step model:

> 1st- That there are large disputes pending between zemindars and ryots regarding the degree in which rent may be enhanced by reason of the increase during recent years in the value of the produce of land;
>
> 2nd- That when these disputes become embittered, then, besides the question of enhancement, other questions become involved, such as the levy of certain cesses, the payment of alleged arrears, the past rate of rent, the area of actual holdings—the end of all this being that the payment of rent altogether in some places is likely to be held in abeyance for some time;
>
> 3rd- That under such circumstances zemindars have sometimes attempted, or may attempt, to collect rents by force, which attempts are forcibly resisted,—the result being breaches of the peace.[25]

The colonial diagnosis of the issue as one of vagueness in property laws led to a lengthy discussion in bureaucratic circles about necessary reforms to agrarian property rights in Bengal. In 1881 the colonial government circulated a draft Tenancy Bill, further enhancing security of tenure and offering even greater protection against rent enhancements to the occupancy ryot. Zamindars reacted angrily, proclaiming that the new bill would destroy them.[26] The Tenancy Act of 1885 curbed the zamindar's powers vis-à-vis their tenants and, as Sugata Bose has argued, brought to an end the rent and revenue offensive against the peasantry of Bengal. From 1885 onward, zamindari rents would no longer be the primary mechanism of surplus extraction from the Bengal peasantry.[27]

By the end of the nineteenth century, the majority of the delta's jute cultivators fit into the legal category of "permanently settled occupancy ryot," and thus possessed legal protections against rent enhancements and evictions by zamindars. Attaining the legal category of property rights was not solely about gaining economic security, but also about fulfilling an idealized notion of peasant selfhood premised on secure property rights to the land they labored on. Further, and more significantly, peasant households fashioned themselves into property-holding subjects through acts of consumption: enhanced property rights were a colonial legal product that was consumed through expensive and lengthy lawsuits financed by jute profits.

Dress, Dwellings, Diet

For colonial and bhadralok observers of the agrarian delta, peasant prosperity was apparent in their dress, dwellings, and diets. W. W. Hunter's *Statistical Account of Tippera* stated that "the general prosperity of the people is shown in their houses, in their food and clothing."[28] Regarding cultivators in Mymensingh, Hunter noted: "The people of the District are making rapid progress toward improvements of many kinds. A common husbandman now-a-days is much better dressed, has fewer unsatisfied wants, and more knowledge of what tends to promote his comfort, than people of his class had twenty years ago."[29] The collector of Noakhali similarly associated prosperity with clothing and housing: "This improvement [in material conditions of cultivators] is seen both in their dress and in their dwellings."[30]

These "improvements" in dress, dwellings, and diets consisted of the increased expenditure in hats, melas, and ganjes on imported cloth, metal utensils, corrugated iron roofing, kerosene lamps, gourmet fish, seasonal fruits, and the occasional confectionery. Yet, these "improvements" did not entail experiments with Western forms of dress and domesticity. Despite the increased consumption of various commodities, peasant households' clothing, housing, and food retained strong elements of continuity with the past. Even as it was constructed out of the consumption of global commodities, the peasant habitation of modernity was resolutely agrarian and local.

Clothing

Manchester cloth or, in the language of colonial trade statistics "European piece goods," was the most significant commodity imported into the Bengal delta. The first jute boom, sparked by the Crimean War, was accompanied by a sharp spike in Calcutta's cloth imports, which increased in value from .5 million to 8.25 million rupees between 1855 and 1875. While not all of this increase was attributable to consumption in the jute tracts, jute-growing districts consumed more cloth per capita than the rest of the province.[31] The second jute boom of the 1880s and 1890s followed the expansion of the railway network into the delta. Railway traffic in European piece goods between Calcutta and the delta increased sharply, at an average annual rate of 11.5 percent on the Northern Bengal State Railway and 7.1 percent on the Eastern Bengal State Railway between 1882–83 and 1891–92, and an average rate of 5.6 percent on the Dacca State Railway between 1886–87 and 1891–92.[32] The final and decisive jute boom of the 1900s was not accompanied by a comparable increase in imports of Manchester cloth: the delta's cloth imports increased at an annual rate of only 1.5 percent between 1905–6 and 1912–13.[33] This was partly due to the Swadeshi boycott of cloth, but also because jute earnings were being invested in other consumer goods. By the 1910s peasant expenditures on clothes, largely Manchester cloth, accounted for a full 10 percent of peasant households' annual expenditure, regardless of whether the family was living in "comfort" or "extreme indigence."[34]

The increased consumption of cloth did not, however, result in a revolution in peasant fashion. Both before and after the jute boom, peasant costumes remained largely unchanged: a *lungi* or sarong with a *chadar* or shawl for men and a *sari* for women. Unlike urban South Asians, men had not adopted trousers and buttoned shirts and women did not wear petticoats and blouses along with saris. Instead of a change in fashion, the increased consumption of cloth meant that peasant men and women owned more changes of clothes, and were better able to replace worn and torn clothing. When colonial officials or urban bhadralok noted that peasant wealth is reflected in clothing, they were not speaking about new forms of clothing but newer, cleaner, and less-worn clothes. The absence of change in peasant fashion meant different things for peasant men and women. For peasant men, it implied the wider adoption of a distinctive agrarian Muslim form of dress, associated with the Faraizi movement. The lungi differentiated the delta's Muslims from Hindus, who wear the sarong as a *dhuti*, with the cloth passed between the legs.[35] Haji Shariatallah, the founder of the Faraizi movement, advised Muslims to wear the dhuti without passing the cloth between the legs—that is, as a lungi—because it would facilitate the motions of Islamic prayer. From the colonial perspective, the lungi became a signifier of Muslim difference from Europeans: "externally a *Faraizi* may be known by the fashion of wrapping his *dhuti* or waistcloth round his loins without crossing it between his legs, so as to avoid any resemblance to a Christian's trousers."[36]

For women, the absence of change in clothing accompanied the lack of change in their mobility. Urban women adopted petticoats and blouses and new ways of wearing the sari to appear in public spaces. Peasant women's dress—*sans* the blouse and petticoat—drew prurient and scandalized commentary from the colonial male gaze: "The ordinary dress of a woman . . . is the *sari*, a long piece of cloth fastened round the waist so as to form a petticoat and also a covering for the upper part of the body. It has the great advantage of being cool, but at times leaves little to the imagination, and it is no matter for surprise that men should not like their womenfolk to appear freely in public in quite exiguous attire."[37] B. C. Allen makes an important point: peasant women's mobility was restricted even as jute cultivation expanded. Peasant women's labor, which included threshing rice, stripping jute, and the like, was conducted within the shielded and protected space of the homestead. Peasant women did not visit hats and melas and, when they visited family, they traveled in the covered portions of boats, ox-drawn carts, or, rarely, in palanquins. The increased consumption of cloth meant that peasant women owned more and less-worn and torn saris; they did not, however, own clothes that enabled them to appear in public.

The more substantive changes in peasant fashion were not in clothing, but in ornaments for women and umbrellas and hairstyles for men. Colonial sources noted that increased peasant wealth resulted in an upgrade in women's ornaments—from *lac* to brass and copper, from brass and copper to silver, and from silver to gold. The collector of Bogra observed in the 1870s that ornaments of "lead, glass or shell" had been replaced by "brass ornaments and silver ear-rings." Shambhu Charan Mookerjee stated that in Tipperah in 1882, "the women have all more costly ornaments. . . . Silver clearly predominates."[38] The *Tippera District Gazetteer* stated in 1915: "Gold ornaments have been substituted for silver in the houses of the upper classes, and silver for those of bell-metal or brass."[39] Colonial sources do not, however, indicate whether the use of precious metals in ornaments was accompanied by a change in jewelry design.

The widespread adoption of umbrellas was another sign of peasant fashion. Beyond providing protection from the rain, umbrellas were regular accessories for peasant men in public—at hats and in small towns. The collector of Bogra commented in 1875: "Well-to-do *rayats* constantly walk about with umbrellas."[40] Calcutta's imports of umbrellas increased sharply during the 1880s and reached 3 million umbrellas in 1893–94. Imports tapered off as umbrellas began to be assembled in Bengal from imported fittings of steel ribs and cloth.[41] Peasant expenditure on umbrellas was noted in anticonsumerist pamphlets and poems published during the 1920s, which I discuss in greater detail in chapter 4. One such tract urged cultivators not to spend five or six rupees on an umbrella from Ralli Bros but to make their own umbrellas at home.[42] These anticonsumerist tracts also dwelt on peasant men's hairstyles, castigating them for spending money on fancy "Albert cuts" in towns rather than getting cheaper haircuts from the village barber. The Albert cut was a distinctive hairstyle that became popular in towns and villages following the visit of Prince Albert Victor to South Asia and Calcutta during the winter of 1889–90.

Despite these changes in peasant fashion—newer and cleaner clothing, gold and silver jewelry, umbrellas, and hairstyles—to Europeans, peasant men and women often appeared poorly dressed. As the *Dacca District Gazetteer* commented: "Well-to-do Muhammadans often spend a good deal on their wardrobe, but fortunately the villagers have not yet become imbued with any desire to squander money on dress and an old man whose clothes would disgrace a scarecrow will sometimes admit that he has sold his jute for as much as Rs. 500."[43] In reality, though peasants were spending a considerable portion of their income on clothing, peasant dress was not recognizably modern to European eyes. Instead of experimenting with European fashions with their increased purchases of machine-made imported cloth, jute-cultivating men and women adopted forms of dress particular and specific to Bengali and Muslim peasants.

Housing

Even as they recognized peasant homes as indicative of prosperity, colonial officials were struck by the bareness of their interiors. The *Tippera District Gazetteer* stated: "Cultivators even when well to do have still less [than zamindars]. A box or two to hold their clothes, a wooden stool, some mats on which they sleep on the mud floor and that is all."[44] Peasant belongings appeared "cheap and tawdry" to colonial officials, as the *Mymensingh District*

Gazetteer also noted: "The tin lamps, the earthenware pots, the wooden *hoo-kahs*, the two penny half penny ornaments and toys which he brings back from the *hat* are all of the most *tawdry and cheap* manufacture."[45] These absences were not indicative of poverty, but rather the peculiarity of tastes. J. C. Jack ascribes the bareness of peasant homes to aesthetic preferences:

> A wealthy Bengali . . . has as little furniture as a member of the poorer classes. Cupboards are rarely to be found even in the houses of the most wealthy; linen is usually kept in boxes or chests, often richly decorated with brass work. A Bengali always eats off the ground, from a sheet or mat and squatting on his haunches. He will not eat off a table. . . . If he sits on a chair at all, he selects a very low stool, for to sit on a chair of the ordinary size is to him not at all restful; when he is tired and requires a rest he will squat on his haunches. . . . To beds there is not the same objection, but of all articles of furniture bedsteads are the most expensive and cheap bedsteads are of little use. In truth the absence of internal decoration and of furniture is not a question of money, but a question of taste. The wealthiest Bengali who is untouched by foreign influences keeps as bare a house as his poorer neighbours and eschews ceilings, painted walls and furniture as completely as they do.[46]

As was the case with peasant fashion, colonial observers did not recognize the considerable peasant expenditure within and atop their homes as modern. As with peasant clothing, these expenditures had created forms of domesticity firmly rooted in the agrarian past and did not entail adopting and adapting new forms of domestic life. Unlike urban South Asians, the delta's peasantry did not construct multiroom homes, with specialized spaces for different activities. The basic design of the peasant home remained unchanged: one-room dwellings constructed around an internal courtyard, or *uthan*. The dwellings consisted of a frame of timber posts and beams supporting a sloping roof, and the number of dwellings varied according to household wealth. Only one of the dwellings was specialized—the kitchen with earthen hearths—while the rest were multipurpose spaces for sleeping, storage, and entertaining.

Peasant households, however, had invested considerably in the interiors and exteriors of their homes, through purchases of new kinds of construction materials, utensils, and indoor illumination. Strikingly, these peasant-purchased commodities were largely metallic: copper, brass, or enameled iron utensils, corrugated iron roofs, tin lamps, and tin or brass trunks. Colonial sources generally ascribe cultivators' preference for metal in terms of

TABLE 2.1. Average Annual Increase in Metals and Minerals Imported into Eastern Bengal, Northern Bengal, and Dacca Blocks by Rail, 1900–1901 to 1905–1906

Metals/Minerals	Percentage increase
Wrought brass/Brass manufactures	8.0%
Wrought iron and steel	27.7%
Iron and steel manufactures	21.8%
Kerosene oil	28.0%

Compiled from Government of Bengal, *Reports on the Trade Carried by Rail and River in Bengal in the Official Year 1900–1901 to 1911–12*, Calcutta, 1901 to 1912. It is not possible to prepare one table on the basis of these reports for two reasons. First, as the tables show, the categories of metals are altered. Second, the partition of Bengal into Eastern Bengal and Assam in 1905 means that the geographic categories of trade are changed.

TABLE 2.2. Average Annual Increase in Metals and Minerals Imported into Eastern Bengal and Assam by Rail and River, 1906–1907 to 1911–1912

Metals/Minerals	Percentage increase
Metals, brass manufactures	22.1%
Metals, wrought iron and steel, bars, sheets, girders	37.8%
Metals, wrought iron and steel, other manufactures, including cutlery	31.4%
Kerosene oil	4.4%

convenience and utility, rather than aesthetics: corrugated iron roofs were fireproof and easier to maintain than thatching, metal utensils were easier to clean, tin lamps burning kerosene oil provided brighter light. Tables 2.1 and 2.2 tabulate the annual average increase of imports of metal and minerals by rail into the jute tracts during the first decade of the twentieth century. Imports, however, had begun much earlier. The traffic in metals on the Northern Bengal State Railway had increased at an annual average of 13.1 percent between 1882 and 1892, by 16.8 percent on the Eastern Bengal Railway between 1882 and 1888, and by 10.8 percent on the Dacca State Railway between 1886 and 1892.

The first jute boom of the 1870s led to peasant investments in their homes. The Collector of Noakhali described the improvements in peasant housing in 1875: "Houses, which used to be built of straw, bamboos, and reeds on low marshy lands, are now constructed on well-raised lands and of better and more durable materials."[47] These materials did not yet include metal but rather higher quality timber and thatching. A rural poem from a later period associated jute prosperity with timber frames: "Say brother, there is no crop like jute / The one who deals in jute has seven huts / And his four-roofed house is built with strong Joanshahi timber."[48]

Corrugated iron began to be used during the second and third jute booms, from the 1890s onward, and by the early twentieth century, corrugated iron roofing became the definitive symbol of peasant prosperity. The survey and settlement report for Tipperah of 1916 states: "Though rice covers a larger area than jute, jute is really the most important crop. All cultivators depend on it entirely for comfort and largely to provide the money to purchase rice. The extension of its cultivation has increased the prosperity of tenants greatly and the spread of *expensive houses roofed with corrugated iron clearly shows this*."[49] The subinspector of madrassas in Sirajganj, Mokhtar Ahmed Siddiqi, wrote in his pamphlet on the history of Sirajganj: "The jute trade has improved the conditions of ordinary people so much that there is no poverty in these parts. In every village and in every neighborhood *we see many tin houses—only because of jute*."[50] Gobindo Chandra Das, an unknown poet from Sirajganj, rhymed in his 1914 poem, the *Jute Song*: "Those who did not have straw hovels / now their houses are covered / four-cornered, eight-cornered, shiny tin."[51]

Metal utensils entered peasant households earlier, from the first jute boom onward. The collector of Bogra observed in 1875: "Those who used to do very well with earthen pots and pans now have vessels of brass and copper. Vendors of these vessels say they now sell as many at a single fair as they formerly sold at three."[52] By the early twentieth century, copper and brass utensils were commonplace in peasant homes. The *Tippera District Gazetteer* noted: "For cooking and eating, they use brass and bell-metal pots and pans, plates, and bowls of enameled iron and cheap but ugly imported pottery."[53] Further, the absence of metal was a clear sign of poverty, as J. C. Jack commented on Faridpur: "in the poorer homesteads the most obvious signs of poverty will be holes in the walls of the huts and the absence of brass plates, pots and jars."[54]

Tin lamps were yet another form of metal that had become commonplace in peasant homes. Kerosene lamps had become ubiquitous during the late nineteenth century, and all peasant households—from the rich to the poor—used kerosene oil for illumination.[55] "His cottage is brightly and cheaply lit by a rude kerosene lamp. He kindles his fire with Swedish safety matches which have driven the English product from the market," a colonial report in 1891 noted.[56] The *Dacca District Gazetteer* commented: "For lamps the cultivators use little tin pots filled with kerosene or earthenware saucers with the wick floating in the oil."[57] Beyond lamps, the tin cans used for storing and transporting kerosene oil were another source of metals introduced into peasant homes. Empty cans were widely used as receptacles for a variety of household goods and a metalworking industry had emerged that reshaped oilcans into domestic goods. According to the *Mymensingh District Gazetteer*: "The only new industry is the manufacture of steel trunks painted in gaudy colours which are so conspicuous in the shops of Mymensingh and Netrakona. Tinsmiths in the same shops also make lamps, chiefly from empty kerosene tins. It is impossible to imagine what people did without these tins when only local vegetable oils were in use. Besides providing receptacles for paint, lime, grain, and all sorts of other commodities, they are made into furniture, roofs, and walls of houses and boats."[58]

The written archives' silence on the place of metal in peasant aesthetics means that it is difficult to conclude that the increased consumption of metal in peasant domestic spaces constituted a form of metallic modernity, akin to that described by Nira Wickremasinghe in reference to the consumption of sewing machines, bicycles, and gramophone players in colonial Sri Lanka.[59] Whether or not peasant dwellings constituted a metallic modernity, they were certainly a habitation of modernity, specific to peasants in the agrarian delta, crafted out of the consumption of metals financed by sales of fiber. As with peasant fashion, colonial commentators did not recognize peasant homes as modern. Colonial officials and middle-class Bengali observers were struck by the changes that had not taken place rather than those that had: they focused on the absence of chairs and tables and the lack of specialized rooms for sleeping and entertaining.

Food

As with peasant clothing and housing, peasant diets remained largely unchanged even as jute-cultivating households purchased more of their foods from markets. The continuity in peasant diets was noted in the *Tippera District Gazetteer* in 1915: "Since then [1881] there has not been much change in the food of the people, but in other respects the standard of comfort is rising."[60] Peasant meals were much the same in the 1900s as they had been in the 1800s, based on rice, vegetables, fish, and spices—with milk and meat as occasional luxuries. During the 1870s the peasant diets consisted "chiefly of common rice, pulses, *kachu* (a species of yam), vegetables of different sorts, salt, oil, fish, and occasionally milk. Milk is more a luxury than an ordinary article of food."[61] This was unchanged in the 1910s: "The peasant has three meals a day. In the early morning the rice (*pantha bhat*) left over from the preceding day is eaten cold with a little salt and some burnt chilies and perhaps a little fruit if in season. The midday and evening meals have rice as their foundation and with this is taken dal of different kinds, or fish, or vegetables. Milk is a luxury and not one of the staple foods."[62] Even as peasant households purchased more of their foods from markets—particularly their main staple, rice—peasant diets did not experience anything like the changes in working-class diets in Europe, where sugar had become a major calorie source.[63]

The expansion of jute did accompany the rise of a new intoxicant, tobacco, though tobacco never displaced the primary intoxicant almost universally consumed by peasant men and women—the betel nut and betel leaf. Tobacco consumption was already widespread during the 1870s: in Noakhali "many men, and some women and children, smoke; but the habit is not universal in the District. The stimulants, betel-leaf and betel-nut are in common use."[64] With the expansion of jute cultivation during the nineteenth century, however, peasant households, particularly men, switched from smoking homegrown or locally grown lower-quality tobacco to smoking higher-quality Rangpur tobacco.[65] Further, peasant households were smoking manufactured cigarettes rather than loose tobacco from hookahs: the *Tippera District Gazetteer* noted the "increased demand for crockery, cigars, cigarettes and perfumery."[66] Eastern Bengal and Assam's imports of manufactured and unmanufactured tobacco rose sharply during the 1900s, increasing by an annual average of close to 50 percent between 1905 and 1912. Tea, on the other hand, had not made substantial inroads into peasant households by the early twentieth century, despite the concerted colonial campaign to introduce South Asians to Britain's favorite beverage. The *Tippera District Gazetteer* stated that, "tea is now taken in the towns, and outside them by well-to-do persons," but rarely consumed by peasant men and women.[67]

The most significant changes in peasant diets were not in the structure of meals, the primary sources of calories, or intoxicants, but in the occasional expenditures on specialty, gourmet foods: confectioneries, seasonal fruits, bottled drinks, and luxury fish. These purchases were made during visits to rural hats and annual melas and were more likely impulse purchases rather than planned expenditures. Interestingly, such treats were rarely consumed at the hat, but were brought home and shared with the entire family. J. C. Jack wrote that, in Faridpur: "Even if he buys some soda-water or lemonade or sweetmeats, of which he and his children are inordinately fond, neither he nor they will consume them at the market. If he buys fruit, mangoes or lichis, one or two may be eaten at the market." Purchases of such treats spiked during harvest time or after sales of jute, when peasant households were flush with cash: "In the harvest season nine out of every ten cultivators returning from the market will carry an earthen jar full of sweetmeats and at least a pair of the best fish obtainable, whatever may be their price; if the large jack-fruit, which is not unlike a melon and a great favourite with the cultivator is in season, he will carry home two or three also."[68]

These purchases of "the best fish obtainable" are noteworthy, because colonial commentators maintained that most of the fish consumed by peasant households was not bought in markets but was caught by men and boys of the household. Peasant men purchased prized varieties, usually caught by professional fishermen in the larger rivers, rather than the varieties available to amateur fishermen in ponds and streams near the homestead. Increased peasant purchases of fish can be traced back to the first jute boom: in Tipperah, fish prices rose in the 1870s due to the "improved condition of the people, and the larger demand for fish which has arisen in consequence."[69] Jute cultivators' demand for prized varieties of fish would keep their prices high. In his account of Sirajganj, Mokhtar Ahmed Siddiqi complained that jute cultivators were driving up prices of *hilsa*, the quintessential Bengali fish, beyond the affordability of salaried professionals: "They [jute cultivators] pay one taka, one and half takas for a simple *hilsa*, while bhadraloks, salaried men and businessmen do not dare to pay more than 10 or 11 annas for the same fish."[70]

The consumption of bottled drinks, sweets, seasonal fruit, and luxury fish was a form of gourmet consumption, more concerned with enjoyment and pleasure than the simple fulfillment of caloric needs. These were impulsive purchases, prompted by vendors cries and by the sights and smells of fish, fruits, and confections at hats and melas. These purchases transformed rural markets and fairs into spaces of pleasurable consumption, where peasant men and boys indulged in impulsive purchases of luxury foods. The significance of hats and melas as spaces of pleasurable consumption was revealed during the Swadeshi movement, when peasant households vigorously defended these spaces from Swadeshi activists' occasionally violent attempts to prevent the sale of imported goods at marketplaces.

Swadeshi, 1905–6

The colonial state's administrative decision to partition the province of Bengal into two halves, Bengal and Eastern Bengal and Assam, was met with vigorous opposition among the mostly Hindu urban bhadralok in Calcutta and in eastern Bengal's small towns. The urban bhadralok perceived the partition decision as an attempt to cripple Bengal culturally, politically, and economically. In response, they launched a concerted and organized movement against partition—the Swadeshi movement. This was one of the earliest attempts at nationalist mass mobilization, as urban nationalists sought to enlist the support of the so-called peasant masses. Unfortunately for Swadeshi activists, mobilization consisted of enrolling consumerist jute cultivators in a program of economic boycott—of abstaining from the consumption of imported commodities.

The Swadeshi program of economic boycott was informed by a nationalist economic discourse focused on India's impoverishment and deindustrialization through colonial rule. The poverty debate, Bipan Chandra has demonstrated, was the primary issue for nineteenth-century Indian nationalists. Dadabhai Naoroji, the Grand Old Man of Indian Nationalism, spent a lifetime calculating and proving India's poverty.[71] Moreover, the devastating famines of the 1870s and the 1890s that swept parts of central, western, and northern India were considered to be definitive proof of Indian poverty. Indian nationalist thinkers argued that the colonial economic relation—the exchange of primary commodities for manufactured goods—had impoverished India. In his economic history of British India, R. C. Dutt documented the demise of Indian industries, particularly the textile industry.[72]

In this nationalist discourse of colonial impoverishment through primary commodity production, jute cultivators were an embarrassing anomaly. In their rhetorical defense against the nationalist charge of impoverishment, officials of the colonial state frequently drew attention to jute cultivators' apparent prosperity. An 1892 memorandum on material conditions of the peasantry, claimed that jute "pours a flood of wealth into Central and East Bengal . . . [and] it would be difficult to over-state the influence for good on the material condition of the peasant exercised by the vast and ever-growing volume of international trade."[73] In their attempts to counter colonial claims and to square jute cultivators' prosperity with national impoverishment, nationalist thinkers recast jute cultivators as economic villains who were enriching themselves at the expense of their communities and the nation. Nationalists charged jute cultivators with forsaking their communities for their colonial masters, diverting land away from the production of rice, food, oilseeds, and dairy for local communities to produce fiber for distant mills and factories. Chandrashekhar Kar's poem *Shekal-ekal* (Those days, These days) attributed reduced supplies of fish and milk and the adulteration of *ghee* to the spread of jute cultivation onto land formerly left fallow for cattle to graze:

> [Those days] there were fish in the canals and lakes, rice on the fields
> Cows would give plenty of milk
> There was no jute cultivation anywhere in the country
> There were fields of grass here, there, and everywhere.[74]

Nationalists accused jute cultivators of polluting Bengal's water bodies, through rotting stalks in standing water and, to add insult to injury, using their jute profits to purchase medicines to protect themselves against the diseases that they were causing to the rest of the community. Nikilnath Roy's pro-Swadeshi pamphlet *Sonar Bangla* (Golden Bengal), published at the peak of the Swadeshi movement, explicitly accused jute cultivators of selfishly aggrandizing themselves at the expense of the nation, by substituting grain with fiber, starving their fellow countrymen, and by polluting the delta's water:

> From outside it seems that in this life-struggle [jute production], our cultivators are winning. But what is happening inside? The cultivation of rice has been reduced to such an extent, that ordinary people are experiencing starvation every year. . . . It is true that a few cultivators may have made some money, but there is no doubt that lack of rice cultivation has driven ordinary people and even some cultivators to hunger and death. On top of that, the rotting of jute in rural waterbodies has destroyed the health of these areas and the very cultivators who grow jute are spending their money on quinine and other foreign medicines. . . . Only if everyone can survive equally out of this, can we say that we are winning this life-struggle. Otherwise there is no value to victory.[75]

The biggest crime perpetrated by jute cultivators, however, was their consumption of imported commodities. In Swadeshi economic thought, the consumption of imported goods—particularly cloth—had deindustrialized and impoverished India. While the pollution of water bodies, the increased prices of rice, milk, mustard oil, and fish, and the adulteration of ghee were local issues, deindustrialization was a national problem. Jute cultivators were not only guilty of forsaking their communities for global markets and wreaking ecological damage on local water bodies, but they were also guilty of impoverishing the entire nation.

The Swadeshi program sought to revitalize India's economy by directing its energies inward, within the nation's territorial boundaries. Swadeshi economic thought was influenced by Friedrich List's idealized autarkic self-sufficient national economies, where flows of capital and commodities were contained within territorial borders.[76] Enmeshed in global commodity flows, jute cultivators, therefore, were anathema to the Swadeshi economic ideal. Swadeshi activists sought to realize their economic vision through a consumer boycott of imported commodities, their only policy option given the colonial state's unwillingness to erect protective tariffs. These were, of course, the very commodities that were critical to peasant projects of self-fashioning. Unsurprisingly, the economic boycott failed to gain traction in the jute tracts, especially during a period of booming jute prices and expanding jute cultivation.

Between 1905 and 1906, in scores of rural marketplaces throughout rural eastern Bengal, Swadeshi activists attempted to prevent the sale and purchase of imported articles.[77] During the first half of 1906, activists picketed against the sale of foreign merchandise in numerous markets in the jute tracts, especially in Pabna, Rangpur, Mymensingh, Dacca, Faridpur, and Tipperah districts.[78] Rumors that colonial authorities had enforced the ban on imported goods and that imported salt and sugar contained pig and cow bones circulated in these areas.[79] The boycott was also enforced through intimidation and coercion. P. C. Lyons, the senior bureaucrat in the Home Department, reported that schoolboys were being organized by their teachers to "picket the shops and prevent the sale of European goods by forcible interference with both purchasers and sellers."[80] Swadeshi picketing was sometimes met with forceful resistance, leading in several instances to violence.

These clashes between Swadeshi activists and traders and consumers were depicted as episodes of communal violence, between mostly Hindu activists and mostly Muslim traders and consumers. Lyons perceived the danger of communal clashes in February 1906, when he wrote: "And, in all places, the members of the Muhammadan community were more specially subjected to oppression of this kind [forcible purchase of Swadeshi goods], until, at the time that the agitation reached its height, a danger had arisen of organized reprisals, which would have raised trouble of a very serious nature. Muhammadans form 60 per cent of the population of Eastern Bengal, chiefly belonging to the cultivating class."[81] Religious difference certainly played a role in Swadeshi conflicts, and Swadeshi activists had alienated Muslims with the use of explicitly Hindu slogans and symbols.[82] Religion and caste figured in the enforcement of boycott, as in the punishment of a Brahmanbaria shopkeeper, who "under grave provocation, struck a Brahmin boy picket, [and] was made to tender an apology, shave his head, and give away ten pairs of English cloth, which were carried in procession through the streets to the accompaniment of patriotic songs and finally burnt."[83]

The economic element of anti-Swadeshi resistance boiled down to the financial effects of the boycott—causing a rise in prices and forcing peasants to consume more expensive locally made goods. As P. C. Lyons pointed out, "The effect of the artificial demand for country-made goods was to raise prices very greatly, and the cultivators have suffered heavy pecuniary losses from the ostracism of imported articles."[84] The economic dimension of anti-Swadeshi resistance was not about finance; it was about defending rural markets as spaces of pleasurable and indulgent consumption. This was apparent in the anti-Swadeshi resistance at the Nangalband fair near Narayanganj during April 1907. The Nangalband mela accompanied a Hindu bathing festival that regularly attracted over a hundred thousand pilgrims. As in other hats, melas, and ganjes, Swadeshi activists roamed the fairgrounds brandishing sticks, *lathis*, and attempting to prevent stallholders and consumers from dealing in imported goods. When they forced a small boy to return a German-made looking glass that he had purchased for an anna or two and another boy to return a small box labeled "Made in Germany," consumers and shopkeepers confronted the men and snatched away their lathis. These protests were met with a concerted show of Swadeshi force. A large crowd of young men descended on the bazaar brandishing lathis, and looted and forcibly closed down traders' stalls.[85] The defense of small boys' consumption of German-made looking glasses and small ornamental boxes was not about the financial impact of the Swadeshi boycott—it was an attempt to protect the mela as a space of pleasurable consumption, of the indulgent purchase of small European-manufactured toys by peasant boys. I will describe two episodes of market-related clashes during the Swadeshi movement, when peasant men and women sought to defend marketplaces as pleasurable spaces: in a small rural hat in Brahmanbaria and at a mela in Jamalpur.

Mogra Hat, Brahmanbaria

The Swadeshi movement arrived in Tipperah in the persons of A. Rasul and Bipin Chandra Pal and through the medium of a mass meeting. On February 23, 1907, Rasul presided over and Pal addressed a meeting of a mostly Hindu middle-class audience consisting of pleaders, schoolteachers, and schoolboys.[86] The meeting resolved to oppose the partition of Bengal, to boycott foreign-made goods, government education, and legal services, and to promote scientific agriculture and sanitary improvements. They also decided to form a Tipperah People's Association, headquartered in Comilla and with branches all over the district. A conference was held at Kasba, a small town in the Brahmanbaria subdivision, where it was decided to start eighty branch committees in the jurisdiction of the Kasba police station.[87] On March 17, 1907, the first of these branch committees met in Mogra, a hat or market town, twenty-nine miles north of Comilla, very close to the Agartala railway station on the Assam Bengal Railway and in the Chakla Rawshanabad estates owned by the maharaja of Hill Tipperah. At this meeting it was resolved to disallow the sale of foreign goods at the twice-weekly bazaar at Mogra, particularly Liverpool salt which was traded in significant quantities.

On March 18th, a public meeting was held in Mogra. The next day, a Tuesday and a bazaar day, Swadeshi activists went around the market warning vendors not to deal in foreign goods. On the next bazaar day, Saturday the 23rd, Swadeshi activists tried to physically stop a Muslim trader, who had come from Brahmanbaria, from selling Liverpool salt. In the ensuing row, two men were injured and the Brahmanbaria trader's stall upturned.[88] Fearing that there would be an escalation of violence on the following hat day, the 26th, D. H. Wares, the subdivisional officer (SDO) of Brahmanbaria arrived in person, accompanied by two of his inspectors, one Muslim and one Hindu, and a small contingent of village *chaukidars*, or village police. Over the course of an eventful afternoon, Wares had to intervene twice: once to separate "about 300 Muhammadans . . . and about half the number of Hindus [who were] thrashing each other with lathis and throwing stones at each other," and then to defuse the situation between "perhaps a couple of hundred Hindus endeavoring to guard [the bazaar] against a larger number of Muhammadans."[89]

There was no looting involved; this was a show of force. As the district magistrate of Tipperah noted, "both sides came . . . prepared to fight."[90] It seemed that the Muslims, being in the numerical majority, were prepared to carry on the fight. On March 27th, a group of Muslims attacked seven

Hindu shops and several stalls at a small hat in Ghatiara, between three and four miles from Mogra, and part of the Sarail zamindari. On March 28th, a group of five hundred Muslims collected to attack the village of Binauti, three miles south of Mogra, and home to a number of wealthy, "respectable" Hindu families. D. H. Lees, district magistrate of Tipperah, received an anxious call for help from these prominent Hindus and arrived in time to avert violence. The arrival of twenty-five armed Gurkhas on the 26th and a further contingent of fifteen armed policemen on the 27th had ensured that an uneasy peace prevailed.[91]

The colonial authorities did take one further measure to defuse the situation—they reasserted the doctrine of free and unrestricted trade. They arranged with the maharaja of Tipperah Hill State to have the following notices circulated in Mogra hat and surrounding areas:

> It is hereby notified that in Hats, Bazaars and Melas . . . there is full liberty for all persons to buy and sell any article they please. In case of any interference in this connection information should be given by the aggrieved party to the sub-manager of the district concerned.[92]

A similar notice was issued in Ghatiara and surrounding villages, this time by the collector of Tipperah, in his role as the manager of the Sarail zamindari:

> Allegations having been made that in certain bazaars and other places undue pressure has been put on sellers as well as buyers not to deal in certain articles, it is hereby notified that in all bazaars, hats, melas, etc. in the Sarail estate, full liberty exists for people to buy and sell what they please. If there is any interference in this respect, information should be given by the aggrieved party to the undersigned.[93]

Janmashthami mela, Jamalpur

A two-month-long mela was held on the outskirts of Jamalpur town in celebration of Janmashthami, or Krishna's birth. As in Nangalband near Narayanganj, Swadeshi volunteers patrolled the Jamalpur fairgrounds, brandishing lathis and "endeavouring to prevent the sale of European goods." On April 21, 1907, the same day as the assault on traders at the Nangalband festival, Swadeshi activists launched a full-blown attack—with men, lathis, and an elephant—on traders at the Janmashthami fair. R. Nathan, the commissioner of Dacca, described the Swadeshi assault in the following manner:

Things went on smoothly to 3 or 3-30 P.M. At this time some two hundred zamindari servants, pleaders, mukhtears and volunteers, with lathis, with an elephant, marched round and entered the Mela shouting "Bande Mataram." The volunteers wore conspicuous badges. They molested the shopkeepers and destroyed a certain amount of European toys and sweetmeats and scattered some Liverpool salt.

As in Mogra, mostly Muslim shopkeepers and consumers struck back against mostly Hindu Swadeshi activists. As Nathan proceeded to narrate: "The shop-keepers and the Muhammadans attending the Mela became enraged and attacked the volunteers, using sticks and booth poles and lathis which it is said were snatched from the volunteers. The 'volunteers' scattered and fled. . . . The Muhammadans pursued striking and shouting . . . and endeavoring to get at the fugitives." They continued their attack—targeting Swadeshi shops selling domestically produced goods, the zamindar's court, and, more egregiously, a Hindu temple: "Ten Muhammadans entered the Durgabari in pursuit of fugitives and . . . partly damaged the image which had been prepared for the [Janmasthami] festival and did some other damage. . . . [They also] entered three *swadeshi* shops, and damaged some of the stalls. . . . They pelted the cutcheries of the . . . Gauripur estates and of the Ramgopalpur estate."[94]

Peace was restored in Jamalpur through an agreement between Hindu and Muslim "leaders" in the town—salaried professionals, landholders, and substantial traders who claimed to represent their respective communities. The two parties signed a form stating that they "deeply deplored . . . [the] unfortunate disturbances [that] have occurred in the town of Jamalpur . . . are exceedingly desirous to prevent their renewal and to restore quiet . . . [and] will use to the utmost their influence on their communities to promote peace."[95] Notably, the Muslim leaders asked for an end to "Swadeshi oppression." As Nathan recounted: "At the request of the Muhammadans I asked the Hindus if their promise included "swadeshi" oppression, and in the presence of the Muhammadans they replied that it did."[96]

Events at the hat and the mela followed a similar pattern. In both Mogra and Jamalpur, violence commenced with Swadeshi activists' assault on consumer goods: Liverpool salt at the hat and European toys and sweetmeats at the mela. This assault was met with shopkeepers' and consumers' resistance. Mostly Muslim consumers and traders retaliated against Swadeshi activists, seizing their lathis and chasing them out of the mela and the hat. They then continued their attack, targeting Hindu-owned and *Swadeshi* shops, Hindu authority figures, and even Hindu religious sites. In Mogra, they attempted to attack the homes of wealthy Hindus and, in Jamalpur, they attacked the zamindar's *kutcherry* and the Durgabari temple. Peace was restored when the colonial state intervened, by announcing that "full liberty exists for people to buy and sell what they please" in Brahmanbaria and brokering an end to "Swadeshi oppression" in Jamalpur between Muslim and Hindu "community leaders."

Nationalists and imperialists saw these conflicts through the prism of communalism rather than consumerism, as conflicts informed by religious differences rather than differences in economic ideas regarding market-based consumption. Swadeshi leaders interpreted their failure to "mobilize" peasant support in terms of the inability of primarily Hindu elites to appeal to the religious sentiments of the mainly Muslim peasantry. Hence, their efforts to garner Muslim support were often couched in the language of religion. A pamphlet circulated through the jute tracts that combined the image of the nation as the mother goddess with appeals to stereotypes of Muslim masculinity: "Mussalmans, mother entertains high hopes in you. Strong as you are, broad as your chests are, strong as your arms are, fear not to die, to save our mother from dishonour. Say once 'Din!' 'Din!' 'Allah ho akbar' and take possession of the towns by whatever means you find to hand, lathi or sword, sticks or guns, or anything."[97]

Appeals to Muslim masculinity—broad chests and strong arms—could not mitigate the nationalist elite's antipathy toward market-dependent jute cultivation. The program of economic boycott was premised on a nationalist economic discourse that vilified jute cultivators' market-entangled lives. Swadeshi activists envisioned an autarkic and self-sufficient economy where the circulation capital and commodities were contained within the nation's territorial limits. Nationalists accused jute cultivators of forsaking the national community: they produced inedible fibers for distant markets instead of foodstuffs for proximate consumers and they purchased goods manufactured in distant factories instead of South Asia's local products. Swadeshi activists carried this message of economic nationalism into the jute tracts during a consumerist boom fueled by high jute prices. Unsurprisingly, jute cultivators were not responsive to Swadeshi appeals to forsake global commodity markets for the sake of an imagined national community. Instead, they responded with hostility.

World War I

If the nationalist economic discourse lost the battle of economic ideas among jute cultivators, does that imply that British ideas of a laissez-faire economy were victorious? Were jute cultivators more responsive to the colonial government's doctrines of free trade, to proclamations of the liberty to buy and sell as posted around Brahmanbaria after the Mogra riots? If the colonial government believed that jute cultivators were doctrinaire free traders, they would be disabused of this idea by incidences of looting in eastern Bengal's rural markets in December 1917 and January 1918. The crisis of World War I shook the market-based consumerist livelihoods of jute-cultivating households. As jute prices plummeted and the prices of peasant-consumed articles spiked, consumption stopped being pleasurable and market entanglements became stressful. Rather than a means of self-fashioning, peasant consumption now focused on the struggle to secure subsistence. Widespread instances of looting demonstrated that peasant politics had shifted focus, toward ensuring the viability of their market-based livelihoods.

During December 1917 the government reported 91 cases of looting in rural marketplaces in eastern Bengal and another 28 during January 1918. A majority of these incidents took place in the jute tracts of eastern and northern Bengal: 22 of them in the jute regions of Rangpur.[98] Similar incidents took place in the jute-growing region of Purnea, in the province of Bihar, and in the Sylhet district in Assam: Sylhet was in the Meghna valley, adjacent to Mymensingh and Tipperah, and ecologically, economically, and culturally similar to those important jute-growing districts.[99] The government stated: "There can be no doubt that the main cause of these disturbances is the high price of salt and cloth, which people attribute to the greed of shopkeepers. The discontent is accentuated by the low prices obtained for paddy and jute."[100] In several instances, looters claimed that the government had given them permission to loot shops charging excessively high prices: "An absurd idea had got abroad that Government would not be adverse to people taking the law into their own hands and compelling the vendors of cloth and salt to bring down their prices."[101]

The government decided to respond in December 1917 by enlisting the support of prominent locals "who can explain to their tenants and others the economic causes of the high prices and the futility of the looting."[102] The difficulty of attempting to control riots through economic theory became apparent to the state when cases of looting did not abate during January 1918.

The situation "eased" in February and it was "attributed partly to the fall which had taken place in the price of salt and partly to the promptness with which the rioters have been apprehended and placed on trial." Significantly, the government announced that it would bring the prices of salt and cloth under control. Looting came to an end with price controls—the very opposite of the proclamation of "full liberty for all persons to buy and sell" in Mogra in 1905.

The cases of looting also took place in a particularly vulnerable period in the crop calendar, during December and early January, just before winter rice or aman was harvested. The situation eased in late January and February, after the aman harvest. The government feared that violence would recur once more, in the "hot weather" as the aman crop was depleted and before the aus and jute harvest came in: "It is . . . far from improbable that disturbances may break out again in the hot weather, when the resources of the cultivating classes will be depleted owing to the poor prices which they have received both for jute and for rice."[103]

During the decades after World War I, global commodity markets decisively turned against cultivators and the peasant politics of consumption came to focus more on hunger and subsistence rather than on pleasure and self-fashioning. During this period of immiseration, anticonsumerist nationalist economic discourses found more fertile ground in the deltaic jute tracts. As I discuss in chapter 5, this was the case during the Khilafat and Non-Cooperation movements of 1921–22, when anticonsumerist nationalist discourses similar to the Swadeshi economic message found greater traction among jute cultivators during a time of low jute prices, unfavorable commodity markets, and widespread hunger.

Conclusion

The nineteenth-century era of relative prosperity, driven by expanding jute cultivation, food security, and favorable global commodity markets, manifested in the peasant consumption of a variety of goods and services: property rights, cloth, ornaments, metal utensils, kerosene oil, corrugated iron, German-made toys, sweets and confections, seasonal fruits, and luxury fish. These forms of consumption, I have argued, were critical elements in peasant projects of self-fashioning, and in crafting a distinctively agrarian, Muslim, and Bengali habitation of modernity. Peasant consumption cannot be reduced to narrow economic self-interest. Their desire for secure property rights in a landscape of limited zamindari power was driven not solely by economic and financial motives but also by an idealized conception of peasant claims to property. Peasants' desires for various commodities in rural marketplaces were not only motivated by their utility or affordability but by the desire to construct new kinds of dress, dwellings, and diets—distinctive Muslim clothing, metallic homes, and the occasional indulgence in gourmet food. Peasants' vigorous resistance against the Swadeshi program of boycott was not just about the financial costs imposed by the boyott, but also an attempt to protect rural hats and melas as spaces of pleasurable consumption where men and boys purchased sweets and toys. The onset of a rapid and thorough process of peasant immiseration during and after World War I, however, brought an end to this period of consumerism. After World War I, peasant market engagements were focused primarily and even exclusively on securing subsistence, on staving off hunger. The nineteenth-century politics of consumption gave way to a twentieth-century politics of hunger.

Peasant market entanglements were accompanied by a physical infrastructure that enabled vast quantities of peasant-produced fiber and peasant-consumed cloth, accessories, construction materials, utensils, illumination, and foods to circulate in and out of peasant homesteads. The circulation of peasant-produced and peasant-consumed commodities took place through the interface between steam-powered transport technologies of railways and river steamers and an existing infrastructure of country boats and ox wagons. Intermediary market towns—the mofussil—were located at the intersection of these transport infrastructures. Mofussil towns grew and expanded along with the jute trade during the late nineteenth and early twentieth centuries as spaces where peasant-produced fibers were assorted, bulked, and packaged en route to Calcutta. The towns mentioned in this chapter as sites of Swadeshi mobilization and anti-Swadeshi resistance—Brahmanbaria, Narayanganj, and Jamalpur—were important, fast-growing market towns connected by rail and steamer to Calcutta. The next chapter focuses on the circulation of commodities and the emergence of the mofussil as a significant space for peasant material lives and political action during the late nineteenth and early twentieth centuries.

3

The Spaces of Jute

METROPOLIS, HINTERLAND, AND *MOFUSSIL*

PEASANT-PRODUCED fibers traveled through the delta's river and railways, westward to the jute mills and seaports of Calcutta. En route to Calcutta, the fibers changed hands, traveled on ox carts, country boats, steamships, and railway wagons, and were bought and sold, stored, bulked, and assorted in river-port and railroad market towns. As it passed through layers of inter-mediary traders, jute changed in form, from small lots of peasant produce of variable quality to standardized units of quantity, quality, and price. The built-up capital through which jute circulated—steamships, railways, jetties, docks, and warehouses—connected the delta's jute tracts to metropolitan Calcutta, home to half the world's jute mills and almost all the jute presses in Bengal. The flow of fiber transformed the delta into Calcutta's hinterland and, conversely, Calcutta into the delta's metropolis. This chapter shifts focus from production and consumption to jute's circulation through the delta's landscape, and examines how commodity transformed the delta's spaces and spatial relationships.

The relationship between the hinterland and the metropolis was mediated through intermediary market towns, the mofussil (see map 2).[1] At the turn of the twentieth century, these towns housed only 2 percent of the delta's popu-lation and were very small: only Narayanganj and Sirajganj had populations of more than 20,000 in 1900. However, they were growing rapidly along with the jute trade: by 12.7 percent during the decade of the 1890s. Growth was most pronounced in railway and river markets that specialized in the jute trade: the populations of Chandpur, Narayanganj, Jamalpur, and Madaripur increased by more than 20 percent between 1890 and 1900, and Narayanganj's population doubled between 1880 and 1900. New market towns emerged along recently constructed railway tracks and were enumerated for the first time in the 1901 census: Akhaura in Tipperah, and Domar, Haldibari, and Nilphamari in Rangpur district. Like most colonial publications of the period, the 1901 census celebrated the growth of small towns as manifestations of the jute tract's prosperity: "the country is prosperous and trade is increasing, and the most progressive towns are those connected with the export trade in jute."[2]

Mofussil jute markets grew up along the delta's waterways and railways, connecting peasant farms to Calcutta. Small village-level traders known as *farias* or *beparis* sold fibers purchased from peasant smallholders to mahajans, more substantial capitalists usually acting as agents of jute balers in these markets. During the nineteenth century, intermediary jute traders invested in mofussil towns, building warehouses, river docks, railway sidings, and *kutcha* presses—hand-powered screws that packed fibers into bales of four to six maunds. The first section of this chapter shows that superimposing coal-powered trains and river steamers over the delta's existing infrastructure of oar- and sail-powered boats shaped patterns of mofussil growth in the delta.

As was usually the case in the British Empire, the colonial state accompanied colonial capital. Mofussil towns housed not only the warehouses and baling presses of jute traders, but also the paraphernalia of the colonial state. The forward institutions of the colonial state were those of revenue extraction and law and order. The most visible signs of colonial authority in the hinterland were mofussil courthouses, police stations, and land administration offices. In the late nineteenth and early twentieth centuries, the colonial government established a different type of government institution—the developmental. The Agriculture Department, formed in 1885, extended into the hinterland at the behest of global jute capital, in an effort to "know" and "improve" peasant jute production. In the second section, I examine the increasing penetration of the state into the delta through the activities of the Agriculture Department.

The third section will explore the mofussil as a site for nationalist politics, especially as metropolitan nationalists attempted to mobilize the hinterland's peasant masses into the Swadeshi movement. Metropolitan activists introduced Swadeshi ideology into the hinterland through whistlestop tours of eastern Bengal's mofussil towns, traveling on the very railways and steamers that conveyed jute and other commodities, and addressing public meetings in the very towns that served as centers of the jute trade. Local Swadeshi activists were drawn from the mofussil bhadralok, and were mostly Hindu—lawyers, schoolteachers, doctors, clerks, traders, and zamindari employees who resided in the jute towns. While the towns were mostly Hindu and middle class, the surrounding countryside was overwhelmingly peasant and Muslim. Attempts to enforce the Swadeshi economic program of boycott pitted the mofussil town against the surrounding countryside. Swadeshi-related conflicts in the jute tracts, I argue, took place between the overlapping categories of Hindu and Muslim, bhadralok and peasant, and town and countryside.

Circulation

When jute first emerged as a major commodity, the bulk of fiber was transported to Calcutta by oar- and sail-powered wooden boats, traveling through the canals of the mangrove jungles of Sundarbans and entering the metropolis through the Nadia canal and, to a lesser extent, the Midnapore and Hidgellee canals. These boats were loaded with fiber in riverside market towns, known as ganjes, located on major rivers, and connected to jute cultivators' homesteads through the delta's network of rivers and canals. The two primary centers of nineteenth-century jute trade were Sirajganj and Narayanganj. Sirajganj was on the banks of the Jamuna, the major tributary of the Brahmaputra river system, and collected jute from northern Bengal and western Mymensingh. Narayanganj was on the confluence of the Buriganga and Dhaleswari rivers, and collected jute from eastern Mymensingh, Dacca, and Tipperah. Two very different capitalist communities built and operated the jute warehouses, docks, and presses in these towns. Marwari capital concentrated in Sirajganj, and Armenian and Greek merchants—later joined by British firms—dominated Narayaganj's jute trade.

Sirajganj and Narayanganj collected jute from smaller towns, like Pabna, Mymensingh, Kishoreganj, Jamalpur, Munshiganj, Bhairab Bazaar, Brahmanbaria, and Chandpur. These towns dealt with considerable quantities of fiber, though they rarely dealt directly with Calcutta—for the most part, they supplied the larger marts of Sirajganj and Narayanganj. The notable exception was Madaripur, in Faridpur district and on the banks of the Kumar, close to the Sundarbans route to Calcutta. A collection point for jute cultivated in Faridpur district, Madaripur sent jute directly to Calcutta: an average of 18,000 tons of jute was shipped from Madaripur to Calcutta between 1877 and 1880.[3]

Sirajganj's importance as a river mart preceded the rise of jute as a major global commodity. In 1854 an American missionary described a brief visit to Sirajganj: "As we approached Serajgunge [traveling from Pabna, up the

Jamuna] the forests of masts reminded me of the shipping of New York or Liverpool. We were ten hours and half passing by them, as they were moored to the bank, two, three, or five deep. I computed them at the time above 600, but was afterwards informed they were more than a thousand."[4] Sirajganj's preeminent position in Bengal's trade was secured by its location in a network of rivers. However, the river routes that underpinned the early years of the jute trade were soon overlaid by expanding railway routes. Sirajganj would lose its position as the "emporium of Bengal jute" to Narayanganj, as railways arrived too late in Sirajganj—in 1915, with the opening of the Sara-Sirajganj line. Narayanganj, on the other hand, was connected by rail as early as 1885, when the Dacca-Mymensingh line began operations.

The railway arrived in eastern Bengal in 1870, when the Eastern Bengal Railway line was extended to Goalundo, connecting Calcutta to the confluence of the Padma and the Jamuna, the point where the Ganges and Brahmaputra river systems merged. Beyond Goalundo, the Eastern Bengal Railway operated two steamer services: one running north, up the Brahmaputra to Sirajganj and then to Diburgarh in Assam, and the second going east to Narayanganj and then to Chandpur on the banks of the Meghna. The rivers were not cooperative with these first attempts to connect rivers and railways—in 1875 floods washed away sections of railway track and the town of Goalundo itself. After that, Goalundo was no longer a fixed point on a map, but a "wandering terminus" shifting frequently to avoid the unpredictable and unstoppable rivers. The town consisted solely of "a very large bazar and railway and steamers officers' quarters which follow the terminus in its wanderings."[5]

Goalundo also struggled to become a transshipment point for jute, where fibers were off-loaded from boats and reloaded onto railway wagons. The *Report on the Internal Trade of Bengal for 1876–77* noted with concern: "It is evident that the railway has not succeeded in displacing the waterways of Bengal as the favored channel for the supply of this important staple to Calcutta. And yet almost the whole of this jute passes by the railway station of Goalundo."[6]

Between 1870 and 1872, more than half of Calcutta's jute arrived by country boat: 8.5 million maunds by country boats, 6 million by railway, and 2 million by river steamer.[7] Railways would only displace rivers gradually, as tracks were extended further and deeper into the delta. Between 1876–77 and 1889–90, arrivals of jute in Calcutta by boat rose from 3.8 million maunds to 4.5 million maunds. On the other hand, arrivals by railway more than doubled from 3.4 million to 8.4 million maunds and by river steamer almost quadrupled from 860,000 to 3 million maunds (see table 3.1).

TABLE 3.1. Arrivals of Jute into Calcutta (in maunds of 40 kg), 1876–1890

	By boat	By rail	By steamer
1876–77	3,839,000	3,382,000	858,000
1877–78	4,784,000	3,978,000	1,072,000
1878–79	5,803,000	3,008,000	1,208,000
1879–80	4,456,000	4,331,000	1,481,000
1880–81	4,086,000	3,701,000	1,340,000
1881–82	4,570,000	5,784,000	4,570,000
1882–83	5,974,000	7,001,000	2,086,000
1883–84	4,908,000	3,252,000	1,888,000
1884–85	4,911,000	4,876,000	2,757,000
1885–86	4,113,000	4,544,000	2,959,000
1886–87	3,661,000	5,290,000	2,789,000
1887–88	4,013,000	6,773,000	2,959,000
1888–89	4,819,000	7,429,000	3,219,000
1889–90	4,492,000	8,399,000	3,054,000

The Northern Bengal State Railway opened in 1878, connecting Calcutta with Assam, and traversing Rangpur district, the primary jute district of northern Bengal. The Northern Bengal Railway successfully captured the jute trade, and led to a rapid increase in jute cultivation in north Bengal. As an official report observed, "the easy communication afforded by the railway has given a powerful impetus to the development of the jute trade in this district [Rangpur]."[8] Quantities of jute loaded onto railways in north Bengal towns increased rapidly during the 1880s: in Rangpur from 740 tons in 1879–80 to 9,900 tons in 1889–90, in Domar from 7,700 tons to 13,440 tons, and in Haldibari from 1,810 to 12,000 tons. By 1880 two Calcutta firms were operating in the towns of Rangpur and Domar, and over the following years more followed. In the early twentieth century, Domar was described as "a large jute-exporting centre, containing jute presses."[9] The Northern Bengal State Railway initially bypassed Sirajganj, and Rangpur jute that was previously dispatched to Calcutta via Sirajganj was now consigned directly to the metropolis in railway wagons at railway stations along the line.

In 1885 the Eastern Bengal Railway opened a Dacca branch, connecting Dacca, Narayanganj, and Mymensingh. Narayanganj's connection to the hinterland was now overlaid with rail routes, giving Narayanganj an edge over Sirajganj in its river-steamer service. In 1889–90 Narayanganj sent 65,200 tons of jute to Calcutta by steamer flats, while Sirajganj sent just 38,800 tons. Sirajganj retained its importance as a center of the country-boat trade: that same year, Sirajganj sent more than 32,100 tons of jute to Calcutta by country boat against the mere 6,800 tons dispatched from Narayanganj. As coal-powered rail and steamer displaced oar- and sail-powered boats, Narayanganj eclipsed Sirajganj as the delta's jute emporium. When Sirajganj was finally connected by rail in 1915, it had already been surpassed by Narayanganj as Bengal's premier jute mart. Sirajganj's decline began in 1897, when an earthquake destroyed the Serajgunge Jute Company and shifted the rivers. As the *Imperial Gazetteer of India* commented in 1908: "Sirajganj has of late somewhat declined in impor-tance owing to the damage done by the earthquake of 1897, and to a change in the course of the Brahmaputra, which is now three miles distant from the town."[10] Connected by railways and steamers to cultivators' homesteads and to Calcutta's jute mills and seaport, Narayanganj grew rapidly. The town's population more than doubled between 1881 and 1901: in 1901, 24,472 resided in Narayanganj. In 1908 there were 53 jute packaging factories with a total of 73 presses and 6,000 workers in Narayanganj.[11] On the other hand, there were only 14 presses in Sirajganj and another 5 in the neighboring jute town of Bera.[12] While Narayanganj's population had doubled between 1881 and 1901, Sirajganj's population had increased only slightly, from 21,037 to 23,114.[13]

European capital concentrated in Narayanganj. The large number of Euro-peans residing in Narayanganj made it the model colonial "upcountry" market town.[14] According to the *Imperial Gazetteer of India* of 1908: "Narayanganj has the appearance of a Western rather than of an Eastern town, and has not unjustly been called the model municipality of Bengal."[15] European traders formed the Narayanganj Chamber of Commerce in 1904, and up until 1912 rep-resented "the jute interest" in the Bengal Legislative Council. The dominance of the European-dominated NCC in local municipal politics, to the exclu-sion of Indian traders, lasted into the 1930s. In 1926 Tarit Bhushan Roy of the Bengal Mahajan Sabha, an association of mofussil Bengali traders and finan-ciers, complained in the Legislative Council that the Narayanganj Chamber of Commerce dominated the Narayanganj Municipal Board despite the fact that the Indian commercial community paid about one-third of municipal taxes.[16]

The Assam Bengal Railway was inaugurated in 1892 and connected the southeastern port of Chittagong to Assam's tea plantations. The ABR traversed the Tipperah jute tracts and passed along the Meghna. In 1903 a branch line from Laksham to Chandpur was opened. As the terminus of the EBR steamer running from Goalundo, Chandpur had already emerged as an important jute town. The Census Report for 1901 ascribed the 37 percent growth in the population of Chandpur subdivision (not just the town) to "the development of trade in Chandpur town."[17] The branch line offered an alternative seaport to the delta's jute—Chandpur was now connected by railway to Chittagong port. The Assam Bengal Railway was heavily interested in promoting Chittagong, and promised that the Laksham-Chandpur branch would make it the "port for all jute from Narainganj and the country north of that place."[18] Calcutta jute interests were initially fearful that the Chandpur branch of the ABR would divert jute away from Calcutta to Chittagong, and the Bengal Chamber of Commerce, the Indian Jute Mills Association, and the Calcutta Baled Jute Association publicly opposed the project as it would "compete with a long-established private enterprise."[19]

The ABR captured a sizable portion of the jute trade: in 1903–4 their wagons carried 45,000 tons of jute.[20] However, Calcutta jute interests' fears did not materialize. Though Chittagong's exports of jute increased marginally, the bulk of Chandpur's jute trade was with Calcutta. The EBR ran two steamers daily from Chandpur to Narayanganj and Goalundo. The steamers would arrive from Calcutta in the morning; after their arrival, two trains would depart—one north for Assam and the other south for Chittagong; and the steamers would return to Goalundo and Narayanganj the following morning.[21] The network of river steamers and railways spurred the growth of Chandpur as a jute mart: in 1910 there were seven European and two Indian firms operating jute presses in the town.[22]

The Assam Bengal Railway also led to the growth of Akhaura, a town served by both the railway and the river Titas, a tributary of the Meghna. The 1901 census reported that Akhaura was "coming into importance as the railway station for Brahmanbaria subdivision."[23] By 1908 jute presses had been established in the town.[24] In April 1910 a branch line of the ABR from Akhaura to Ashuganj on the banks of the Meghna and opposite the important jute mart of Bhairab Bazaar was opened. Akhaura became *the* railway junction town of Tipperah district, connecting Tipperah's jute tracts to Narayanganj and Calcutta. In 1937 the King George VI Railway Bridge across the river Meghna—connecting the Ashuganj and Bhairab Bazaar stations—was opened to traffic. The Assam Bengal Railway was now directly connected to the Dacca section of the Eastern Bengal Railway, and to the hinterland's premier jute emporium, Narayanganj. By the time the railway bridge opened, a series of significant jute trading stations had emerged along the ABR's tracks, notably in Chandpur, Akhaura, Brahmanbaria, and Ashuganj.

The overlaying of different transport infrastructures and the enormous growth in the jute trade in the late nineteenth century led to distinctive patterns of small-town growth in the jute hinterland. Along with concentrating capital in warehouses and presses in the major jute marts of Narayanganj, Sirajganj, and Chandpur, jute merchants established smaller purchasing agencies deeper inside the hinterland. Their move deeper into the hinterland was driven by competition, as jute traders attempted to gain an edge against their competitors. The Narayanganj Chamber of Commerce noted in 1916, "With increasing competition [Narayanganj] balers went further afield and established buying stations in smaller places in the interior."[25] The NCC was referring solely to large European jute-baling firms, who, according to an estimate in the *Capital*, operated at least five hundred purchasing stations in eastern Bengal.[26] However, the hinterland trade was dominated by indigenous jute merchants—mahajans—rather than European purchasing agencies. The majority of mahajans were Marwaris from Rajasthan, and some Bengali traders, particularly from the Saha community, also participated in the jute trade. Similar to European balers, mahajans also went "further afield" as the volume of trade increased and competition intensified. Marwari traders were usually the first to begin operations in towns just connected to railways, and dominated the jute trade in towns along the Northern Bengal State Railway, in Rangpur, Domar, and Haldibari.

Another aspect of the growth of mofussil market towns during the late nineteenth century was the establishment of kutcha baling presses—hand-powered screws that would pack jute into bales of about five maunds or two hundred kilograms. In the 1870s Calcutta received almost solely "hanked" or "drummed" jute—"stricks of fiber" that had been "rolled into the shape of a drum and tied with three strings."[27] By the early 1900s almost all of Calcutta's imports of jute from eastern Bengal arrived kutcha-baled. Narayanganj had the largest number of kutcha presses in the delta and there were also pressing facilities in smaller jute marts throughout the hinterland. Marwari merchants (and a few Bengali traders) moved into the kutcha-baling trade during the late nineteenth century. In the early years of the jute trade, baling was a preserve of European capital; by 1900 the majority of jute-baling firms were Marwari concerns.[28] Between 1870 and 1900 kutcha baling had transformed from a primarily metropolitan and European to a mostly mofussil and mostly Indian business.

Mofussil market towns were settings for encounters between farias and beparis—village-level petty traders—and mahajans or balers' agents. The mahajan operated either on his own account or on the account of a jute baling firm and either owned a warehouse, or rented one from an *aratdar*—a warehouse owner. Balers' agents, on the other hand, were salaried employees of Calcutta or Narayaganj-based baling firms. These mostly Bengali men were appointed in either the Calcutta headquarters or Narayanganj offices of jute baling firms for a monthly wage to conduct the firms' purchases in a mofussil market.[29] The balers' agent, the registrar of the cooperative societies, argued in 1927, was in effect another intermediary trader between farm and factory instead of simply the balers' representative "as his salary is not fixed on the principle that it represents the whole of his remuneration."[30]

Farias and beparis were village-level jute traders, often peasant households with larger landholdings who had invested accumulated capital from jute production into the jute trade. The district officer in Jalpaiguri, in northern Bengal, described "the *paikars* . . . [as] generally well-to-do Muhammadans of this district."[31] According to the Narayanganj Chamber of Commerce, "*beparis* were generally the large boat owners of their villages."[32] Farias and beparis were familiar and local individuals: J. M. Mitra, registrar of the cooperative societies in Bengal, described farias and beparis as "familiar figures in the village. The faria is usually a resident of the village and is well known to the cultivators."[33]

At the start of the jute season, in August, farias and beparis rowed their boats between peasant homesteads and rural hats buying up jute. Once their boats were filled to capacity, beparis rowed and sailed to the nearest riverine market town and sold their entire cargo to a particular mahajan. Beparis operated either on their own accounts, or on advances from a more substantial merchant in a nearby market town. Mahajans advanced money to beparis on the "condition . . . that the latter must bring to the *mahajans* all the jute they can get from the raiyat. The money is not realized from season to season, but is allowed to be in the hands of the *beparis*, one *bepari* sometimes having an advance of Rs. 5,000 or Rs. 10,000, and occasionally no less than Rs. 20,000."[34] In other words, advance contracts were meant to secure the mahajans' supply of fiber, not squeeze profits out of beparis by specifying sales prices or extracting interest payments.

The transaction often took place in "floating bazaars," where the mahajans' and agents' boats maneuvered through a throng of beparis' jute-laden boats. Negotiations were conducted through brokers, known as *dalals*. The dalal showed the mahajan a sample of the fiber and then negotiations would begin in earnest. Dalals and mahajans bargained in silence and in secret, drawing the Bengali character for numbers as prices on each other's palms, which were hidden under cloth. If an agreement was reached, the dalal would hand the mahajan a sample, and the mahajan's assistant would record the agreement and the faria's particulars. The faria would return to the mahajan's warehouse with his entire boatload of jute, where quality would usually be disputed and prices renegotiated. Jute would be weighed out, though the purchasers' maund was often more than the standard forty kilograms. Further, a variety of deductions in weight and/or price would be charged to the bepari. The mahajan's workers would then make up drums of jute, by doubling up and rolling together a maund of jute stricks and tying the whole together with rope. Jute would be transported to Calcutta or to mofussil kutcha presses in one-maund drums.

Colonial capitalists viewed these hinterland transactions with intermingled fascination and anxiety. The teeming masses of jute-laden beparis' boats along riverbanks and the hustle of floating bazaars as mahajans' boats made their way through the crowd was the stuff of the colonial exotic—a traveler's fantasy of India. At the same time, the hinterland market was a murky space, where inscrutable natives operated in indecipherable and potentially dangerous ways. What was taking place underneath the cloth? What exactly was a maund? What were the charges and deductions made in transactions? While drawn by the exotic, the travelers' gaze could not penetrate through the activity and they felt that important things were being concealed from their sight. The silent negotiations and the hands hidden under a piece of cloth captured British anxieties about impenetrable and indecipherable mofussil markets. Below, I cite two instances of colonial capital's anxieties about hinterland transactions traders, the first from 1873 and the second from 1915.

In the winter of 1872–73, George Burnett, a Dundee "jute expert" who had recently arrived in Calcutta to assist in establishing the Champdany jute mills, took a tour of the jute-growing districts of eastern Bengal. His account of the tour was published in the pages of the *Dundee Advertiser* and reprinted as a pamphlet titled *The Jute-Growing Districts and Markets of India*. Burnett's descriptions of jute transactions in Sirajganj combined the traveler's gaze—"the floating bazaar is an interesting and amusing scene"—with capitalist anxieties. His account dwelt at length on how hand signals kept the seller and onlookers ignorant of prices, on how variable weights and the array of charges and deductions inflated prices paid by mills, and how the mahajan's drum "serves only to conceal the defects" and "renders . . . the trade . . . liable to the deception arising from concealed defects."[35]

In the decades following Burnett's tour, the volume of jute traded in hinterland markets increased tremendously and European balers employed indigenous staff to conduct operations at remote purchasing stations. The increased penetration of their agents into the countryside did not allay colonial capitalists' anxieties. In May 1915 *Capital*, the mouthpiece of Calcutta's British merchant interests, published an article that focused on the "purchasing Babu," the employee of the baling firm posted at mofussil purchasing stations. The *Capital* alleged that the purchasing babu was, "at the most moderate estimate of robbery," stealing four thousand rupees from his European bosses. The article portrayed the purchasing babu as the archetypal wily native of colonial fantasy, using his knowledge of the mofussil markets' arcane ways to manipulate weights, qualities, and prices to cheat his European bosses of their rightful share. The purchasing babu was also an effeminate Hindu who feared the more masculine Muslim beparis and farias. As the babu tells the author of the article, "present day Beparis very shrewd; if weighman weigh excess, he catch scale and stop if, and if I do *teri beri* [cheat him] he come with big bamboo to smash my head! He rough Mahomedan, I poor *dal bhat* Bengali Babu, what I do to him?" Unable to do *"teri beri"* with "rough" Muslim bepari, the "cunning native purchasers" cheated their European bosses. The imaginary babu informs the author: "Sahib in my hand, I no in Sahib hand! He not know Bengali man. We can buy and sell Sahib, his father, grandfather, and his fourteen generations, and he not understand how!"[36]

Jute manufacturers depended on peasant smallholders and indigenous capitalists in the deltaic markets to deliver their raw materials in sufficient quantities, of suitable qualities, and at remunerative prices. Manufacturers' anxieties about jute cultivation and trade in the hinterland increased as capital was poured into jute mills in Dundee, Calcutta, Continental Europe, and the United States. Would cultivators be able to satisfy the increased consumption of the mills? Would the quality of fiber deteriorate, driving up production costs and decreasing the value of the manufactured product? Would cultivators and middlemen drive up prices of raw materials, cutting down on mills' profitability or allowing jute substitutes into the market? Anxious about the impenetrable and indecipherable hinterland and the wiles of cunning indigenous intermediaries, colonial capitalists turned to the colonial state.

The State

The massive rise in the jute trade during the late nineteenth century took place concurrently with the increased penetration of the colonial government and its institutions in the jute-producing hinterland. In addition to the facilities of the jute trade, mofussil towns housed the paraphernalia of the colonial state. The colonial administration manifested itself through a hierarchy of administrative towns with metropolitan Calcutta at its apex, and then district headquarters, subdivisional towns, and police stations. While police stations, or *thanas*, accommodated a constabulary force of the colonial police, district and subdivisional towns contained full complements of the state's law and order and revenue-extraction institutions—courthouses, police stations, jails, and the offices of land administration and revenue departments. These towns also accommodated the colonial "man on the spot"—district magistrates and subdivisional officers, autocratic figures with wide-ranging powers to govern the hinterland. Railway development and river-steamer services also housed railway administration, ticketing offices, and the railway and river police.

Administrative and market towns did not always overlap. The most important jute towns were not located in district headquarters, but in subdivisional headquarters—Narayanganj was a subdivisional town under Dacca, Sirajganj under Pabna, Chandpur under Comilla, and Madaripur under Faridpur. The colonial state created the new subdivision of Narayanganj in 1882, only after the town had already emerged as a significant center of the jute trade.[37] Some of the most important jute towns were not even subdivisional headquarters—Akhaura's subdivisional headquarters was Brahmanbaria and Domar's was Nilphamari. Akhaura and Domar housed only railway offices and railway police, rather than the usual complement of colonial services that were located in Brahmanbaria and Nilphamari.[38] The attempt to combine state institutions and trade facilities in Goalundo failed spectacularly, as the entire town was washed away in a flood within five years of its establishment. After the flood, subdivisional and railway officers were moved inland to the town of Rajbari, and, as discussed earlier, Goalundo became a "wandering terminus." In 1908 Rajbari had a deputy magistrate collector (who combined judicial and revenue collection responsibilities), two munsiffs, and a jail accommodating up to fifty-eight prisoners.[39]

Perhaps the most visible manifestations of the colonial state's penetration into the mofussil were courthouses and police stations. In the previous chapter, I argued that the expansion of the colonial judiciary into the delta during the late nineteenth century was driven by peasant households' consumption of legal services, financed by revenues from jute sales. Indigenous capitalists in hinterland markets also used mofussil courthouses to enforce contracts. European jute capitalists, on the other hand, preferred to contest legal battles over hinterland transactions in metropolitan courts in Calcutta, rather than in the district courts in the mofussil. When proposals to partition the administration of Bengal were floated in 1903, colonial jute capitalists supported the scheme with the caveat that the Calcutta High Court would retain jurisdiction over the partitioned province of Eastern Bengal and Assam.

In addition to legal institutions, the state penetrated the hinterland through its police force. The Indian Police Commission of 1860 created an administrative structure for a mofussil police force, with a district superintendent in charge of the district, an inspector over a several police stations, and a head *daroga* in charge of a police station.[40] The colonial police force was augmented steadily over the remainder of the nineteenth century, with the establishment of new police stations and the addition of railway and river police. The mofussil police force, however, was thoroughly incapable of preventing or investigating crime. As David Washbrook has argued about late nineteenth-century India that "the essential development of an efficient and centrally-disciplined police force, to protect 'legal' rights, safeguard the emancipation of the individual from community constraint and impose the rule of law, was neglected."[41] Washbrook contends that the modernization of the police took place in the early twentieth century and was primarily directed at suppressing the anticolonial nationalist movement rather than in preventing crime.

The delta was a difficult place to police. The commissioner of Dacca division complained in 1882 that "resignations" were frequent as police work was "distasteful and hard" and policemen "see in the towns of Dacca and Naraingunge men of the laboring classes earning a good deal more than they do."[42] In 1884 constables in Noakhali and Tipperah districts complained: "the beats are . . . unduly large, which is another way of saying that the municipalities are unsuited to police as being too rural." The commissioner of Dacca reported in the same year that it was difficult to police the EBR terminus at Goalundo, "where the so-called town stretches over six square miles of country. . . . In the collections of scattered hamlets, of which Bengal municipalities generally consist, real watch and ward is impossible, and the police can do little more than report crime and keep order."[43] Piracy on the delta's extensive waterways was similarly difficult to investigate. E. C. Ryland, assistant inspector general of police, railways, and rivers, described river dacoities: "These occurrences take place on dark nights, on big rivers and people have no idea in what direction the dacoits have gone after the occurrence."[44]

Surprisingly, the inadequacies of the colonial government's provisions for security in the delta did not disturb colonial jute capital. During the jute season between July and October, millions of rupees in cash were disbursed throughout the hinterland's market towns. European jute capitalists provided for their own security: they employed private armed guards to protect their property in mofussil towns and, though instances of petty theft abounded, there were very few instances of armed robberies of jute traders' mofussil facilities. Further, jute capitalists' steam-powered boats were immune from river pirates, as they could outrun dacoits' oar- and sail-powered boats. The largest jute-purchasing firms employed expensive motorboats to distribute cash among its hinterland purchasers.[45] Armed robberies on riverways affected smaller traders relying on country craft—the farias and beparis—much more than they did larger capitalist concerns. In meetings with business interests to discuss an expanded river police scheme in 1905 and 1906, the colonial government found European jute traders to be vaguely supportive but somewhat indifferent.[46] Colonial capitalists felt that the government was "over-reaching," and urged a less ambitious and expensive scheme. Responding to the seeming apathy of Calcutta jute capitalists, E. C. Ryland found it necessary to impress upon his audience that "there is a great deal of crime [on waterways] . . . which does not come to the knowledge of people in Calcutta, and in which you are perhaps not, therefore, much interested, but it seriously affects the poorer classes. . . . They suffer to a great extent. To us perhaps they would be small sums, to them they are fortunes."[47]

Colonial capitalists did not lobby the government for provisions of law and order in the mofussil, for the judicial and police services to enforce contracts and protect their property. Instead, they asked the government to intervene in peasant production and hinterland trade. The lasting legacy of colonial jute capital with regard to state formation in the hinterland was neither the delta's legal system—a product of peasant consumption of legal services—nor its police force, oriented toward suppressing anticolonial nationalist movements. Instead, it was in government agencies that worked to "improve" peasant production in order to increase output and improve quality and to provide forecasts of the probable outturn of jute. State formations in the hinterland were the outcome of colonial capital lobbying the state to provide information, improve quality, and increase production of fiber.

Upon his return to Calcutta from the mofussil in the winter of 1873, George Burnett wrote a memorandum to the lieutenant governor of Bengal, George Campbell. Burnett's memorandum urged the creation of a program for "foster[ing] . . . the jute industry."[48] His primary concern was with peasant production, which he characterized as careless and lazy. In Burnett's narrative of jute, Bengal's cultivators had done nothing to "improve" the plant since finding it growing wild in the delta. He depicted cultivators as unintelligent and unthinking, mechanically producing poor-quality and low-yielding plants, and recommended that the colonial government set up "model" farms to devise and disseminate best-production methods among cultivators. He was also scathingly critical of the multitude of charges and the irregularity of weights used in hinterland transactions. Arguing that such practices ate into manufacturers' profits and denied cultivators a fair price for their produce, Burnett urged the state to "endeavor to eliminate middlemen." Last, Burnett was concerned about price instability, and asserted that the sharp rise and fall in prices between July and November 1871 had caused significant losses to Dundee jute manufacturers. Price instability, he suggested, could be reduced through government-published forecasts of jute acreage and probable yield. An "energetic and intelligent" collector in Dacca had assured him that the government would be able to provide a reasonably accurate forecast.[49]

Jute manufacturers and traders constantly lobbied the Calcutta government to intervene in the delta's jute cultivation and trade along the lines proposed by Burnett. They urged Calcutta to improve production, forecast yields, extend jute acreage, regulate markets, and designate quality grades. In 1874, jute spinners in Dunkirk urged the Government of India's "attention [to] . . . three special points, viz., the establishment of a Government scale of marks or brands, the frequent change of seed and greater care in the preparation of jute for the market."[50] In October 1885, the Dundee Chamber of Commerce lobbied the Government of Bengal to furnish "statistics of the probable outturn of the jute crop . . . between the seasons of sowing and reaping."[51] The Calcutta Baled Jute Association (an association of raw jute exporters) and the Dundee Jute Importers' Association petitioned the government to "improve" peasant cultivation so as to ensure better quality fiber.[52] Between 1906 and 1914, as global jute-manufacturing capacity rose sharply, a variety of international jute interests lobbied the colonial government to oversee the extension of jute cultivation so as to avoid shortfalls in supplies to the growing numbers of mills across the world.[53]

The government was generally responsive to capitalists' demands to intervene in peasant production. Campbell was sympathetic to Burnett's 1873 memorandum. Burnett's program of "fostering the jute trade" fit in with Campbell's theory of "positive government," which has been characterized by Peter Robb as a form of liberal developmentalism.[54] Upon receiving Burnett's memorandum, Campbell issued an "Official Note" on jute, expressing his desire for information about "Bengal's greatest commercial staple . . . where and how it is grown; from what plants; what are the qualities and varieties; how it is prepared for the market; how brought to market; and through what hands it passes, &c., &c." More complete information about jute cultivation and trade in the hinterland would, Campbell argued, underpin a program of positive government in the hinterland. "The Americans are actively prosecuting the experimental growth of Jute," Campbell said, "while we are, as a Government, doing nothing to extend it." He wanted to know "whether the quality of the fibre can be improved by careful preparation, and what are the best processes for its preparation." He stated: "The necessities of the Jute trade must have a very great influence on all our plans for roads, railways, and canals."[55]

Campbell acted promptly on Burnett's recommendation to establish experimental jute farms in the interior of the jute tracts. Just four days after receiving Burnett's memorandum, Campbell's office sent a letter to the commissioner of Dacca division informing him of "the desires of His Honor to see a farm established in this division for the experimental cultivation of jute and preparation of the fibre for market."[56] Within weeks, D. R. Lyall, the collector of Dacca described by George Burnett as "energetic and intelligent," had selected a plot of eighty bighas near the Dacca cantonment and had estimated a budget for establishing an experimental jute farm there.[57] The project was approved in less than a week, and the government immediately sanctioned money for initial and working expenses.[58]

The government began publishing jute forecasts in 1887, through the Agriculture Department that had been formed just two years previously as part of the colonial state's response to the devastating famines in central and western India.[59] The Agriculture Department's primary purposes were to "know" and "improve" peasant production: to "collect and embody in convenient forms of the statistics of vital, agricultural and economic facts" and to bring about "the general improvement of Indian agriculture with a view to increasing the food-supply and general resources of the people."[60] Despite its origins as a famine-prevention institution, in Bengal the department focused its energies on commercial fiber rather than subsistence grain. They did so at the behest of colonial capital.

In October 1885 the Dundee Chamber of Commerce requested the government of Bengal to publish forecasts of the probable jute crop sometime between its sowing and reaping. The Government of Bengal responded promptly and positively, stating that they would pilot a scheme for the "collection and publication of information regarding the area sown with jute and the prospects of the crop as it approaches maturity."[61] The provincial government's decision met with approval from the central government "The Governor-General in Council concurs with His Honor the Lieutenant Governor . . . that attempts to prepare crop estimates should in the first instance be confined to jute."[62] In 1887 the provincial government proudly noted its service to Scottish jute manufacturing: "Mr. Finucane [the director of agriculture] was able, in response to a call from the Secretary of State, to make to the satisfaction of the Dundee Chamber of Commerce, a forecast of the outturn of this year's crop."[63]

The Agriculture Department produced its first rice forecast in 1891, but even after that, considerably greater departmental resources would be devoted to forecasting the outturn of fiber rather than grain. As department officials admitted in 1894, "these forecasts are not particularly intended to indicate the approach of famine" and "were intended to supply information to the commercial public."[64] The department's jute forecast had become an international event, reported in the commercial pages of newspapers and magazines in London, Dundee, New York, Hamburg, Paris, and so forth. The publication of the forecast would have an immediate effect on jute prices. However, it was based on nothing more scientific than colonial district and subdivisional officers' guesses as to the probable acreage and output of jute. As the forecast came to play an increasingly important role in markets, its lack of accuracy came in for sharper criticisms.

In October 1903 the Dundee Jute Importers' Association and in December 1903 the Syndicate of the Jute Industry in Paris wrote to the colonial state complaining about the unreliability of forecasts and discrepancies between initial and final forecasts.[65] Dundee complained, "the forecasts . . . instead of being reliable guides, have proved misleading and have caused considerable loss to those interested."[66] In response, the department introduced a new scheme for estimating the probable outturn of jute in 1913, where information was provided by village panchayats, proclaiming it a "great improvement over the old system of guess work."[67] However, the panchayat's figures were never cross-checked and the system proved equally faulty. During the 1910s and 1920s, a variety of schemes for forecasting were tried out, usually in consultation with Calcutta and international jute capitalists. None of these schemes would prove satisfactory, and traders ultimately came to disregard government forecasts, relying on their own estimates instead.

The Agriculture Department's attempts to bring about "the general improvement of Indian agriculture with a view to increasing the food-supply" also—remarkably—focused on fiber rather than grain. The department had decided early on to leave "even . . . the introduction of the most promising improvements" to a later date when "a very much more intimate and thorough acquaintance with the agricultural facts and circumstances . . . [had] been obtained."[68] In 1902 they finally commenced a program of scientific agriculture based out of agricultural research stations throughout the jute hinterland. As part of this program, the department conducted investigations into different varieties of jute in Bengal, collecting sample seeds. In 1905 Robert S. Finlow was appointed as the Agriculture Department's first jute expert.[69] Finlow served as fibre expert for more than a decade before becoming director of the Agriculture Deparment, a position he held into the 1930s. Under Finlow's leadership, the department attempted to improve jute yields and to extend jute cultivation into new parts of British India, primarily through producing better-quality seeds and distributing them among farmers.

These activities were carried out at the behest of the global jute capital and their concerns during the early 1900s, particularly their concern that, as global jute manufacturing capacity rose, the demand would outstrip the supply of fiber. In 1905 the American consul in Bombay wrote, "The jute producing districts at present are restricted in the provinces of Bengal and eastern Bengal, and it is said that these will soon have reached the limit of their productive power, and that they will be utterly unable to keep pace with the enormous increase demanded."[70] In June 1914 the Indian Jute Mills Association sounded a warning of a commodity famine: "Extensive additions to the consuming power, both in India and elsewhere, will come into play during the next few months, and unless material increases take place next year in both acreage and yield, it will be impossible for consumers to secure their requirements of the raw material."[71]

R. S. Finlow admitted the validity of capitalists' concerns that demand was outstripping supply in a 1906 note: "Although it would appear that the area under jute cultivation and the weight of fibre produced are expanding considerably year by year, yet it also seems equally certain that the demand for the fibre is outstripping the supply."[72] Finlow and his department decided to extend jute cultivation to other parts of British India. This was a priority task for the Agriculture Department. The inspector general of agriculture stated in September 1906: "The most important work of the year has been the investigation of the possibilities of the *extension of jute cultivation* into other parts of India."[73] Finlow also advocated seed development and improved agricultural practices—particularly fertilization with manure—to increase yields.[74]

Under Finlow's leadership, the Agriculture Department commenced an intensive examination of jute varieties from across Bengal, and even developed their own seeds, which they claimed provided better yields. The department established "seed multiplication farms" and distributed these seeds among cultivators. Between 1918 and 1926 the government sold between 1,000 and 2,000 maunds of seed annually to jute cultivators. Though this was a rather small quantity, the department's seed multiplication and distribution activities were useful in extending jute cultivation to other parts of British India. In 1926 the Agriculture Department received funding from the London Jute Association, 20,000 rupees annually for five years, to distribute seeds in parts of Bengal, Bihar, and Assam where jute was not grown. M. Azizul Huque, the representative of Nadia, a non-jute-growing province in western Bengal where the department's seed distribution program was particularly intensive, complained in March 1930: "The Fibre Expert is entirely devoting himself to jute experimentation. They are always trying to produce jute where cultivators cannot possibly take to jute owing to the conditions of the soil."[75]

In carrying out these programs of jute forecasting, agricultural research, and seed production and distribution, the Agriculture Department considerably increased its presence in the delta and its mofussil towns. The extension of the Agriculture Department into the agrarian hinterland is an important phenomenon in the history of state formation in the delta. Its presence in the countryside increased sharply during the twentieth century. In the 1920s the department came to employ a full-time staff charged with estimating forecasts for output. From 1942 onward, jute cultivators were individually licensed to grow fixed quantities of fiber through the department's agencies in the mofussil. The Agriculture Department would emerge as a focal point in state-peasantry interactions in the jute hinterland.

Politics

In 1905, during a period of high prices and rapid increases in jute cultivation and trade, the government partitioned the province of Bengal, thus separating the administration of the hinterland from that of metropolitan Calcutta. The viceroy of India Lord Curzon's spatial rearrangement of the Bengal administration in 1905 was informed by the configurations of hinterland and metropolis that had been wrought by the circulation of jute. The plan was not merely a cynical ploy to divide and rule South Asia's Hindus and Muslims, as has been alleged by Indian nationalist historiography, but also a well-conceived territorial plan. The new province of Eastern Bengal and Assam comprised the jute tracts of the delta and the tea plantations of the hills, and was provided with a more proximate provincial capital in Dacca and a more "natural" outlet to the sea through Chittagong.[76] Curzon's plan was an attempt to solve the rising administrative burden on metropolitan Calcutta as the scale of state operations and functions in the deltaic hinterland expanded. The government's oft-repeated explanation for partition was that Bengal was too large a province to be under a single administration. Further, partition was a developmental plan for the underdeveloped hinterland—an attempt to increase and improve state administration, revenue collection, enforcement of law and order, extraction of resources, and transportation infrastructure in the relatively "backward" delta. Economically and administratively, the spatial rearrangement of the administration of Bengal made sense to Curzon and his colleagues.[77]

Opposition to the partition focused on preserving Calcutta's position as the delta's metropolis. When the government announced its plans to partition Bengal in 1903, a flurry of petitions poured in from eastern Bengal protesting the separation of hinterland from metropolis. For the petitioners, partition implied the severance of ties with a well-developed metropolis that served as the seat of commerce, culture, and administration for eastern Bengal. The "loss of Calcutta," as many petitioners pointed out, would lead to economic dislocation and civilizational decline—the latter exacerbated by its attachment to Assam, which was seen as "uncivilized" and home to "savages."[78] Petitioners wrote at length about Calcutta's civilizing effect on the backward hinterland, due to Calcutta's Bengali literary scene, headquarters of government administration, education system, and opportunities for middle-class careers. As a memorial from Noakhali argued, their district's connections with Calcutta had enabled "the most backward district in Bengal . . . to steadily work up to the high ideal set up by other enlightened parts of Bengal." The petitioners feared that the transfer to Assam, "a backward province with a lower form of administration" would destroy Noakhali's civilizational progress.[79]

These concerns about civilizational decline from the loss of Calcutta were accompanied by fears of economic dislocation. In the eyes of the petitioners, the hinterland had prospered from its material connections with this great "Metropolis of India," to use a phrase from a memorial from Fatehpur, Mymensingh. Opponents of partition feared that the severance of commercial ties with Calcutta would impoverish Bengal. Mahim Chandra Bhaumik from Mymensingh wrote: "Calcutta is a great centre of commerce, where people of almost every country in the world are making large profits by the import and export of goods. No other place in Bengal or Assam can be so convenient to a trader or offer so lucrative a market to him as Calcutta. On its transfer to Assam, East Bengal will lose its commercial prosperity."[80]

Eastern Bengal's traders and zamindars were among the most vocal and active opponents of partition. Many of them had invested considerable sums of money in Calcutta, particularly in Hatkhola bazaar, a wholesale jute market in the metropolis. In a December 1905 report, the government noted: "The most ardent workers in spreading the agitation [against partition] from Calcutta were the brothers of the Roy family of Bhagyakul, who in addition to being land-owners in Dacca have large trade interests, particularly in jute."[81] The Bhagyakul Roys operated a steamer service between eastern Bengal and Calcutta and had considerable investments in Hatkhola bazaar. Sita Nath Roy was president of the Congress-affiliated Bengal National Chamber of Commerce and wrote and spoke at length against the partition proposal. The petitions received by the colonial government from eastern Bengal pleaded the case for Dhaka and Mymensingh traders and their investments in Calcutta. The following petition from Sahadevpur in Tangail was emblematic of an oft-repeated concern:

> In Calcutta, a very large number of merchants from Dacca and Mymensingh carry on trade in which they have made large investments. They have built houses in Calcutta by spending lakhs of rupees. If they are compelled to remove all these from Calcutta to Chittagong, they will have to undergo very heavy loss. . . . All the jute is sent to Calcutta. But if they are to send the jute to Chittagong, their expenses will be much greater and their profits will be greatly reduced.[82]

While eastern Bengal's hinterland jute traders, led by the Roy family of Bhagyakul, wholeheartedly opposed Curzon's spatial rearrangement of the province, European jute capital lent his partition plans conditional support. The Indian Jute Mills Association did not think that partition would affect their mills' supplies of raw material: "the bulk of the crop will be attracted to Calcutta, regardless of any rearrangement, or redistribution, of the provinces in which it is grown."[83] The Bengal Chamber of Commerce noted that a simple administrative partition would not lead to a diversion of trade: "Trade will always follow the cheaper route, regardless of the jurisdiction under which it is carried on."[84] The BCC offered the partition plan conditional support. First, they said they would oppose state subsidies to divert trade away from Calcutta to Chittagong: "[the BCC] would strongly deprecate any attempt to force trade in the direction of Chittagong by the expenditure of State revenues in creating and maintaining what would be distinctly unfair competition between the Assam-Bengal Railway and the existing means of communication both by rail and river between the jute and tea districts and Calcutta."[85] Second, the BCC insisted that the Calcutta High Court should continue to maintain juridical authority over the newly created province of Eastern Bengal and Assam. In other words, European capital refused to fight their legal battles in hinterland courts. The second of these objections was more serious. "The Bengal Chamber of Commerce," the government concluded, "saw no objection from a commercial point of view to the transfer . . . but strongly objected to the proposals generally without a guarantee that the jurisdiction of the High Court over the transferred districts would not be interfered with in the slightest degree."[86] Curzon readily provided the chamber its guarantee.

Curzon's 1905 partition of Bengal and the opposition to it was informed by spatial ideas about the relationship between the eastern Bengal hinterland and metropolitan Calcutta. While the colonial government talked up plans of developing Dhaka and Chittagong and providing better government services in the hinterland, opponents of partition in eastern Bengal spoke of the loss of the hinterland's connections with metropolitan Calcutta. Supporters and detractors of Curzon's partition did not distinguish mofussil towns from the rest of the hinterland. The importance of the mofussil in the partition of 1905 was not as a conceptual spatial category, but as the stage for the antipartition Swadeshi movements, as the meeting place between metropolitan nationalists and eastern Bengal's peasant masses.

The mofussil was a crucial element in the spatial practices of nationalist politics. The attempt to mobilize the countryside was conducted from the metropolis and took place through the mofussil. The Swadeshi movement arrived in eastern Bengal in the persons of metropolitan politicians, who undertook whistlestop tours of the jute tracts. Between 1906 and 1909 Swadeshi leaders like Bipin Chandra Pal, Aurobindo Ghosh, and Abdullah Rasul undertook extensive tours of eastern Bengal, stopping to speak in towns

like Chandpur, Brahmanbaria, Narayanganj, Sirajganj, and so forth.[87] During
the course of the Swadeshi movement, over five hundred meetings were organized in eastern Bengal's mofussil towns protesting partition and promoting
Swadeshi. The colonial government kept a close watch on these meetings, and
were fearful of the oratory powers of nationalist leaders, particularly Bipin
Chandra Pal. Audiences attended these meetings not just to listen to oratory,
but also to see or catch a glimpse—do *darshan*—of famous figures. Nolini
Kanta Gupta accompanied Aurobindo Ghosh on a tour of Eastern Bengal
and Assam in 1909 and reported that "village folks . . . came in crowds just to
hear him [Ghosh] speak and have his *darshan*."[88] As the inspector general of
police noted in January 1905, "The strength of feeling in the Mufassil and the
progress of the Swadeshi movement varied considerably. . . . The determining
influences were probably the attitude of the local zamindars and *visits to the
towns of certain leading agitators*."[89]

Nationalists' speaking tours were successful in mobilizing support among
mostly Hindu salaried professionals in mofussil towns: schoolmasters,
pleaders, doctors, zamindari *amla*s (employees), and clerks. Mofussil towns
housed a small but growing population of the professional salaried middle
classes that formed the core of Swadeshi support in the hinterland. Many
of them had recently arrived from Calcutta or other parts of Bengal. In 1907
the Mymensingh magistrate collector, L. C. Clarke, reported that Swadeshi
activists in Jamalpur consisted of "the less permanent Hindu residents of the
town, I mean pleaders, doctors and zamindars' servants who have only been
here a few years or less." He further stated that the "more permanent residents
. . . have no sympathy with the 'Bande Mataram walas' as they call them."[90] The
mostly Hindu mofussil townsmen were at the frontline of the Swadeshi movement, occasionally sharing the platform with visiting nationalist politicians.[91]
While investigating picketing at the Nangalband fair, the collector of Dacca
met with local Swadeshi leaders: a doctor and a pleader from Narayanganj and
a pleader from Narshingdi.[92]

In the previous chapter, I described clashes at the Janmasthami mela near
Jamalpur town and Mogra hat in Brahmanbaria subdivision between mostly
Hindu Swadeshi activists and mostly Muslim jute cultivators over the boycott of imported goods in the hinterland's hats and fairs. In this chapter, I will
return to the events in Jamalpur town, following the clashes between mostly
Hindu Swadeshi activists and mostly Muslim stall owners and consumers at
the fair on April 22, 1907. On April 21 and 22, 1907, Swadeshi volunteers—
consisting largely of students—attempted to prevent the sale of European

goods at the fair. On the afternoon of April 22, "some two hundred zamindari servants, pleaders, mukhtears, and volunteers, with lathis, with an elephant, marched around the stalls and entered the Mela shouting Bande Mataram." They attacked stalls and destroyed "European toys and sweetmeats and scattered some Liverpool salt." The mostly Muslim visitors and shopkeepers at the fair attacked the volunteers, chasing them along the streets of Jamalpur to the river, the railway station, and the Durga temple, where an image for the Janmasthami festival was defaced.

This incident, I argued in the previous chapter, was a manifestation of the politics of jute cultivators' consumption. Over the following days, it transformed into a clash between the mostly Hindu town and the mostly Muslim countryside. Jamalpur was an administrative and market town, a subdivisional headquarters that was on the Mymensingh-Jamalpur-Jagannathganj railway line, connecting Mymensingh district to the Jagannathganj steamer station on the Brahmaputra. By eastern Bengal's standards, it was a fairly large town, with a population of 17,965 according to the 1901 census. The town, however, was dwarfed by the surrounding countryside: the population of Jamalpur thana was 282,000 and of the entire subdivision, 673,000.[93] During Swadeshi clashes, the town and the countryside were engaged in a prolonged battle with, on occasion, mostly Muslim cultivators from the countryside encircling and besieging mostly Hindu middle-class townsmen.

On the evening following the destruction at the Jamalpur Durgabari, Muslim cultivators from the surrounding countryside laid siege to the town, in a calculated show of strength apparently to prevent reprisals against fellow Muslims and an attack on the town's mosque in retaliation for the defacement of the image at the Durgabari: "Muhammadans of the outskirts and of the other side of the river . . . assembled in considerable numbers on the opposite bank of the river and some crossed: others collected from the railway side. They shouted for a long time, but finally were reassured and dispersed."[94] Tensions between mostly Hindu townsmen and mostly Muslim villagers, however, continued to simmer. On the night of April 27th, at around 9:30 p.m., a group of young Hindu men, including a mukhtear's (lawyer's) son and the son of the superintendent of a nearby zamindar's cutchery, shot at another group of men. The reasons behind the shooting were unclear to M. A. Luffman, the police superintendent at Jamalpur, but Genda Sheikh, a Muslim, was hit in the thigh. Luffman described what followed: "The news that a Muhammadan had been shot spread like wildfire and the Muhammadans from the surrounding country began to pour into the town in large numbers."[95]

During the following days, Muslims from the surrounding villages wandered the streets of Jamalpur ostensibly providing support for their coreligionists in the town. The Dhaka commissioner, R. Nathan, wrote on May 2: "At first there were a good many Muhammadans from outside the town, and they tended to collect in groups. I made the leaders tell them that they must go away, and during the past three days the streets have been quite normal." Nathan also reported that the town had been emptied of the mostly Hindu middle-class Swadeshi activists—"the majority of the Hindus of the Pleader, *zemindari amla* and *bhadra log* classes have left the place."[96] The bhadralok was a composite figure—Hindu, townsman, and salaried professional—and the term neatly collapses the overlapping religious, class, and spatial categories that informed Swadeshi conflicts in the jute tracts. Swadeshi mobilization pitted Hindu against Muslim, salaried middle class against peasant, and town against country.

The Jamalpur incident was reported in sharply religious terms by the Calcutta nationalist press. A Mymensingh journalist of the *Hitabadi* sent out a telegram to Calcutta describing the events: "Hindus menaced by 1000 Muhammadans, shops all closed and town absolutely deserted. Anarchy and lawlessness prevail. Magistrate and District Superintendent of Police are there; but are doing nothing, and appear to be egging on the rioters. Hindus leaving by every train. 200 respectable females left packed in cattle trucks, soiling their clothes and the platform, a pitiable spectacle."[97] Jamalpur was the epitome of the metropolitan nationalists' failure to generate support in the mostly Muslim countryside through mostly Hindu mofussil political activists.

This was in stark contrast to the nationalist fantasy of unity preceding violent clashes. The Bengal Provincial Conference in Mymensingh, Jamalpur's district headquarters, immediately preceded the Janmasthami incident. The nationalist press celebrated the Mymensingh Provincial Conference as emblematic of unity behind the nationalist cause, especially noting the presence of Muslim landlords and cultivators on a nationalist stage. A. K. Ghaznavi, a prominent Muslim landlord from Tangail, chaired the meeting and three jute cultivators—Sheikh Nazer-udddin, Sheikh Azim, and Sheikh Yokubali—addressed the meeting. As the nationalist press proudly noted, the Hindus, Muslims, zamindars, and ryots shared a common platform at the Mymensingh conference.

The platform did bring together the overlapping categories of peasant and middle class, Muslim and Hindu, and countryside and city. Bhupendranath Basu, a Calcutta-based Congress politician, with no social or familial connections to Mymensingh district, presided over the meeting. Radharaman Kar, a Calcutta jute baler and member of the Calcutta Baled Jute Association, moved a resolution opposing government legislation to prevent the watering of jute—the practice of wetting jute before packing in order to increase its weight. Swadeshi activists insisted that such practices were rare and expressed concern that such legislation would lead to legal harassment of hinterland jute traders. The three Muslim peasants—Sheikh Nazer-udddin, Sheikh Azim, and Sheikh Yokubali—spoke in support of Kar's motion. The official report on the meeting did not reproduce their actual statements but made the following observation: "Their [the cultivators'] rustic speeches made a great impression on the vast audience. The simplicity with which they refuted the accusations of mixing water and sand surprised the whole audience. Their speeches were a magnificent success. None ever expected such simplicity of eloquence."[98] This, then, was how metropolitan nationalists imagined peasant participation in the nationalist movement: the peaceful, reasonable, and possibly even "eloquent" participation of "rural rustics," in rehearsed and orchestrated mofussil events, presided over by metropolitan political and economic interests. This nationalist fantasy of metropolitan mobilization of the rural hinterland would be powerfully punctured by marketplace clashes throughout the hinterland.

Conclusion

The circulation of fiber through the built-up capital of railway tracks and stations, river ports, warehouses, and kutcha presses underpinned the emergence and growth of the mofussil, small towns serving as intermediary spaces between metropolitan Calcutta and the jute-growing agrarian hinterland. Mofussil towns were centers for wholesaling peasant-consumed commodities and for bulking peasant-produced commodities on their journeys between metropolitan Calcutta and the peasant homestead. The pattern of distribution of mofussil market towns was determined by superimposing steam-powered transport technologies over the delta's existing infrastructure of oar- and sail-powered boats and ox-drawn wagons. In addition to serving as centers of trade, mofussil towns were also centers of state administration, and housed courtrooms, police stations, revenue offices, and schoolhouses erected by the state. The expansion of the jute trade was accompanied by the increasing penetration of the state and, I have argued, the Agriculture Department was the forward institution of the state in its attempts to serve global capitalist interests in the jute-producing hinterland. During the late nineteenth century, these mofussil towns emerged as spaces of encounters between the hinterland peasantry and agents of metropolitan capital and the state.

The mofussil provided the stage for metropolitan nationalists to mobilize peasant masses during the Swadeshi movement. This attempt failed and sparked a revolt by mostly Muslim cultivators in the countryside against mostly Hindu bhadralok in the towns. For Aurobindo Ghosh, the failures of Swadeshi mobilization were explained by the mofussil's incapacity for autonomous and independent political thought and action. Writing in 1910, Ghosh described the mofussil as a politically and intellectually backward space that was under the thrall of Calcutta. He wrote that the mofussil Hindu middle classes who constituted the frontline of the movement "always waited for an intellectual initiative and sanction from the leaders in Calcutta." The "greater independence" and "higher organization of life, resources, activity in this great centre of humanity" made Calcutta a vibrant center of higher intellectual thought: "Calcutta is to Bengal what Paris is to France. . . . It is from Calcutta that Bengal takes its opinions, its inspirations, its leaders, its tone, its programme of action."[99]

Calcutta's intellectual and political dominance over mofussil towns was challenged after World War I, when mofussil towns emerged as independent centers of intellectual production and political action. The mofussil middle classes increased in numbers and changed in religious composition. Educated Muslim men, with close family and social ties to the surrounding countryside, took up professional employment in the hinterland towns. Far from being under the thrall of metropolitan culture, this mofussil middle class developed a distinctive political culture, challenging the intellectual supremacy of Calcutta. This mofussil political culture came into its own during a period of immiseration, as ecological disasters, fluctuating commodity markets, fragmented landholdings, and rising debt burdens drove peasant households into penury. The following chapter examines the processes of immiseration that set in after World War I and impoverished the countryside. Chapter 5 examines the emergence of a new Muslim middle class during this era of immiseration and the ways in which it transformed the cultural and political life of mofussil towns.

4

Immiseration

WORLD WAR I sparked a process of thorough, rapid, and utter immiseration of the jute-cultivating Bengal peasantry. Between World War I and World War II, a combination of market shocks, ecological disasters, fragmenting landholdings, and a crushing debt burden drove the majority of jute cultivators into destitution, hunger, and starvation. Discourses on jute cultivators' consumerist prosperity were replaced by descriptions of peasant hunger, disease, and nakedness. The poet Nagendrakumar De described the Bengal peasant in a poem *Bograr Kahini* (The Story of Bogra) in 1927: "Half dead, and wearing nothing but a loin cloth / Can't get food, the loincloth wrapped body is skin and bones."[1] The unclothed and unfed Bengal cultivator was a far cry from the nineteenth-century descriptions of peasant prosperity that manifested in clothing, food, and housing. The corrugated iron roofs that symbolized jute prosperity earlier in the century had lost their luster. The survey and settlement report for Rangpur, conducted during the depression decade, noted that, in "the principal jute area [to the southeast of the district] the country is open evincing by its large tin-roofed homesteads and orchards of graceful betel-nut palms, *evidence of past prosperity*."[2]

The first section of this chapter describes the processes of immiseration that set in during and after World War I. Impoverishment was driven by a combination of diminished landholdings, unfavorable and rigged commodity markets, frequent and recurrent ecological shocks, and high levels of indebtedness. The second section focuses on the depression decade of the 1930s, on how jute cultivators coped with the prolonged collapse in jute prices. The final section examines the tragedy of the Great Bengal Famine of 1943–44, when the inflationary pressures of World War II and colonial policies drove up the price of subsistence rice far faster than that of jute, and jute-cultivating peasant smallholders and agricultural wageworkers—themselves former peasant smallholders who had lost their farms through debt—starved. During the famine period of 1943 and 1944, between two and four million people died of hunger or hunger-related causes. In the century since the beginnings of commercial jute cultivation, Bengal's jute cultivators had gone from consumerist prosperity to market-driven hunger and starvation.

Immiseration

Peasant households' vulnerability to shocks stemmed from their reduced holdings of arable land and their inability to produce—even during years of good harvest—sufficient rice for basic subsistence. The delta's increasing population had resulted in the progressive diminution of peasant holdings during the late nineteenth and early twentieth centuries, as property was subdivided equally among sons. By the early twentieth century, the majority of the delta's peasantry possessed less than two acres of land. In 1929–30, on the eve of the Great Depression and the collapse of agrarian prices, the average holdings of cultivators in the jute tracts ranged from one to two acres (see table 4.1). These are, however, average figures, pulled upward by the small number of households with considerable lands. The median was closer to one acre, or sometimes even less. The survey and settlement report for Mymensingh, conducted between 1910 and 1919, found that 60 percent of peasant households cultivated an average of two acres, 36 percent cultivated five acres, and only 4 percent possessed twelve acres.[3] Peasants' holdings were even smaller in Pabna, where the survey and settlement report found that 36 percent of cultivators held less than an acre, 20 percent possessed between one and two acres, and 12.5 percent had between two and three acres.[4]

TABLE 4.1. Average Landholdings in Jute-Growing Districts, 1929–1930

District	Average landholdings
Dacca	1.52 acres
Mymensingh	2.79 acres when rent is paid in cash 0.86 acres when rent is paid in produce
Faridpur	1.39 acres
Tippera	2.03 acres when rent is paid in cash 0.86 acres when rent is paid in produce
Pabna	1.09 acres
Bogra	2.05 acres

Given the preponderance of agricultural production, peasant households found it impossible to produce sufficient subsistence out of miniature holdings of an acre or less. Indu Bhushan Dutta, the elected councilor from Tipperah, estimated "not more than 25 per cent of the agriculturists can grow sufficient rice for their own consumption. The rest of the people have to buy, even if for a few months of the year."[5] The survey and settlement report for Pabna and Bogra noted: "This condition of land tenure is uneconomic. Even in the most fertile tracts, a holding of 3 *bighas* [1 acre] . . . will not suffice to keep a cultivator with his family in the barest necessities of life. In order to exist he has to take a few extra *bighas* in *barga* [to sharecrop], or to undertake a little labour such as carting jute to market."[6] Many peasant smallholders thus began to produce jute as part of a market-based subsistence strategy, in the hope that proceeds from sales of jute would finance purchases of rice from the market. As the survey and settlement report for Pabna and Bogra stated: "The cultivator grows sufficient paddy to last for 8–10 months and trusts to the profit from jute to provide him with food for the remaining months."[7]

Land fragmentation and market-based subsistence strategies unmoored the supply of jute from its demand, making it difficult for cultivators to scale back jute cultivation in response to a fall in prices. In the nineteenth century, when jute was grown to finance nonsubsistence forms of consumption, the supply of fiber was more responsive to global prices. In the twentieth century, particularly during the depression decade, the relationship between demand, supply, and price no longer held. Cultivators could not respond to low jute prices by slashing acreage, as they were reliant on jute to procure subsistence. Simultaneously, even modest increases in price led to disproportionately greater increases in acreage, as marginal peasants expanded jute cultivation enormously in the hope that high prices would not only support basic subsistence but also support some additional consumption or even pay down outstanding debts.

Unfortunately for jute-cultivating peasant households, global commodity markets turned against them after World War I. In the boom-and-bust economy of the 1920s, the prices of rice and all commodities rose faster and higher than jute in inflationary years, and did not fall as low as jute during price slumps (see figure 4.1). The price scissors—when prices of peasant-produced commodities were far lower than that of peasant-consumed commodities— was particularly wide from the closing years of World War I until 1923. Omkar Goswami has calculated that a peasant household holding three acres of land faced a shortfall of sixteen rupees in 1921–22. Most cultivators held far less than three acres and would face far greater shortfalls. In February 1921, when rice prices rose to new highs, the delta's subsistence jute cultivators were hit hard.[8] Kishori Mohan Chaudhuri, the member from Rajshahi, informed the Legislative Council that the vast majority of cultivators "were in difficulty, not being able to get a market for their jute, and the result was that they were on the brink of starvation, which was partly due, I think, to the shortage of food-grains."[9] Indu Bhushan Dutta (Tipperah) spoke in agreement: "For the last few years, the prices [of rice] have reached the extraordinary limit of Rs. 9 to Rs. 10 per maund at this season of the year. The agriculturist who has to pay this price for his staple food cannot bless the system which causes this high price and spells utter ruination for him and his like."[10] With the exception of the boom year of 1926, the terms of trade between jute and other commodities were never as favorable as they were in 1914.

Further, jute markets were increasingly rigged against cultivators. The year-to-year fluctuations in commodity prices disguised the price fluctuations within the year. Jute prices fell sharply during harvest time, around September and October, and then increased over the winter, once peasant households had sold their stocks of fiber. The Indian Chamber of Commerce testified to the Banking Enquiry Committee in early 1930: "The jute market is always dull

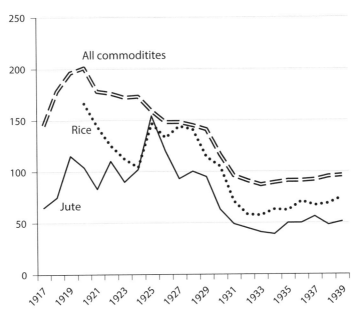

FIGURE 4.1. Price indices of jute, rice, and all commodities in Bengal, 1917–1939 (1914 is base year, when all price levels equaled 100)

in the months of September, October and November. . . . It is only after the first rush is over that the arrivals of jute in the mofussil are to some extent affected by the prices ruling in the market."[11] Jute purchasers began to act like cartels, withholding purchases to suppress prices. Narayan Chandra Ghosh, SDO of Netrokona in Mymensingh district, stated: "It sometimes appears that the agents of firms and companies, dealing in the export trade, stop buying of jute whenever there is a tendency towards increase in the buying rate."[12] Purchasers' ability to influence prices was related to cultivators' reduced bargaining power, as peasant households were forced to sell to secure household subsistence and could not withhold fiber for any length of time. Mofussil jute purchasers were well aware of this, holding off purchases until hunger drove peasants to accept whatever prices were on offer.

Under these conditions, cultivators could not benefit even during years of high jute prices and, instead, the benefit of high prices accrued to traders and middlemen with the financial wherewithal to withhold fiber and bargain for prices. The relatively higher prices in 1926 had benefited wealthier inhabitants of the agrarian delta rather than the direct producers of the fiber. The Narayanganj Chamber of Commerce reported to the Banking Enquiry Committee, "the middlemen or wealthier inhabitants of the village do all the holding of jute for better prices by financing the *raiyat* during the period for which the jute is held, and this has become more prevalent since 1926 when they made fabulous profits and put up corrugated iron sheds all over the country in order to store up their holdings, thereby minimizing the risk of fire."[13] The Agent of the Imperial Bank in Dacca reported: "The wealthier inhabitants, not necessarily cultivators, in the interior however are increasingly inclined to speculate and buy under the market price from their own raiyats if they are zamindars. Numbers of the latter classes made fortunes during the high price year—1926."[14]

Adding to peasant households' woes, as Iftekhar Iqbal has shown, the delta's ecology deteriorated rapidly in the early twentieth century.[15] This was an unintended consequence of the east-west orientation of railway lines, linking the agrarian hinterland to metropolitan Calcutta, that blocked the delta's natural north-south drainage. Railway lines were constructed with high embankments and relatively few openings to allow drainage—the former to protect railways during the delta's annual flood and the latter to reduce costs. These railway embankments caused untimely, more severe, and prolonged flooding; the standing water became a breeding ground for malaria-carrying mosquitoes and a conduit for waterborne diseases like cholera and black fever.

Further, the delta was invaded by the water hyacinth, the "lilac-killer." Initially imported as an ornamental plant, the water hyacinth spread throughout the delta, choking waterways and invading farmlands with standing crops. Railway embankments and water hyacinth were jointly responsible for numerous crop failures and the rapid spread of waterborne diseases during the early twentieth century.

The two railway lines responsible for the greatest damage in the Bengal delta were the the Akhaura-Ashuganj line on the Assam Bengal Railway, opened in 1915, and the Sara-Sirajganj railway line in northern Bengal, opened in 1918. The important jute-growing area of Brahmanbaria in Tipperah and along the banks of the Jamuna in northern Bengal was particularly flood-prone during the 1910s and 1920s. Serious floods occurred in Brahmanbaria in 1915–16, the year the Akhaura-Ashuganj railway line opened, leading to "real famine" according to the survey and settlement report for Tipperah. Floods recurred in Brahmanbaria in 1919, 1924, and then again in 1929. Floods had occurred in Tipperah prior to railway construction though, according to the Tipperah survey and settlement report of 1919, "it seems that . . . they [floods] have been more frequent and violent than ever before."[16] In addition to frequent and devastating floods, there was a permanent decline in productivity in many areas abutting the railways, where high embankments caused water to pool and stagnate. In the low-lying areas in eastern Brahmanbaria, "the cultivators seem to have lost much of the winter rice crops every year since the railway embankment on the Branch Line to Asuganj was completed."[17]

Disease and death constituted yet another external shock to peasant households that increased in frequency during the 1910s and 1920s. Ihtesham Kazi has illustrated how the construction of railways was followed, often immediately, by the outbreak of malaria epidemics in the eastern Bengal districts of Pabna, Mymensingh, and Tipperah and that stagnant pools of water, caused by railway embankments, provided fertile breeding grounds for malaria-carrying mosquitoes.[18] The Annual Report of the Sanitary Commissioner of Bengal for 1922 calculated that the incidence of malaria in eastern Bengal had more than doubled in the previous decade.[19] *Kala-azar*, or black fever, was another waterborne disease that took on epidemic proportions in the period. An investigation by the Public Health Department in 1919 found that 54 percent of surveyed villages in Mymensingh, 30 percent in Dacca, and 15 percent in Tipperah had cases of kala-azar.[20] In addition to malaria and kala-azar, epidemics of smallpox and cholera were reported from throughout the delta.

"More railways, more malaria" became a common saying in Bengal. Legislators on the Bengal Council frequently attributed epidemics to high railway embankments. In 1926, Emdadul Huq—the member from Tipperah— informed the council that, "it is a well known fact that in Bengal the high railway embankments and water hyacinth have jointly contributed to spread malaria and kala-azar by interfering with the natural drainage and choking up all the bils and canals."[21] In March 1930 Tamizuddin Khan, a member from Faridpur, spoke poignantly of the destruction wrought by waterborne epidemics in eastern Bengal: "the areas which were once flourishing and prosperous and teeming with a smiling population are now de-populated hot-beds of malaria and other disease."[22]

Frequent and recurrent market and ecological shocks buffeted a marginal and vulnerable peasantry in the years during and after World War I. For a peasant household cultivating less than an acre of land such shocks translated into hunger and, possibly, starvation. In the agrarian economy of the Bengal delta, there was only one safety net available to a peasant household that had experienced the shock of unfavorable prices due to volatile markets, crop failures due to floods, or sickness and death due to epidemics—high-interest emergency loans from moneylenders. As the Bengal Provincial Banking Enquiry rightly concluded, indebtedness in the agrarian delta arose out of poverty: "there is a kind of poverty, which while not amounting to insolvency, nevertheless makes for precarious and uncertain living. It is this latter class of poverty, which is the real cause of indebtedness among agriculturists in Bengal."[23] The "precarious and uncertain living" of the delta's agriculturists drove peasants to undertake high-interest emergency loans in addition to the regular annual debt required to finance cultivation.

TABLE 4.2. Monthly Interest Rates in Munshiganj, Dacca, 1929–1930

	General loans	Petty loans
November–December	2%	3%
December–January	2%	3%
January–February	2%	3%
February–March	3%	4%
April–May	5%	6%
May–June	6%	7%
July–August	7 to 8%	Anything up to 16%

Evidence of S. Basu, SDO Munshiganj, to the BPBEC, BPBEC, vol. II, part I, 1929–1930, p. 194

The availability and price of loans fluctuated sharply according to the harvest calendar and incidences of seasonal hunger: interest rates were generally at their highest when peasant households' cash needs were greatest. As variations in monthly interest rates from Munshiganj subdivision in Dacca district (table 4.2) demonstrate, interest rates rose sharply in March and peaked during May and June, reaching monthly rates of up to 16 percent for petty loans. May and June were about the time that cultivators with smaller holdings would be running out of stocks of winter or aman rice, harvested in December and January, and were awaiting their aus and jute harvests. These marginal cultivators required petty loans to stave off hunger until they harvested spring or aus rice and jute in August and September. In saving themselves from starvation, these peasant households dug themselves deeper into poverty.

In addition to petty loans to tide them over seasonal hunger, peasant households took on emergency loans during times of crisis: when prices were low, when crops failed, when floods were prolonged, or when a member of the household was sick or dying. Emaduddin Ahmed, chairman of the Rajshahi District Board testified to the Royal Commission on Agriculture in 1926 that "the highly lowering down of the prices of jute" was one of the causes of agricultural indebtedness.[24] M. Fariduddin, Khas Mahal officer in Faridpur, testified to the Banking Enquiry Committee in 1929: "when they [cultivators] do not get a good harvest they have to incur debts to meet their ordinary wants."[25]

Interest rates on emergency loans were considerably higher partly because moneylenders were taking advantage of peasant desperation and also because the much greater demand for loans drove up the price of credit. In his evidence to the Banking Enquiry Committee, Bhabesh Chandra Roy, SDO of Naogaon in Rajshahi, reported that interest rates varied proportionately according to the "urgent necessity of the borrower." Umesh Chandra Chakladar, vice chairman of the Mymensingh District Board, reported that if the monsoon rains fail or are delayed, "credit is invariably dear in every quarter."[26] Mohammad Khayer Ali's long poem about the floods in north Bengal in 1922, *Bonya Kahini* (Events of a Flood) was especially critical of moneylenders who, taking advantage of the situation, raised their interest rates too high: "A few moneylenders take advantage / and increase interest rates very high . . . All the mahajans of the country / They are sucking the blood of farmers."[27] The debt burden of peasant households rose steadily during the postwar years and interest payments were a major recurrent expense in household budgets. These ever-increasing interest demands kept peasant households trapped in poverty. Unable to build up assets or savings during the infrequent years of favorable harvests, health, and market prices, peasant households lurched from one crisis to the next, forever falling into deeper debt.

Other major sources of credit, besides the professional moneylenders, included wealthier and more substantial peasant households, village shop-keepers who offered small amounts of consumer credit, and local traders who provided produce loans against standing crops. The latter form of credit—known as *dadan*—which was nonexistent during the more prosperous pre–World War I years, had become more common after World War I, though it was still far from widespread. During the 1920s, consumer credit from shopkeepers and petty loans from wealthier peasant households were more common sources of credit than dadan and were at least as widely used as loans from professional mahajans. For the most part, moneylenders were not inter-ested in taking possession of peasant assets and arable lands. Instead, they pre-ferred to receive regular interest payments. However, as the 1920s progressed, the increasing incidence of marginal cultivators with occupancy rights being reduced to sharecroppers, or *bargadars*, was reported from the delta. Muazzam Hossain, deputy collector in Mymensingh, testified to the Banking Enquiry Committee in 1926 that in the eastern parts of the district "a very large pro-portion of the raiyats . . . now work as bargadars."[28] B. B. Dutt testified that in Brahmanbaria, the jute-growing subdivision of Tipperah, "good farmers were being converted into *bargadars*."[29] The depression decade of the 1930s witnessed a rise in creditors' confiscation of peasant arable lands, the spread of produce or dadan loans, and ultimately the departure of the professional mahajan from the agrarian economy.

The Depression Decade

The onset of the global Great Depression in 1930 led to an extreme and prolonged fall in prices. Jute prices dropped from close to 9 rupees per maund on average between 1926 and 1929 to about 3 rupees per maund in 1930. The average price of jute during the 1930s was less than half the average price of the 1920s.[30] The value of the total jute crop in 1930–31 in Bengal was less than 200 million rupees, against an average of 500 million rupees over the preceding decade.[31] The prices of all commodities collapsed during the depression decade, but jute prices fell faster and lower than that of peasant-consumed commodities (see figure 4.1). Unlike previous market collapses, low prices persisted for the entire decade of the 1930s, and only recovered with the beginning of World War II.

The depression decade of the 1930s provided the final push into destitution for a significant portion of the delta's jute-cultivating peasantry. Omkar Goswami has calculated that permanently settled occupancy ryots with three acres of land—far more than the average landholding in the delta—were simply not able to make ends meet during the 1930s.[32] The survey and settlement report for Rangpur presented household budgets of more substantial peasant households with larger landholdings. A family with six acres of land was living just "above starvation," earning 150 rupees from the produce off their land. "In normal times," the report noted, "it should be reasonably prosperous." A family with almost thirteen acres of land was living in "comfort," but hardly in luxury: "[Their] expenditure is all in necessities." This family "would be normally prosperous but has been badly hit by the slump in price of jute."[33]

The market shock of the depression was accompanied by severe ecological shocks. Flooding occurred across the jute tracts, notably in Brahmanbaria, where severe flooding had become especially frequent after the construction of the Akhaura-Ashuganj spur for the Assam Bengal Railway, and in Bogra, in northern Bengal. The early rise of floodwaters during May and June of 1929 in Brahmanbaria led to the total destruction of spring rice and the premature harvesting of jute on lowlands to prevent the total loss of crops. The damage to spring rice and jute was compounded by the loss of a portion of the winter rice by water hyacinth. According to the government's estimates, "distress"—the colonial euphemism for extreme hunger—continued until March of 1930.[34] According to official estimates, flooding had affected 250,000 people, 50,000 of them severely, and covered over 250 square miles. When Ashrafuddin Chaudhuri, the member from Brahmanbaria, alleged in the Legislative Council that flooding had caused famine and starvation deaths, the government responded that there was "distress in some of the areas affected by floods" and that deaths were due to disease, not starvation.[35] There was severe flooding in Bogra in two consecutive years—1930 and 1931. Low jute prices after the harvest during August and September 1930 had already pushed peasant households into hunger, when floods struck, destroying "14 *annas* [14/16th] of the standing *aman* [winter] paddy." To compound peasant households' woes, floods recurred in July and August 1931, when the Brahmaputra overflowed its banks, and destroyed the expected bumper crop of aus paddy.[36]

Buffeted by market and ecological shocks, the jute-cultivating peasantry turned to their usual safety net—high-interest emergency loans from moneylenders. However, the depression had caused a liquidity crisis, with mahajans' sources of credit drying up. Rather than advancing further loans, mahajans decided to call in outstanding debts and even take possession of peasant lands. Sugata Bose has demonstrated that moneylenders' refusal to advance loans and, further, to call in outstanding debts led to anti-moneylender riots in Kishoreganj and Dacca during the early years of the Depression.[37] These riots consisted of bands of peasants attacking moneylenders' homes and demanding and destroying deeds for outstanding loans. If moneylenders produced the deeds, their lives and property were spared. If they did not, attacks turned violent, with several episodes of moneylenders being killed. As Bose emphasizes, peasants were not protesting high interest rates—they were protesting moneylenders' attempts to call in debts and renegotiate outstanding loans. The Bengal Agricultural Debtors Act of 1936 spelled the end of the professional moneylender in agrarian Bengal. The act provided for the establishment of debt settlement boards that renegotiated peasant households' outstanding debts with moneylenders. Unable to lend at their previous high rates of interest and to continue to extract interests out of the peasantry, the mahajan departed the agrarian economy.

Average levels of debt per family had increased quite sharply in the jute tracts between 1929 and 1934, by 113 percent in Mymensingh, 81 percent in Dacca, and 42 percent in Tipperah.[38] The increase in debt was due to new forms of produce loans that emerged in the depression decade. With the departure of the professional moneylender, wealthier peasant households with more substantial landholdings and intermediary traders entered the credit market. The former offered small loans secured against peasant property and the latter offered produce loans, where cultivators would agree to deliver a portion of their future harvest to the creditor at a fixed price far below prevailing market rates. Further, marginal cultivators also subsisted by selling off parcels of arable land, thereby reducing their already uneconomic landholdings. The depression further impoverished an already destitute peasantry, increased their debt burden, reduced their ability to negotiate prices, and transformed "permanently settled occupancy ryots" with secure property rights to sharecroppers. When the next price shock arrived, with the inflationary pressures of World War II, marginal jute cultivators and sharecroppers had no resources left to fall back on and millions of them starved to death.

Famine

The beginning of World War II jolted the agrarian delta out of its prolonged depression. The war and colonial inflationary war policies led to a rise in prices across the board, but jute prices did not rise nearly as quickly as the price of rice. The price scissors of World War II was extreme and hit an agrarian economy with far fewer assets and absolutely no safety net. Rice prices increased sharply in the first quarter of 1943, from 12.5 rupees in January to 30 rupees in March.[39] As Amartya Sen has argued, the rise in prices was not due to poor harvests and declining food availability but, instead, was due to grain speculators who turned local shortfalls in production into a price bubble. Marginal cultivators who depended on sales of jute to finance rice purchases were affected by rising rice prices. Jute prices had risen concurrently with rice prices during the winter and spring of 1942 and 1943, but more slowly and not as steeply. The price of jute increased from between 6.5 and 9.5 rupees a maund in July 1942 to between 14 and 17 rupees a maund in July 1943; jute prices only doubled while rice prices had almost quadrupled.

The increase in jute prices only took place after November 1942, at which time peasant households had sold their jute to intermediary traders. When aman stocks ran out in the spring and monsoon season of 1943, peasant households did not have enough cash from the previous year's jute sales to purchase rice. Nor did they have recourse to emergency loans, as professional moneylenders had departed the agrarian economy following anti-moneylender legislation during the depression decade. The poorest and most vulnerable inhabitants of the agrarian delta starved. Refusing to allow any distractions from the war effort and actively spurred on by Winston Churchill's racist attitudes toward Indians, the colonial government refused to recognize the famine and undertook no relief measures. The colonial state stood by as commodity markets wrought death in the Bengal delta. During the famine years of 1943 and 1944 around three million of the poorest and most vulnerable inhabitants of the delta died from starvation and hunger-related causes.[40]

TABLE 4.3. Peasant Families' Sales of Land, April 1943 to April 1944 (percentages out of total number of peasant families in each landholding category)

	Sold all arable land	Sold part of arable land
Less than 2 acres	240,000 (6.1%)	300,000 (7.4%)
Between 2 and 5 acres	20,000 (1.2%)	250,000 (15.3%)
More than 5 acres	4,000 (0.4%)	110,000 (12.5%)

Starvation deaths were highest among landless agricultural laborers, those earning a living from a trade or a craft, and among women and the elderly.[41] Those who survived did so because they had either grown enough rice for household subsistence or received gifts and loans of grain from kin and neighbors, or because they had sold their assets (see table 4.3). Many marginal peasant households that had managed to hold on to some arable land during the hardships of the depression decade ended up landless. Close to a million peasant families sold all or part of their arable lands—and over half of those families were marginal cultivators with less than two acres of land. Additionally, 670,000 peasant families mortgaged arable land, out of which about 103,000 families also sold some of their land.[42] In their desperate attempts to stave off death from starvation, large numbers of peasant households were rendered landless and joined the rapidly expanding ranks of impoverished landless laborers and sharecroppers in the Bengal delta. While nineteenth-century prosperity had resulted in more secure peasants' rights to the lands they tilled, twentieth-century immiseration witnessed the conversion of former occupancy ryots into landless laborers and sharecroppers.

Conclusion

The nineteenth-century peasant politics of consumption came to an end with World War I. Projects of peasant self-fashioning through the consumption of cloth, metals, and gourmet foods were not applicable in a context where the vast majority of cultivators were barely scraping together subsistence from markets. A new peasant politics of austerity and market asceticism replaced the politics of consumerist desires that had dominated the nineteenth century. This politics of market asceticism was informed by ideas of Islam as a worldly religion that provided a program for the ethical practice of market-entangled lives. The next chapter discusses the emergence of discourses of an agrarian form of Islam that related peasant poverty to the failure to practice Islam in the everyday activities of work, buying and selling from markets, patriarchal authority over the household, and good neighborly relations.

Peasant immiseration was also accompanied by the rearrangement of the spatial relations of metropolis, hinterland, and mofussil. The few peasant households that did not experience immiseration were critical toward these transformations. These peasant households had used profits from the earlier jute boom to diversify their livelihoods away from purely agrarian pursuits. They had invested in moneylending, in acquiring intermediary tenures like *taluks* and *jagirs*, in trading peasant-produced and peasant-consumed commodities, and in their sons' education. As the bulk of the peasantry was rapidly reduced to destitution, this small segment prospered. Many of them established professional careers and businesses in mofussil towns. The next chapter will show how mofussil towns transformed from islands of metropolitan culture surrounded by a hostile hinterland to spaces that were autonomous and independent of the metropolis and closely connected to the countryside.

The remaining chapters examine the post–World War I peasant politics of immiseration, up to and beyond independence, partition, and the creation of Pakistan in 1947. The politics of immiseration was not simply a function of unfavorable markets and the deteriorating terms of trade between peasant-produced and peasant-consumed commodities. Instead, the changing conditions of markets created new forms of peasant life that focused on ensuring the viability of market-entangled livelihoods and transformed the spatial relations of hinterland, metropolis, and mofussil. These changes, in turn, gave rise to new forms of peasant political action.

5

Agrarian Forms of Islam

THE POLITICS OF PEASANT IMMISERATION

PEASANT IMMISERATION was accompanied by new forms of peasant politics. Prior to World War I, peasant politics was concerned with the possibilities and pleasures of consumption. After World War I, it was concerned with the viability of market-entangled livelihoods. The looting of rural marketplaces during 1917 and 1918 was an early instance of this new politics of immiseration, as markets transformed from spaces of self-fashioning and pleasure to sources of scarcity and hunger. The peasant politics of immiseration manifested in diverse forms during the following decades: in collective action against the colonial state and its agents during the Khilafat movement in 1921–22, violence against Hindu elites and villagers in Pabna in 1926, attacks on Hindu moneylenders and traders in Kishoreganj and Dacca in 1930, votes for the Krishak Praja Party during the 1937 elections, the forced conversion of Hindus in Noakhali in 1946, and widespread support for the Pakistan movement and the Muslim League during the 1946 elections. Markets did not determine peasant political action in a straightforward, deterministic fashion: peasant households did not swing from violence to acquiescence according to fluctuations in global market prices. Instead, this era of immiseration gave rise to new forms and discourses of peasant self-fashioning and transformed spatial relations of metropolis, mofussil, and hinterland that, in turn, informed the content and form of peasant political action.

Paradoxically, peasant immiseration was accompanied by an efflorescence of mofussil intellectual life and a growing unity between mofussil towns and the hinterland. The 1920s witnessed a boom in mofussil print and publishing: new presses were established, newspapers proliferated, and small-town poets, essayists, novelists, and pamphleteers published extensively. The burgeoning mofussil printing and publishing industry was sustained and supported by a new community—Muslim men with origins in the jute-cultivating hinterland who had moved to the towns to take up professional employment or to start small businesses. These men were the products of the pre–World War I jute boom, as some peasant householders successfully invested jute profits in their sons' education and in establishing businesses in mofussil towns. These newly arrived mofussil Muslim men overturned Aurobindo Ghosh's 1910 assertion that "Calcutta is to Bengal what Paris is to France, it is from Calcutta that Bengal takes its opinions, its inspirations, its leaders, its tone, its programme of action."[1] Their opinions, inspirations, and programs of action were rooted in the jute tracts' peasant society, not in metropolitan Calcutta.

Many mofussil Muslim men authored, read, and financed the publication of poems, pamphlets, essays, and newspaper editorials about peasant immiseration. They addressed the causes and solutions of peasant poverty through discussions of Islam that provided an ethical guide and moral compass to market-entangled lives. They formulated a discourse of agrarian Islam focused on the viability of market-entangled peasant lives, urging ceaseless labor, austerity in consumption, and patriarchal authority as means to balancing peasant household budgets. Their texts reached beyond the limits imposed by the delta's abysmal literacy rate, and circulated between the mofussil print economy and hinterland oral cultures. The primary genre of agrarian Islamic discourses was the *boyan*: a long poem consisting of rhyming couplets printed on cheap paper, loosely bound with thread, and sold at a low price in mofussil and rural markets. The poem was then performed at rural and mofussil public places—in hats, melas, bazaars, and in front of courthouses. Thus the printed boyan was the spoken poem, written down, printed, mass-produced, so as to be read aloud once again.

This chapter begins with a narrative and analysis of the Khilafat movement of 1920–22. The movement was launched in protest against Britain's abolition of the Ottoman Caliphate and its conquest of the Muslim holy lands in Arabia during World War I, and it subsequently joined Gandhi and the Indian National Congress's Non-Cooperation Movement. The Khilafat/Non-Cooperation movement was formative in the peasant politics of immiseration that emerged after World War I, creating a mofussil political sphere that was autonomous from the metropolis and closely integrated into the countryside, and informing discourses of agrarian Islam. The second section examines the intellectual and cultural efflorescence in mofussil towns during a period of agrarian immiseration, focusing on the emergence of a mofussil Muslim intelligentsia and its connections to the burgeoning small-town print and publishing industry. The third section explores the mofussil Muslim intelligentsia's writings on Islam and poverty, demonstrating that these texts constituted a discourse of agrarian Islam that circulated between towns and the countryside and oral and print cultures.

Khilafat, 1920–22

In stark contrast to the failures of Swadeshi mobilization, the delta's mostly Muslim jute cultivators were committed and energetic participants in the Khilafat movement. In fact, their enthusiasm far exceeded the expectations of nationalist leaders and political elites, who were often more concerned with controlling and disciplining peasant enthusiasm than in mobilizing peasant support.[2] Swadeshi failure had accompanied a period of peasant prosperity and intense consumerism. The Khilafat movement coincided with a period of acute economic crisis. Jute prices fell by 10 percent in 1920 and a further 20 percent in 1921. Simultaneously, rice prices remained stubbornly high, and the ratio of jute to rice prices reached extreme lows. The movement came to an end as the economic situation improved in 1922, when jute prices rose by 33 percent and rice prices fell by 13 percent.[3] The correlation between the terms of trade between jute and rice and peasant political action should not, however, lead us into economic determinism, with peasant politics alternating between rebellion and acquiescence as global commodity prices fluctuated. This was the colonial argument put forward to discredit anticolonial nationalism. P. C. Bamford, senior colonial official and author of the state narrative of the movement, wrote: "when the economic pinch was so severe and the listener so ignorant and gullible, it need be no matter for surprise that the propaganda [by activists] proved effective." He triumphantly noted: "There is . . . no greater proof of the hollowness of these agitations than the manner in which they succumbed to improved economic conditions."[4]

Historians have filled in the alleged "hollowness" of peasant movements during the Khilafat/Non-Cooperation movements. Peasant support for the Khilafat movement in the delta's jute tracts reflected Muslim peasant households' long-standing extraterritorial loyalties to a global Muslim cosmopolis that long predated the movement and nationalist mobilization. It was also built upon peasant understanding of Gandhi's message of "*swaraj* within a year" as a utopian and millenarian promise of the imminent end of the unjust

British Raj and the impending arrival of a moral and just society.[5] However, the millenarian appeal of swaraj and Muslim jute cultivators' extraterritorial loyalties, while enormously significant to peasant political action, did not mark the Khilafat movement out as a formative moment in a new post–World War I peasant politics of immiseration. The Khilafat movement was formative in two respects. First, it marked the entry into national politics of mofussil Muslims with close connections to the countryside and thus provided for a completely different spatial organization of metropolis, hinterland, and mofussil than the earlier Swadeshi movement. Second, it provided the intellectual and material contexts for the development of agrarian Islamic discourses during the 1920s. The Khilafat cause informed mofussil thought on the relationship between peasant immiseration, economic salvation, and Islamic practice and the movement relied on the circulation of printed texts between mofussil towns and hinterland villages.

The Khilafat movement originated among the Urdu-speaking Muslim intelligentsia of northern India and was led by the Aligarh- and Oxford-educated brothers, Shawkat Ali and Mohammad Ali. While the movement was not indigenous to the delta, the popularity of the Khilafat cause predated the arrival of the men from Aligarh. Abul Mansur Ahmed (1898–1979), who was born into a well-to-do jute-cultivating peasant household in Dhanikhola village, Mymensingh, remembers how Italy's attack on Libya and the Ottoman Empire, on "our Khalifa," in 1911, when he was thirteen, angered him. He supported Germany against Britain in World War I because he believed the Kaiser was Muslim—a belief that was confirmed by the Ottoman Empire joining the war on the German side. Ahmed recounts how he felt that Britain's victory in the Great War only proved to him "that the Muslims have no greater enemy than the English."[6] In his memoirs of his childhood in Kishoreganj, also in Mymensingh, Nirad Chaudhuri remembers that, "when Britain declared war against Turkey in November 1914, a mullah hoisted the Turkish flag in a field near Kishorganj and proclaimed it as the Caliph's territory. He was, of course, promptly arrested."[7]

The formal Khilafat movement arrived in the delta from north India with the establishment of Khilafat committees in mofussil towns in 1920; educated Muslim men—many of them recently arrived in towns—joined immediately. Abul Mansur Ahmed was a student at Dacca College who, upon finishing his studies, returned to his childhood village home, Dhanikhola, as a Khilafat volunteer. Tamizuddin Khan (1889–1963) was born into a much poorer peasant

family than Abul Mansur Ahmed, but had excelled in his education. He earned
a bachelor's and a master's degree in English from Presidency College, Bengal's premier institute of higher education, and also successfully completed a
Bachelor of Law degree. He was Faridpur's first "Muslim Honours graduate"
and returned to the district in 1915 to establish a successful legal practice.[8] Like
Ahmed, Khan was an early member of the Khilafat movement. Khan describes
how the British Empire's treatment of the Ottoman Caliphate had "created an
upheaval in me. I was overpowered with a sense of shame and anger and fired
with a zeal to do something."[9] A senior and popular Muslim lawyer, Khan joined
the Faridpur District Khilafat and Congress Committees, and was promptly
elected vice president of the former and general secretary of the latter.

These mofussil Muslim men began their work of organizing in earnest even
before Gandhi persuaded the Indian National Congress Party to officially
adopt the Khilafat/Non-Cooperation movement at the Nagpur Conference
in December 1920. Throughout 1920, they organized mass meetings, where
mofussil Muslim professionals delivered speeches combining a condemnation
of the British occupation of the Muslim holy cities with a critique of colonial
economic exploitation. Ismail Emanuddin of Tipperah informed a prayer
meeting at the jute port of Narayanganj that the European capitalists were
profiting from the jute trade while clerks and coolies did not have "sufficient
money even to meet the demands of nature."[10]

The Khilafat and Congress Committees also organized a boycott of the
1920 council elections, the first elections to be held under the Government of
India Act of 1919. Tamizuddin Khan was among several mofussil Muslims who
withdrew their candidacy and put up a "fake candidate"—a cartman named
Birbal—to prevent the pro-government candidate from winning. Khan's plan
failed as Abdul Karim, the pro-government candidate in Faridpur, successfully
bribed Birbal to stand down, allowing him to be elected uncontested.[11] Fake
candidates achieved greater success elsewhere, particularly in Noakhali, where
the Khilafat movement "was responsible for the election by large majorities
over well-known local men of six persons of no social status who were induced
to stand by the non-co-operators."[12]

Khilafat and Non-Cooperation activists also resorted to Swadeshi forms of
activism: a consumer boycott of Manchester cloth and a program to reduce
jute cultivation. These movements failed to garner peasant support but, in
stark contrast to the Swadeshi movement, neither provoked a peasant back-
lash. Activists arranged public bonfires of British cloth and extensively promoted the use of *khaddar*. Tamizuddin Khan even began a business importing

domestically manufactured Swadeshi cloth into Faridpur. The lack of peasant resistance probably indicates the dire economic conditions of the time: few peasant households were purchasing much beyond bare necessities.[13] An even bolder attempt to prevent jute cultivation, launched in February 1921 just before jute sowings commenced, similarly failed to spark peasant political action either in support or in opposition. In Noakhali, a group of student activists plowed up jute fields and in one instance played soccer on the cleared ground.[14] The lack of peasant resistance to the destruction of jute fields probably reflects the extremely low prices of jute in the early 1920s. Peasant households were already replacing jute with rice as the terms of trade between fiber and grain had deteriorated: the 1921 jute acreage was about 40 percent lower than the previous year. Cultivators may have even appreciated the free labor of activists in clearing the jute fields in time for the land to be resown with aus paddy.

During the first half of 1921, jute cultivators' actions were overshadowed by other more spectacular protests: the mass withdrawal of students from government schools, recurrent strikes in the jute mills surrounding Calcutta, the mass exodus of tea-garden workers from Sylhet in Assam, and a coordinated strike by railway and steamer workers in the jute tracts. Mofussil Muslim Khilafat activists were, however, busily organizing Muslim jute cultivators, even as the more senior leaders were in jail. While in jails in Fardipur and Dacca, Tamizuddin Khan met many fellow mofussil Muslim Khilafat activists— including Khalilur Rahman of Madaripur, and Syedul Haq and Shamsul Haq of Mymensingh—and he formed a close and enduring friendship with a Hindu fellow prisoner, Surendranath Biswas.[15]

Between June and November 1921, when the jute cultivators' movement began in earnest, Khliafat and Congress Committees had organized 4,265 mass meetings throughout Bengal.[16] Volunteers had spread out in the delta's villages, working to implement a Gandhian program of rural regeneration. Among them was Abul Mansur Ahmed, just twenty-two years old at the time, who had returned to his childhood village of Dhanikhola from college in Dhaka. Ahmed and his comrades established a village society—*palli samaj*— that raised and managed funds; established a high school and a technical school to teach weaving and spinning; created arbitration facilities to settle disputes; and distributed cotton seeds and encouraged cotton cultivation to sustain home-spinning and weaving. To Ahmed, the Khilafat movement's enormous popular support was evident in the enthusiasm with which people donated grain or small sums of cash to the palli samaj.

Toward the end of 1921, the colonial state began receiving reports of peasant households not cooperating with colonial policemen, surveyors, and tax collectors. From Mymensingh it was reported that jute-cultivating peasant households were refusing to cooperate with police investigations and that there was a general belief that the British government had lost its authority.[17] Cultivators in Bogra did not cooperate with surveyors who were compiling records of property rights and reassessing rents of peasant holdings. Peasant communities refused to sell food to surveyors and declared that anyone who did would be socially boycotted and barred from the coming utopia of swaraj. When the British settlement officer went to Dakumura hat to help surveyors procure rice, he was attacked:

> The people there at first behaved respectfully and showed him the place where the rice was being sold. While he was awaiting the arrival of the shopkeeper a crowd collected and remarked in his hearing that they would not sell the rice. Meanwhile the owner of the stall arrived and said that the rice was for sale and that he would sell it, but he was shouted down by the crowd which had increased and had assumed a hostile attitude. Eventually Mr. McPherson was attacked by the crowd, receiving two severe blows on the back of his head from a thick stick and also several blows from an oar. He was forced to run and stumbled into a paddy field near by. Rescued from there by a Mahomedan, he was taken back to the *hat* where he was pelted with clods of earth.[18]

Near the end of 1921, a concerted peasant movement for the nonpayment of *chaukidari* taxes—a local tax levied on landholders to pay for chaukidars, or the village police—and zamindari rents spread throughout the delta, in the districts of Tipperah, Mymensingh, Faridpur, Dacca, Pabna, and Rangpur. When colonial authorites attempted to enforce warrants and arrest villagers for the nonpayment of rents and taxes, they were attacked. Assemblies of peasant men attacked contingents of armed policemen with sticks, bricks, and clods of earth, and tried to snatch away their guns. At Haripur Fulchari thana in Rangpur in April 1922, a British officer attempting to collect the chaukidari tax was forcibly confined by villagers and armed police dispatched to quell rebellious villagers were attacked with lathis and clods of earth. The police fired back, killing one and injuring two protestors.[19] Similar episodes took pace in Sirajganj, Nilphamari, Rangpur, and Noakhali, where contingents of policemen fired on assemblies of peasant men, and injured or killed peasant protestors. The refusal to pay taxes and rents turned into a revolt against colonial state authority. In the jute market town of Nilphamari in northern Bengal, villagers and townsmen attacked a group of thirty-two policemen:

> In view of the disturbed state of the locality due to aggressive activities of the volunteers, thirty-two armed police were sent to Nilphamari in Rungpur district on 28th December. They did a route march through the town. A halt was made in the bazaar, where an altercation ensued between a policeman and the servant of a local gentleman. A crowd speedily collected and began throwing missiles at the police, threatening them with lathis. March was continued to Police-Station followed by crowd who became increasingly menacing and broke through ranks of police. Three policemen eventually fired in the air, causing crowd to halt. Eight policemen were injured; and six of the public were slightly injured by slugs, while two others received severe, but not dangerous wounds, probably caused by kukries.[20]

Peasant resistance to the colonial state's displays of power through police contingents spelled the end of colonial authority over swaths of the jute-producing hinterland. A colonial report summarized the success of peasant noncooperation with the state:

> The political situation at the beginning of 1922 was still volcanic. The forces of lawlessness and disorder which had been so wantonly aroused towards the end of the previous year continued to engender in increasing measure among the masses a widespread contempt for authority which manifested itself in the boycott and intimidation of loyal supporters of the Government, active molestation of Government servants, persistent tampering with the police, dissuading of chaukidars from serving in their normal duties and a growing refusal to pay the chaukidari tax as a first chapter in the book of civil disobedience. . . . The most disquieting development, however, in the mufassal was the increasing display of contempt for the police, and a tendency to attack them in the discharge of their duties, which resulted on several occasions in serious collisions.[21]

In May 1920, at the height of the peasant revolt against colonial authority, Gandhi brought the movement to a halt.[22] The Congress withdrew from all Non-Cooperation–related activities and the Khilafat Committees lost vigor. The peasant movement, though, did not come to an abrupt stop. In Tipperah, the colonial state was unable to reassert its authority until July and, in Pabna, Dinajpur, and Rangpur, the Khilafat movement was transformed into antiza-mindar and anti-moneylender movements. In Pabna, in August 1920, a group of peasant men attacked a contingent of armed police deputed to enforce the collection of taxes: six peasant men were injured when the police opened fire.[23] However, by the end of 1922, the peasant movements had largely been quelled and the colonial state had regained its authority over the jute tracts.

The Khilafat movement of mofussil Muslims limped on for a while after Gandhi's cry of halt. Abul Mansur Ahmad describes the end of his village society in Dhanikhola: "Our enthusiasm did not last more than a year. *Swaraj* had not come within the year, as Gandhi promised. And then he withdrew civil disobedience [*sharbojonin ain omanno*] because of the troubles [*hangama*] at Chauri Chaura." With the decline in enthusiasm, the young volunteers began to experience difficulties: students were leaving their alternative school and rejoining the government school, they were unable to sell their homespun cloth or pay salaries to weaving and spinning instructors, and villagers gradually stopped donating grain or money to the movement.[24] Released from jail, Tamizuddin Khan returned to Faridpur town and, after a few months, resumed his law practice.

Gandhi's promise of swaraj was highly significant to jute cultivators' protests. Peasant households took Gandhi's promise that swaraj would be attained with a year at face value, and understood it in utopian and millenarian terms: swaraj promised the impending end of the unjust British Empire and the imminent arrival of a just and moral society. The utopian and millenarian moment of the Khilafat movement—when the impossible seemed not only possible but also imminent—was characterized as "wild talk" by the colonial state. Colonial officials spoke of "*wild* talk of swaraj and rumours [that] were current of the impending or accomplished abdication of the Sarkar" and of the "promises of the *wildest* character [that] were freely made to ignorant peasants,—for example, rent-free lands, cheap clothes, cheap food and free railway passes."[25] Ideas of Gandhian swaraj were wedded to a deep sense of grievance at Britain's occupation of Mecca and Medina and the harsh terms of surrender imposed on the Ottoman Caliphate. The colonial state noted that "the cultivators talked glibly of Kemal Pasha, the king of the Hedjaz, and political trials."[26] Peasant protests during the Khilafat movement were not driven merely by prices, but were also related to Muslim jute cultivators' long-standing extraterritorial loyalties to a global Muslim cosmopolis and to their utopian and millenarian reading of Gandhi's concept of swaraj.

Moreover, the Khilafat movement was a new and formative moment in peasant politics of immiseration in the post–World War I jute tracts. First, it brought into prominence a new community of political actors—mofussil

Muslim professionals, born and raised in the jute-growing countryside, who had recently taken up professional employment in small towns during the 1910s. Their ties of blood and soil to the countryside transformed the relationship of metropolis, hinterland, and mofussil. Mofussil towns no longer appeared as islands of metropolitan politics and culture surrounded by a largely hostile countryside—as was the case during the Swadeshi movement. These towns were now much more closely integrated into the countryside and, contrary to Aurobindo Ghosh's assertion of Calcutta's dominance, demonstrated autonomy and independence from metropolitan Calcutta.

Mofussil and hinterland connections were also forged through the circulation of printed texts between mofussil small towns and hinterland villages. Poems and songs integral to the Khilafat movement were printed, mass-produced, and performed orally. Abul Mansur Ahmed and his comrades would wander the village roads at night, singing "Swadesh and Khilafat songs" at the top of their voices.[27] Nirad Chaudhuri described a visit from an "elderly uncle" from "an out-of-the-way village" during the movement, who "besides being the village squire was also a poet and composer." He performed a song he had composed to Gandhi: " 'Who is that is blowing his horn, and from which high peak, to pierce the heart in this manner?' "[28] Khilafat poems were printed in mofussil presses. Muhammad Abdul Hakim Ruhani's poems, written in Chandpur, were printed in Dacca. His poems urged Muslims to join Hindus in ousting the British, celebrated the achievements of Islam and called for a global brotherhood of Muslims, rejoiced in the rise of global anticolonial movements led by "Gandhi, Lenin, and Zaghlul Pasha," and advocated for the adoption of homespun cloth.[29] Ruhani also wrote a poem urging Muslims to go into business and trade—a prominent theme in agrarian Islamic discourses that I discuss below. The significance of printed texts exceeded the printed word. Subscribers to Khilafat funds received a receipt, printed in Calcutta, with a quotation from the Koran in Arabic and Urdu—"Who is he that will lend Allah a goodly loan, then Allah will increase it twice fold to his credit, and he will have as well a reward"—and an English inscription stating: "One Rupee, India, 1920." It did not matter that the text contained no Bengali, and was illegible to most of the mofussil intelligentsia as well as the largely illiterate peasantry: the symbolic value of the printed paper exceeded the words that were printed on it.

The following section examines the cultural and intellectual efflorescence of mofussil towns during a period of agrarian immiseration. The cultural vitality of these towns owed much to the recent arrival of young, educated Muslim men who were born and raised in the surrounding countryside—men like Tamizuddin Khan and Abul Mansur Ahmed. These young men were closely associated with the burgeoning mofussil print industry, establishing and running presses, authoring pamphlets and poems, and financing the publication of peasant-oriented texts. These recently arrived Muslim men constituted a mofussil Muslim intelligentsia, and formed a community of writers, readers, and patrons that sustained the mofussil print industry.

The final section of this chapter explores the discourses of agrarian Islam produced by this intelligentsia. Mofussil Muslim authors produced printed poems, essays, and pamphlets which presented Islam as providing a guide to the ethical conduct of market-entangled peasant lives that would restore prosperity or, at the least, ensure survival. Agrarian Islamic texts focused on the everyday practices of work, buying and selling, patriarchal discipline over women and children, and good neighborly relations. The Khilafat movement, with its blend of Muslim loyalties and Gandhian programs of asceticism and labor, provided an early context for thinking about Islam and peasant impoverishment. Much like Khilafat texts, agrarian Islamic texts consisted of printed songs and poems, occasionally adorned with Islamic symbols, that circulated between print and oral cultures.

Mofussil Efflorescence

Agrarian immiseration in the hinterland was accompanied by the increasing cultural, political, and intellectual vitality of mofussil towns. Even as disease and hunger led to a sharp slowdown in the population growth in rural areas, the delta's small towns continued to grow at a rapid clip during the 1910s and 1920s (tables 5.1 and 5.2). The sources of population growth in mofussil towns during the twentieth century were different from those of the nineteenth century. During the nineteenth century, towns' populations increased with the arrival of bureaucrats, merchants, and clerks from metropolitan Calcutta. During the twentieth century, young Muslim men from the surrounding countryside began moving into towns, thus changing the demography of the mofussil.[30] Recent Muslim arrivals had problems finding accommodation in towns, as town homes were mostly owned by Hindus, many of whom were reluctant to rent to Muslim tenants.[31] These young men from the countryside left wives and children in their villages to live with elderly parents and the extended peasant family, contributing to a growing gender imbalance in the mofussil.[32]

TABLE 5.1. Urban and Rural Populations in Jute-Growing Districts of the Delta, 1891–1931

	Population		Percentage change over the preceding decade	
	Urban	Rural	Urban	Rural
1891	321,548	13,402,298		
1901	380,189	14,600,213	18.2%	8.9%
1911	441,920	16,894,439	16.2%	15.7%
1921	503,698	17,398,284	14.0%	3.0%
1931	576,024	18,585,623	14.4%	6.8%

TABLE 5.2. Population and Growth of Mofussil Towns, 1911–1921

Town	Population (1921)	Percentage increase (1911–21)
Rangpur	19,076	16.1%
Bogra	12,322	35.2%
Sirajganj	25,518	2.9%
Madaripur	25,297	32.6%
Mymensingh	25,287	27.4%
Jamalpur	23,113	9.5%
Kishoreganj	19,518	8.3%
Faridpur	14,503	10.4%
Comilla	25,914	14.2%
Brahmanbaria	23,414	5.0%
Chandpur	15,118	18.9%

The emergence of a mofussil Muslim professional and mercantile class during a period of agrarian immiseration indicates patterns of peasant differentiation during this time. Peasant households that had invested jute profits to diversify out of purely agrarian livelihoods managed not only to survive but also to prosper during the post–World War I crises in the delta's agrarian economy. During the boom of the 1900s, they had invested their jute profits in moneylending, in their sons' education, and in business and trade ventures. Moneylending was probably the most common form of livelihood diversification, followed by purchases of intermediary revenue-collection rights, like talukdaris and jagirdaris. Wealthy peasant households also invested in trading ventures, whether dealing in jute or imports of salt, kerosene oil, and cloth. The most successful jute cultivators expanded into mofussil towns, either through educated sons gaining professional employment or by establishing and expanding business concerns in mofussil bazaars. As the agrarian economy deteriorated and the bulk of Bengal's peasantry experienced extreme immiseration during the 1920s and 1930s, this small minority of peasant households managed to prosper and establish themselves in the delta's mofussil towns.

These Muslim men were participants in the mofussil print and publishing boom of the 1920s. During this period, many new local newspapers were established and many mofussil authors published their first and often only books during this decade. They wrote on diverse topics in multiple genres: political and economic pamphlets; poems, short stories, and novellas; histories of localities, families, or castes; religious instruction for Hindus and Muslims; compilations of laws and regulations; agricultural manuals; and guidebooks for the management of zamindari estates. Even tiny Noakhali, with less than eight thousand residents, had at least two printing presses which turned out at least three weekly newspapers and more than thirty original books during the 1920s. Medium-sized Faridpur, with a population of about fifteen thousand, also had at least two presses and produced at least three newspapers. Mymensingh had perhaps the most vibrant print industry of these towns, and its presses published some of the most widely read pamphlets of the period.[33]

Mofussil newspapers' circulation was limited to the towns and the surrounding countryside, but circles of readership had expanded and constituted a sufficiently large market to sustain such newspapers (see table 5.3).

TABLE 5.3. Some Mofussil Newspapers and Their Circulation, 1925–1926

Town	Newspaper title	Circulation
Faridpur	*The Sonjoy*	1,104
	Faridpur Hitoishini	2,828
Noakhali	*Noakhali Sammilan*	400
Comilla	*Tippera Hitaishini*	800
Brahmanbaria	*Praja Bandhu*	200
Chandpur	*Naba Banga*	465
Pabna and Bogra	*The Pabna-Bogra Hitaishi*	1,100
	Suraj	1,200
Rangpur	*Rangpur Darpan*	700 or 800
Tangail	*Tangail Hitaishi*	700
Sirajganj	*Tajkir*	500

Compiled from the "Indian Newspapers Returns: Statements of Newspapers and Periodicals Published in Bengal," IOR/L/PJ/6/1762, File 4929: Aug 1921–Jun 1927

Recently arrived Muslim migrants were prominent members of a newly constituted mofussil intelligentsia. They wrote political and economic pamphlets, poems, and novellas, and edited newspapers. Authors and editors were drawn from a mofussil professional class, individuals with advanced degrees working as lawyers, doctors, schoolteachers, and clerks in the towns. The costs of publishing pamphlets and running newspapers were usually borne by wealthier individuals—mostly merchants and prominent landholders. The publication of the first edition of A.F.M. Abdul Hai's *Adarsha Krishak* (Ideal Peasant, Mymensingh, 1920) was financed by a jute merchant: Abdul Majid of Shilashi, Gaffargaon. The second edition, expanded and replete with illustrated woodcuts, was financed by the Mymensingh District Board and was dedicated to the board's first elected chairman—Khan Bahadur Maulvi Syed Ahmed Chowdhury, a local zamindar. Ashrafuddin Ahmed's poem *Muslim Bani* (Muslim Declaration), published in Comilla in 1927, was partially financed by Munshi Keramat Ali, the patron of the school in Laksham where Ashrafuddin Ahmed taught. The publication of Shah Abdul Hamid's *Krishak Bilap* (Peasant Lament, Mymensingh, 1921), was partly financed through small contributions, ranging from two to ten rupees, by twenty-one different Muslim men from Mymensingh and the surrounding villages, several of whom held a Bachelor of Laws or Bachelor of Arts degree.[34] The *Noakhali Sammilani*, a weekly newspaper published in Noakhali, had nine owners—four merchants operating in Noakhali town's bazaars, three talukdars, and two zamindars. *Bogurar Katha*, a weekly published in Bogra, was owned by an informal group of shareholders drawn from a broad spectrum of Bogra's Muslim community.[35] This complex of mofussil Muslim schoolteachers, lawyers, pleaders, doctors, merchants and shopkeepers, zamindars, talukdars, jotedars, politicians, legislators, and elected members in municipalities and district boards constituted the circles of authorship, readership, and patronage that sustained the print and publishing boom in the Bengal delta.

The efflorescence of intellectual life in the small towns caught the attention of external observers. A colonial report of 1929 stated:

> Town life [in Eastern Bengal] is centred in important railway or steamer stations, or at the headquarters of the civil administration. In the former, trading interests predominate, and many Indians who have had years of contact with foreign business, show a considerable knowledge of modern commerce and its methods. In the latter, a more official atmosphere prevails. The scholastic, legal and medical professions are strongly represented;

and, with the official classes and land-owners of moderate income, form a society which is in close intellectual touch with the metropolis and, at the same time, has steady contact of a professional or legal character with the country villager. The Calcutta newspapers are read daily, and local and provincial politics are a subject of constant discussion, while a real knowledge of village life and thought is maintained.[36]

While the report's author was correct in noting the rise of a politically conscious and intellectually engaged small-town middle class, he was mistaken in two important respects. First, he placed undue emphasis on the readership of Calcutta papers and the "close intellectual touch with the metropolis" and failed to mention the relatively autonomous mofussil print industry. Townsmen did not merely imbibe Calcutta texts but also consumed and produced texts out of the towns' vibrant print industry. Second, he was mistaken in characterizing the relationship of the mofussil middle class with the "country villager" as being solely of a "professional or legal character." In fact, connections ran much deeper. Many small-town professionals, particularly Muslims, had origins and close family ties to the countryside—the "country villager" was not just a client or patient but was also a close relative. The mofussil Muslim intelligentsia did not take its cues from Calcutta, but constituted an autonomous political domain maintaining relative independence from the metropolis.

The Khilafat movement also provided an early context for mofussil thinking about Islam and agrarian immiseration that informed an emergent discourse of agrarian Islam during the1920s. For the mofussil Muslim intelligentsia, peasant immiseration was the burning issue of the day, and the topic of a significant portion of their literary output. In his foreword to Shah Abdul Hamid's *Krishak Bilap* (Peasant Lament), Sheikh Bashiruddin Ahmed wrote: "The Bengal peasant's sorrows and difficulties have been discussed in civil society (*shudhi shamaj*) for some time. But no one could have thought that the last moment of their lives would come so soon, no one could have foreseen that."[37] Similarly, in his preface to Abul Hossain's *Bangla'r Bolshi* (Bengal's Bolsheviks, Dacca, 1926), Muhammad Fazlul Karim Mullick—a zamindar in Dacca district—wrote that the book would "benefit those who are engaging themselves in serving the country or wish to think about the real condition of the nation."[38]

The mofussil intelligentsia conceived of itself as a civil society, an engaged and conscious small-town elite working for the benefit of an impoverished and backward peasantry. Through poems and pamphlets, they sought to create a program of peasant uplift that portrayed Islam as a guide to ethical practices of everyday life, which promised this-worldly salvation—that is, an escape from poverty—through hard work, austerity, proper patriarchal control of households, and good neighborly relations. Through printed texts, the intelligentsia directly addressed Bengal's Muslim peasantry, urging them to undertake comprehensive programs of self-reform. Much as Khilafat texts had done, texts of agrarian Islam circulated between print and oral cultures, and were far more influential in the jute tracts' politics than would seem possible in the largely illiterate delta. The following section examines a sampling of these texts and demonstrates that agrarian Islamic discourses were primarily concerned with reforming peasant market engagements, balancing household budgets, reducing indebtedness, and enabling capital accumulation.

Agrarian Islam

During the 1920s a new genre of Islamic poetry emerged from the printing presses of eastern Bengal's mofussil towns. These were printed boyans, long poems of several hundred lines of rhyming couplets of even beat that were meant to be orally performed in rural and small-town public spaces—at weekly bazaars and country fairs, and in town centers, railway stations, and river ports. Boyans instructed Muslim jute cultivators in the proper Islamic conduct of everyday life. Poets narrated tales of Muslim peasant life, decried Muslim peasant poverty, and relentlessly mocked Muslim peasants for their stupidity, ignorance, indolence, dishonesty, litigiousness, and dandified mannerisms. Poets urged comprehensive programs of Islamic reform of everyday peasant life—of work, commerce, consumption, attire and hairstyle, patriarchal control over wives and children, and neighborly relations. These reforms, poets promised, would bring Muslim peasants this-worldly salvation, that is, an escape from poverty and, perhaps, even prosperity. The sentiments embodied in these poems constituted a discourse of agrarian Islam.

Discourses of agrarian Islam focused on worldly matters and were largely unconcerned with ritual practices, Koranic exegesis, or discussions of *hadith*. Instead, poets and authors of agrarian Islam mandated reforms in the material realms of work, commerce, and consumption. As Abdul Aziz rhymed in his *Dunia O Akherat Do Jahaner Najat* (Salvation in This World and the Next), published in Noakhali in 1922–23:

Listen all Mussalmans to this truth,
All of a Mussalman's works are worship.
Business, trade and sharecropping
These are nothing but worship.[39]

Agrarian Islamic discourses were concerned primarily with peasant market entanglements. Poets argued that the roots of peasant poverty and the means to this-worldly salvation lay in fiscal responsibility, in balancing peasant household budgets so that earnings from sales of peasant produce exceeded expenditure on market-based consumption. Fiscal responsibility, in turn, entailed hard work, restrained consumption, appropriate attire and hairstyles, and the proper patriarchal control of wives and children. These practices constituted being a good Muslim and a good peasant, and deviations from such practices resulted in impoverishment. Agrarian Islam was deeply concerned with peasant poverty, and most poems began with a paean to the impoverished state of Bengal's Muslim peasantry. Poets argued that poverty resulted from the failure to practice Islam in everyday life, from the peasant patriarch's indolence, frivolity, dishonesty, vanity, and his overindulgence of wives and children. These failures related back to peasant market entanglements and manifested in excessive and unrestrained market-based consumption.

Agrarian Islamic texts were produced as cheap, flimsy chapbooks, printed on low-quality thin paper, loosely bound with thread, and priced at between one and six annas. Texts signaled their Islamic content in the material form of the printed book. Some boyans had Arabic words in their titles, such as Abdul Aziz's *Dunia O Akherat Do Jahaner Najat* and Abul Mohsen Mohammad Asghar Hossain's *Kalamal Haq ba Hok Katha* (True Words, Sirajganj, 1932). Some texts had Arabic inscriptions, in the Arabic script, on their covers; others had "Allahu Akbar" printed prominently in Bengali at the top of the cover page. The first edition of Abdul Hai's *Adarsha Krishak* (Ideal Peasant, Mymensingh, 1920) had the Muslim crescent-moon-and-star symbol on its cover. Some texts had epigraphs in the Arabic script, often the Islamic invocation to begin in God's name, *bismillah ir-rahman ir-rahim*, and occasionally longer quotations from the Koran or a hadith, such as in the second, expanded, edition of *Adarsha Krishak* (Mymensingh, 1922). Texts also signaled their Islamic content by opening from the right, like an Arabic book—Hossain's *Kalamal Haq* signaled its Islamic content in this way, as well as by the Arabic words in its title.

These printed books, adorned with Islamic symbols, circulated between literate and oral spheres.[40] Printed texts and their public, oral performance connected the vibrant print cultures of the delta's small towns to the rapidly impoverishing agrarian countryside. Further, agrarian Islamic texts were produced out of the particular dynamics of peasant differentiation in the Bengal delta. Perhaps the most influential and glossiest agrarian Islamic text was not a boyan but a pamphlet: Abdul Hai's *Adarsha Krishak*. In his introduction to *Krishak Bilap* (Peasant Lament, Mymensingh, 1922), Shah Abdul Hamid celebrated *Adarsha Krishak* as the Bengal peasant's *"buker dhon,"* or heart-wealth.[41] Hai claimed to have written *Adarsha Krishak* to "advise peasants on the way out of poverty" and to present vignettes of "ideal peasant life" as examples to be emulated by the impoverished peasantry. The first and longest vignette is about the ideal farmer Osman, a pious man who works hard all day. He is a man who says: "I will do first and then if I have time, I will advise other people to do the same." At the end of a hard day's work in the fields, Osman returns home to tend his chili plants and betel vines, spin cloth, make his own furniture, and dig a pond by hand, scooping out the earth bit by bit. He also abjures luxuries and vices—Osman does not smoke hookah. He is a benevolent patriarch—he does not beat his wife. And Osman is pious—the only breaks he takes from his days of constant labor are to call out the *azaan* (the call to prayer) from the village mosque and to say his prayers. Through hard work, abstinence, and piety, Osman has managed not just to survive but to prosper. The hardworking and abstemious Osman is the counterexample to the Bengal peasantry:

> Hey Bengal's illiterate peasant brothers, it was just the other day that you had used money from jute sales to build tin houses, borrowed 500 rupees to dig a large pond, borrowed money to pay for the wedding of your adored, piece-of-your-liver son . . . but today almost all of you are taking your families into the jungles of Assam. Shame, shame, shame (*chhi: chhi: chhi:*), weren't you the brave warriors who had won this country.
>
> Know for certain that no one has defeated you; you have defeated yourselves. Greed, cupidity, materialism and ignorance (*lobh, mouho, maya o murkhota*) are your eternal enemies.[42]

The subsequent vignettes present similar tales of labor, production, and asceticism. The second vignette is of an ideal farm called Shahbagh, where two and a half acres of land support rice; jute; a vegetable garden growing potatoes, chilies, garlic, onions, peas, all kinds of other vegetables, and tobacco; betel nuts and vines; fruit trees; climbers that produce gourds and beans; and ducks, chickens, pigeons, and goats. The farm belonged to Shah Ahmed, an educated man who had worked for the Mymensingh District Board and taught at several schools and madrassas before returning to the life of an agriculturist. The third vignette is of a farmer who has two tamarind trees in his house and supplements his income by making tamarind chutney and selling it in a nearby town. The fourth vignette is of a zamindar returning from fishing—having caught a large carp or *rui mach*—and running into two boys returning from the market, one having purchased a gourd and the other having bought *koi* fish, a kind of freshwater perch. The zamindar calls the boys' father—an addict who sold his plow oxen to support his opium habit—over to his house. He lectures the man, saying, "I, a *zamindar*, grow my own vegetables and catch my own fish and you, a peasant, send your children to market to buy the same. You are lazy, so you can't make your rent payments to me."[43]

Hai concludes his book with a twenty-one-point program for *mukti*— freedom. The first point concerns peasant budgets: "Every peasant will keep accounts of revenue and expenditure and will completely desist from all wasteful expenditure." The program aimed at reforming peasant production and consumption: farmers should keep aside enough land to grow sufficient rice for household subsistence; they should plant cotton, sugarcane, date palms, betel vines, and tobacco; they should not visit markets empty-handed but with some goods to sell; they should avoid litigation; they must not sell their land and use cash earnings to buy more land; they should not buy fish but catch their own fish; they should not smoke tobacco or chew betel leaf, unless they grow their own; they should make their own umbrellas from bamboo, rather than purchase expensive imported umbrellas for five or six rupees in marketplaces; and so forth. The peasant patriarch is urged to make burkas for his wife and not spend money on palanquins, and to educate their sons. The program of peasant mukti consisted of the male patriarch carefully balancing the household budget, disciplining household members, and reducing market consumption by working harder to produce household necessities.

Andrew Sartori correctly points to Abdul Hai's *Adarsha Krishak* and its relentless promotion of labor as indicative of a Lockean theory of property. Sartori rightly calls attention to Hai's insistence that Osman's belongings— clothing, furniture, the pond, and so forth—truly belong to him since he made them with his own hands. However, as the twenty-one-point program for mukti makes clear, the point of labor is not so much to claim property as to balance peasant households' budgets—to increase revenue by producing more goods for sale and reduce expenditure by producing instead of purchasing household necessities. Peasants are instructed to make their own umbrellas because they will save five rupees by not purchasing an expensive umbrella in the marketplace. Shahbag is a successful farm because it produces a wide variety of goods for sale, rather than relying on a single cash crop, jute. Emancipation was to be achieved through careful and savvy engagements with markets, and labor was related to peasant households' market earnings and expenditure.

The marketplace orientation of agrarian Islamic texts is made more explicit and more general in the printed boyan, a far more accessible and affordable genre than the glossy and expensive *Adarsha Krishak*. Boyans were not only cheaper—one to six annas as against one rupee and four paisa for the second edition of *Adarsha Krishak*—but they were also performed orally in bazaars and public spaces in rural Bengal. The boyans repeat the same focus on work, abstemious consumption, and balancing household expenditures as *Adarsha Krishak*, but also address peasant life much more broadly, focusing on attire, hairstyles, wives, youths, village leaders, and so forth. As I will argue, even in expanding the field of agrarian Islam beyond labor and consumption, these boyans maintained their focus on the marketplace and peasant household finances. These boyans argued that un-Islamic practices, habits, and comportment lead to financially ruinous market engagements that impoverish peasants. Freedom or mukti was to be achieved by restoring household finances through the cultivation of proper Islamic practices in all spheres of everyday material life.

Most agrarian Islamic boyans open with a lament about Muslim poverty. Abdul Aziz's *Dunia o Akherat Dojahaner Najat* begins: "Looking at Muslims today / *Hai hai*, my heart explodes."[44] Hafez Ashrafuddin Ahmed's *Muslim Bani* opens: "I begin my poem by holding your feet and crying / We Bengalis suffer so much sorrow."[45] Akram Ali's *Keno Lok Gorib Hoy* (Why People Become Poor) opens with the lines: "Seeing the situation of people in this age / My soul becomes restless and frightened / Does not get to eat, no clothes on their backs / Going hungry for a day, two days."[46] The boyans then proceed to identify poverty as a specifically Muslim issue. Aziz goes on to ask and answer a series of rhetorical questions in the opening lines to his poem: Who are the beggars? Muslims. Who lose their lands and homes through debt? Muslims. Whose households are depleted by malaria, cholera, smallpox, and plague? Again, Muslims.

Material deprivation was closely related to moral depravity. Abdur Rahim's *Nurul Islam* characterized the present age as a *kali kal*—a dark age—where people cannot tell right from wrong and do not fear Allah or his prophet.[47] The kali kal was an age of disrespect, dishonesty, cheating, theft, lying, bestiality, and adultery covered over by a veil of false religious practice, by ostentatious prayers, fasts, hajj, and beards. Contrary to Pradip Datta's arguments about the purification of Muslim peasants by the excision of Hindu traits, or Asim Roy's claims about replacing syncreticism with more pure practices of Islam, the poets of agrarian Islam often invoked Hindu ideas, hence appropriating and reinterpreting the Hindu idea of a dark age, *kaliyuga*, to describe a period of Muslim decline.[48]

For agrarian Islamic poets, the Hindu kali kal was a period of Muslim subjugation by "other races" or *bijatis*, a word that could refer to the British, non-Bengalis, or Bengali Hindus. The trope of a once proud people—Abdul Hai's "brave warriors" or Abdul Aziz's "those who had brought the world civilization"—having been reduced to servitude was a common feature of these poems, captured in the image of the Muslim peasant swallowing his pride and going to the Marwari moneylender or Hindu lawyer, head bowed and palms pressed together in supplication. Boyans narrate how the Muslim fall from glory was due to ostentatious consumption, an aversion to business, the inability to exercise patriarchal authority over wives and children, deceit and dishonesty, a lack of unity, and a lack of education. Abdul Aziz's *Najat* consists of five sections, each section corresponding to a reason why Muslims have been impoverished: a loss of faith (*iman*), a lack of unity (*ekota*), an aversion to business and trade, frivolous expenditure, and a lack of education. Abdur Rahim's *Nurul Islam* is similarly composed of five sections, with each section illustrating an aspect of the dark ages: the first concerns a land transaction where the seller attempts to cheat the buyer by not handing over the title deeds upon receiving the cash; the second is about a boatman who steals a portion of the mangoes entrusted to him to transport to a wholesaler in Dhaka; the third narrates the stories of spoiled and wayward sons of indulgent fathers; the fourth concerns an extravagant wedding which leads to a bad marriage, as the young husband and wife have been spoiled by a lifetime of indulgence; and the fifth is about bad-tempered and unveiled peasant wives spoiled by indulgent patriarchs, their husbands and fathers-in-law.

Even as they addressed diverse aspects of everyday peasant life, the boyans were ultimately concerned with the marketplace. Agrarian Islam promoted abjuring consumption and producing goods for household use, always visiting markets with something to sell, not relying on markets for subsistence rice, and so forth. These kinds of market engagement were not just economically sensible—they were Islamic. Mofussil boyans are replete with stories of excessive, frivolous consumption by peasant households. As Abdul Aziz rhymes: "He who spends frivolously / Is Satan's brother."[49] Ashrafuddin Ahmed's *Muslim Bani* narrates a tale of a peasant patriarch who takes a loan of three hundred takas for his son's wedding ceremony and is ultimately driven to destitution by the interest payments. Frivolous expenditure was not simply impoverishing—it was not true to an idealized and truly Islamic self-sufficient and market-independent peasant. The ideal peasant caught his own fish, grew his own vegetables, made his own furniture, spun his own cloth, made his own umbrellas, and did not buy anything from the marketplace—like Osman.

In *Muslim Bani*, Ashrafuddin Ahmed compared the market-dependent peasantry of his times unfavorably to the "independent" peasantry of the past, who made their own mustard oil to rub on their bodies, light lamps, and cook food; cultivated eggplants, chilies, ginger, and turmeric; and were satisfied with homespun cloth. This independent peasantry "lacked for nothing," "never experienced the moneylender's pressures," "would be displeased by unnecessary expenditure," and "maintained their full honour."[50] On the other hand, Ahmed argued, contemporary peasants consumed at will, and were losing their true peasant identity. Contemporary peasants were, Ahmed argues, styling themselves as "babus"—as middle-class, salaried Hindus. He reserved special contempt for peasants with an "Albert cut"—a distinctive hairstyle with a side parting and slightly waved that was named for Prince Albert, Empress Victoria's grandson, who had toured India in 1889–90:

> That Albert on your head, it is a gardener's crooked cut
> So much oil for your Albert that there is crisis of oil in the country
> They don't go to the village barbershop
> They get their fancy haircuts for 2 annas in town.[51]

For Ahmed, Albert cuts, oiled hair, and fancy clothes were forms of "babugiri"—cultivating the habits and appearance of middle-class and Hindu babus. "Babugiri" was implicated in a loss of the peasant ethic and, more significantly, in financially ruinous market behavior. Cultivators had stopped working as cultivators and were not devoting sufficient time to the diverse forms of production that would, Ahmed thought, sustain the ideal and profitable peasant household. Ahmed concludes his poem with a series of instructions that are emblematic of this agrarian form of Islam, akin to Abdul Hai's twenty-one-point program for freedom: don't spend unnecessarily, forsake luxury, work hard to produce useful things, avoid litigation, quit smoking, save money, and accumulate capital.

Babugiri was also closely related to litigiousness—another financially ruinous form of peasant expenditure through lawsuits. Ashrafuddin Ahmed alleged that today's peasants were not to be found working in their fields but in courthouses contesting lawsuits. The image of "babugiri" was captured in Ahmed's description of a farmer, dressed in his newest clothes and oiled Albert-cut hair, running to catch the train: he is on his way to town to meet with his lawyer, a Hindu babu. This dandified peasant was contributing to a breakdown in Muslim peasant unity and, also, Muslim subjugation by Hindus: "The Hindu lawyer, when he gets you, will kick you in the ass / Your son, ignorant *shala*, is thinning the jute field."[52]

To abjure consumption was not, however, to forsake markets entirely. In fact, peasants are urged to engage with markets, not as buyers but as traders. Hence, the farmer who makes tamarind chutney and sells it in the marketplace—one of the vignettes of the ideal peasant in Hai's *Adarsha Krishak*—is praiseworthy. Abdul Aziz identifies Muslim aversion to trade as one of the five major causes for their impoverishment, stating in a couplet: "Those races that forsook commerce / They drowned in this world and the next."[53] Aziz claims those who object to commerce and trade on religious grounds, as being too this-worldly, are traitors: "There is no shame in doing *halal* work / Those who hate this work are traitors."[54] They are traitors precisely because the Muslim aversion to commerce and trade has led to their subjugation by "different races"—that is, Hindus and the British. As Aziz rhymes:

> See, different races through commerce
> Have looted our money
> On the strength of commerce
> They have become gods, and we their subjects.[55]

Marwari merchants, from a trading community with origins in Rajasthan, had moved into the Bengal delta starting in the late nineteenth century to participate in the jute trade. By the early twentieth century, they had carved out a dominant position in the delta's market towns as wholesalers and moneylenders. Mofussil boyans repeated the narrative of Marwari merchants coming from afar with few belongings, and amassing enormous wealth out of peasant labor. The "blood sucking" Marwari merchant was a frequent villain in mofussil Muslim poetry. In *Haq Katha* (True Words), Asghar Hossain locates the

Bengali Muslim downfall in British and Marwari commercial prowess, which enabled the British to conquer India and the Marwaris to suck dry the cultivators' wealth:

> Look, white men from England
> Conquered India on the strength of trade
> And look, Marwaris from Bikaner
> Have come and sucked the wealth of Bengal
> They came with a blanket and a dhuti
> And then built up enormous riches
> Casting the net of commerce, Marwaris
> Have sucked out our blood, flesh and life
> They are the only bloodsuckers here
> We are simple Bengalis, and can't find our way
> For money, we call them uncle
> We salam and call them babu and keep our heads bowed
> We look to them with folded hands
> Try and understand how Lakshmi has left us.[56]

Hossain, like Aziz, urged Muslim peasants to go into commerce. He gave the example of a farmer dividing his substantial holdings among his four sons, each fragmented holding too small to sustain the peasant household. As a solution, he advises the four brothers to go into four types of business, to specialize in trading four different commodities.

The mofussil poets' insistent appeal to Muslim peasants to engage in business was accompanied by their emphasis on ethical business practices. Even as he urged cultivators to go into different forms of commerce, Hossain emphasized how certain forms of commerce were un-Islamic. The jute trade was corrupting because it was characterized by deceit and dishonesty: "In jute, all I see is theft / Look and see for yourselves, men and women."[57] Hossain proceeds to narrate a long list of thefts that take place in jute cultivation and trade: the theft of seeds from a neighbor's field, the theft of a few strands from the peasant homestead to buy a cigarette in the market, the trader's theft when weighing small lots of peasant produce, the grader's bribe in assessing quality, the theft in prices by brokers, and the theft on rails and steamers. In a market practice that was unique to jute, negotiations over price took place silently, with a buyer and seller indicating prices by tracing the figures on each others' palms under a piece of cloth. All this secrecy and dishonesty was geared toward cheating cultivators of a just price for their commodity:

The price of everything is revealed openly,
But with jute the hand is under the cloth.
When jute is sold you are cheated,
Judge for yourself see how stupid you are.[58]

No other mofussil poet goes to such lengths in describing an entire commodity as un-Islamic. For most mofussil poets, the emphasis was on specific dishonest practices—on lying, stealing, and cheating. Abdur Rahim's *Nurul Islam* narrates an incident of a boatman stealing mangoes entrusted to him for transport by a cultivator. The boatman sells a portion of the cargo at another trader's dock by the riverside, though he swore—on the Koran—to deliver the entire cargo intact. When the wholesaler in Dhaka receives fewer mangoes, he does not complain, but makes up the money by cheating customers on weight and price—all the while swearing upon the Koran and by Allah. The point of Rahim's narrative is that an individual act of dishonesty leads to a series of dishonest acts, a sequence of deceit and lies sworn upon the Koran. Hence, the boatman's simple theft of mangoes added up, sequentially, into an entire society based on deceit and dishonesty—the kali kal or dark ages. It was not enough for Muslims to engage in commerce and business, they had to do so honestly and ethically.

Agrarian Islamic boyans were focused on patriarchal authority over wives and children. Quarrelsome wives and daughters-in-law and disrespectful youths, these boyans contended, were the result of a failure to exercise proper patriarchal authority. The most common condemnation of women is through a caricatured image of the bad-tempered (*bodmejaji*), quarrelsome (*jhograte*), and unveiled (*bepurdah*) peasant wife—the female equivalent of the dandified male peasant. Abdur Rahim's dark ages, or kali kal, are characterized by such women, who demand luxuries, scream at their husbands, and neglect their children. These women, Rahim contends, are the products of failed patriarchal authority—of overindulgent fathers and husbands who lavish their daughters and wives with expensive clothes and ornaments. Patriarchal overindulgence also created the wastrel youths who characterize kali kal, lazy and disrespectful boys who smoke cigarettes in front of their elders. This overindulgence is marked by frivolous expenditures—on luxuries for wives and children. Three of the five sections of Rahim's *Nurul Islam* are concerned with the peasant household: with bad-tempered, quarrelsome, and unveiled women; failed marriages; and indulgent fathers and their spoiled brats. The failed marriage, in Rahim's narrative, directly results from a lavish wedding, which creates unreasonable expectations of material comfort for the new bride and conflict around the bride's dowry. Hence, in *Adarsha Krishak*, when Abdul Hai upbraided the Bengal peasant for borrowing money for the wedding of his "adored, piece-of-his-liver son," he was concerned not solely with the household budget, but also with patriarchal overindulgence and its moral effects on women and male youths. The degeneracy of peasant women and youths was, therefore, a product of frivolous consumption.

Some agrarian Islamic texts condemned women's participation in producing for markets—even though it would contribute to strengthening the household finances. The marketplace is an exclusively male space, and women's participation in markets would, mofussil poets maintained, lead to their degeneracy. In *Haq Katha*, Asghar Hossain narrates a lengthy condemnation against poultry and eggs. He begins his diatribe against eggs with the following couplet: "In this world there are too many chickens and ducks / These two things destroy religion and work."[59] Hossain's main issue was that poultry rearing was women's work, leading to women leaving the homestead and male strangers entering the homestead: chickens and ducks compromised women's virtue. Women leave the home to collect feed for their birds, and strange men—egg wholesalers—enter the homestead to buy eggs. Not only do women lose virtue, they are also unable to negotiate a just price for their eggs:

> Invited in, the shopkeeper sits down
> Then the wife brings out the eggs
> Then, brother, see what she does
> For a four-paisa egg, she asks for paisa one-and-half
> Shopkeeper listens and says I will give you a paisa for two eggs
> In that case, says womenfolk, I won't give you any eggs
> Finally, the shopkeeper agrees to the price
> And then these naughty (*paji*) women count out the eggs.[60]

These grasping and frivolous peasant women were responsible for a breakdown in peasant unity—or ekota. In Abdul Aziz's *Najat*, the lack of ekota was one of the five causes of Muslim decline and his example of the breakdown of unity centered on quarrelsome women. Aziz narrates a story about two brothers buying meat for their wives: one wife complains that there are two many bones in her share of the meat, the other wife feels that she is being accused of stealing by putting bones in her share, leading to an intense family squabble, and the disintegration of family unity. Quarrelsome and ill-tempered women were grasping and greedy, dissatisfied and demanding, and they caused conflict between men. Hence, consumption and the lack of Muslim peasant unity were closely interrelated.

Alongside women, the breakdown of *ekota* was due to litigiousness—the tendency of peasants to embroil themselves in litigation against neighbors and kin. For Nurul Islam, litigiousness was a symptom of the dishonesty and deceit that characterized the dark ages. He narrates a tale of an "imandar," a person of faith, who sells a portion of his land to repay the moneylender. The person who buys the land is a "trusting soul" and does not ask for the title deeds. This *imandar* then claims that he never sold the land, and the resulting dispute lands up in the village council and then the district court. At each venue, this imandar swears upon the Koran that he never sold the land. This breakdown in trust through deceit, lies, and lawsuits was, according to Islam, symptomatic of kali kal. As he rhymes: "Uncles and nephews form factions and constantly fight / Uncles and nephews are always in the courts."[61]

For mofussil poets, the marketplace and the household were intertwined spaces, ultimately relating back to consumption. Unrestrained consumption in marketplaces led to the corruption of peasant wives in the household and to a breakdown in Muslim unity in the community. The dandified peasant man who spent recklessly on clothes, haircuts, and lawsuits was also a failed patriarch, overindulging his wife and children, creating the ill-tempered and uncontrollable women and disrespectful youth that characterized kali kal. Agrarian Islam was a religion of restoration: freedom (mukti) and salvation (*najat*) meant restoring Muslim peasants to a past prosperity and a lost glory. This task was to be achieved by peasants themselves, through individual self-reforms in the interrelated spaces of the farm, the household, and the market.

Conclusion

Agrarian Islamic discourses were critical to new projects of peasant self-fashioning, as the nineteenth-century period of prosperity gave way to the twentieth-century era of immiseration. As global commodity markets turned against jute cultivators, projects of self-fashioning through consumption were no longer possible. In this era of immiseration, the ideal Muslim peasant was envisioned as a savvy market operator who worked hard and reduced consumption so as to be financially self-sufficient. The ideal peasant was a man who abjured the pleasures of consumption and did not indulge his wife and children with gifts from the hat. The politics of peasant immiseration was not a hollow market-determined form of politics that merely responded to fluctuations in global prices. Rather, it was a new project of peasant self-fashioning that accompanied the reversal in terms of trade between peasant-produced and peasant-consumed commodities. Mofussil discourses of agrarian Islam were similarly utopian—in terms of imagining the impossible as possible—as the "wild talk" and "wild promises" of swaraj. Agrarian Islam was not an actionable program. It was not possible to work as hard as the mythical Osman and produce all household necessities through your own labor, and injunctions to abjure frivolous consumption simply did not apply to the vast majority of cultivators who were barely scraping together their subsistence. Ultimately, agrarian Islamic texts were less concerned with an actionable program than in portraying idealized peasants and an idealized peasant society, where men were hardworking, honest, and strict patriarchs; women were demure and obedient; youths were respectful; and neighbors were cooperative and friendly.

Peasant politics was also premised on new forms of circulation and connection between mofussil towns and the hinterland. These connections were forged by young Muslim men with origins in the countryside who moved into mofussil towns during the 1910s and 1920s to take up professional employment or administer small businesses. These men connected the countryside to the towns not solely through ties of blood and soil to their patrilineal villages, but also through the production and circulation of printed texts, such as agrarian Islamic texts produced by the burgeoning mofussil print industry. The pre–World War I characterization of the mofussil as beholden to metropolitan Calcutta and isolated from the countryside gave way to a new spatial arrangement: of politically and intellectually vibrant mofussil towns that were autonomous from the metropolis and closely connected to the countryside.

The Khilafat movement was formative in the emergence of a post–World War I peasant politics of immiseration, which was defined by two distinctive characteristics: discourses of agrarian Islam and closer connections between mofussil towns and the countryside. The movement, however, promoted non-cooperation with new forms of electoral and representative politics that the colonial state introduced into the jute tracts after World War I.

The Khilafat movement advocated the nonpayment of chaukidari taxes to newly formed village-level local government and nonparticipation in elections to the provincial legislature—or, as Tamizuddin Khan described in Faridpur, the nomination of fake candidates that discredited the elections. Subsequently, however, electoral and representative politics became enormously significant to peasant politics in the Bengal delta. Colonial reforms carved the jute tracts' towns and farms into territorial constituencies, overlaying the spaces of municipalities, union boards, and constituencies to the legislature on top of the spaces of hinterland, metropolis, and mofussil. The following chapter examines the ways in which interactions between the spaces of representative and electoral politics and the spaces of capital shaped peasant political action during the 1920s and 1930s, and produced the stunning electoral victory for the peasant populist Krishak Praja Party (KPP) during the 1937 elections to the legislature. The KPP's electoral triumph, the chapter demonstrates, can only be understood in the context of the spatial rearrangements and agrarian Islamic discourses that constituted the peasant politics of immiseration after World War I.

6

Peasant Populism

ELECTORAL POLITICS
AND THE "RURAL MUHAMMADAN"

IN THE 1937 elections to the Bengal Legislative Council, the first to be conducted under the expanded franchise and powers of the Government of India Act of 1935, the peasant populist Krishak Praja Party (KPP) emerged as the dominant political force in Muslim constituencies in the jute tracts. The KPP campaigned on reforming tenancy laws, forgiving peasant debt, providing universal healthcare and primary education, controlling floods and epidemics, and guaranteeing two square meals a day for everyone. The KPP's campaign was defined by slogans such as "Abolish Zamindari," "Land Belongs to the Tiller" and "Rice and Dal for Everyone." The KPP's campaign resonated among the delta's jute cultivators, who were being rapidly impoverished by the prolonged depression in jute prices during the 1930s. This chapter explores the KPP's peasant populist politics in the larger context of the limited forms of electoral, representative, and legislative politics introduced into the jute tracts in the decades after World War I.

The KPP's electoral victory took place under the rules established by the British Raj under the Government of India Act of 1935. The act substantively expanded the franchise, numbers of constituencies, and powers of elected representatives created by the Government of India Act of 1919—more popularly known as the Montagu-Chelmsford or Montford reforms. The Montford reforms introduced electoral politics into the agrarian delta for the first time, carving the jute-growing districts into seventeen Muslim and eleven non-Muslim constituencies. A fraction of the residents of these constituencies—less than 2 percent—were entitled to vote, based on the amount they paid in local taxes or income tax. The Montford reforms were meant as a sop to increasingly strident Indian nationalist demands for self-government during and before World War I. The limited reforms, however, angered Indian nationalists, who boycotted elections in 1920 during the Non-Cooperation and Khilafat movements and only participated in subsequent elections during the 1920s to "wreck the reforms from within"—that is, to use their seats in the Legislative Council to actively oppose and block the colonial adminis-tration. The 1935 act attempted to address nationalist disappointments with the Montford reforms. It increased the franchise, from less than 2 percent to 12.5 percent, and substantially expanded the powers of elected representatives in the legislature. Further, the 1935 act also altered the distribution of Muslim and non-Muslim, and rural and urban constituencies, increasing the electoral weight of Muslim peasant voters in eastern Bengal's jute tracts. The redraw-ing of constituencies and the increase in rates of enfranchisement created the conditions under which the KPP, whose support was almost exclusively among the Bengal delta's Muslim peasants, came to lead a coalition govern-ment in Bengal between 1937 and 1943.

Both the 1919 and 1935 acts enshrined the "communal principle," whereby Muslims and Hindus in the same locality voted for different representatives to the legislature. The "communal principle" gerrymandered the delta's jute tracts into a patchwork of constituencies: "rural Muhammadan" and "rural non-Muhammadan" or "urban Muhammadan" and "urban non-Muhammadan" constituencies. The legislatively enacted category of the "rural Muhammadan constituency" gained meaning and significance through the everyday activ-ities of electoral politics. The abstract category of the "rural Muhammadan constituency" was translated into imagined and embodied spaces and peoples—mofussil towns, agrarian villages, candidates, voters, representa-tives, and legislators—through campaign speeches and pamphlets, voting decisions, and policy debates on the floor of the legislature. As this chapter argues, the particular meanings and significances of the rural Muslim as ter-ritorial constituency, voter, representative, and legislator were inflected by discourses of peasant immiseration.

The first half of the chapter examines electoral, representative, and legislative politics in the agrarian delta from the colonial state's introduc-tion of limited electoral politics into the jute tracts between 1919 and 1935. The first section of this chapter shows how the category of the rural Muslim was conceptualized and utilized in elections to the provincial legislature and in legislative debates. The colonial state also introduced elections to local government institutions: local boards and district boards, mofussil munici-palities, and village unions. The second section describes how the formation of the mofussil municipal government sparked debates over the demarcations of town and countryside for the purposes of voting and taxation. The third section investigates Hindu-Muslim violence in Pabna in 1926, examining how electoral competition between Muslim and Hindu elites in a mofussil town culminated in Hindu-Muslim violence that engulfed the agrarian hinterland. Electoral politics, the first section of the chapter demonstrates, animated con-tests between the overlapping categories of Muslim and Hindu, peasant and bhadralok, and villager and townsman that had informed Swadeshi conflicts in the early twentieth century.

The second half of the chapter explores the Krishak Praja Party's peasant populist campaign during the 1937 elections and its subsequent failure to deliver on its campaign promises. The Government of India Act of 1935 considerably expanded the franchise, created many more rural Muslim constituencies in the jute tracts, and granted elected representatives substantial executive power. The Krishak Praja Party, which had been created out of shifting coalitions on the floor of the Legislative Council during the 1920s and 1930s, launched a staunchly peasant populist campaign. KPP candidates promised Bengal's jute cultivators tenancy reform, debt forgiveness, flood control, healthcare, edu-cation, and two square meals a day. In the context of the Bengal delta, their pro-peasant stance was always recognizably Muslim, even without invoking Islam. The conflation of peasant and Muslim in the jute tracts meant that KPP candidates were inoculated against their Muslim League rivals' charges that they were anti-Muslim stooges of the Hindu Congress. Notably, the KPP was also able to convince the jute-cultivating peasantry that they would mobilize state power to reverse peasant immiseration.

The KPP's most potent campaign pledge—"Rice and Dal for Everyone"—was the most difficult to fulfill. While the KPP was notably successful in substantially reducing peasant debt through debt arbitration boards and in curbing zamindari powers through tenancy legislation, they were unable to affect commodity prices. Their attempts to raise jute prices were frustrated and stymied by a cartel of Calcutta-based jute mill owners, surreptitiously and ably aided by colonial bureaucrats. In the market-entangled jute tracts, the inability to increase the price of jute relative to rice meant that the KPP could not solve the delta's perennial problem of *dal-bhaat* (dal-rice). The last section of this chapter examines the inability of the elected provincial government to effectively intervene in global commodity markets. During

1943 and 1944, mere months after Bengal's British governor unceremoniously and undemocratically removed the KPP from power, starvation and hunger stalked the jute tracts.

Before examining how electoral and representative politics transformed the Bengal delta and gave rise to a new form of politics around the "rural Muslim" as a category of constituency, candidate, and voter, it is necessary to describe the peculiarities of colonial reforms. The Montagu Chelmsford Reforms carved Bengal into 34 Muslim constituencies and 42 non-Muslim constituencies. Of the 34 Muslim constituencies, 31 were rural and 17 were in the jute tracts. The rural Muslim representatives of the jute tracts thus constituted a substantial presence in a legislature of 142 members—about 12 percent of the seats. The franchise was highly limited: only men who paid a substantial amount in taxes were entitled to vote, that is, men who had paid more than one and a half rupees in municipal taxes, or one rupee in taxes to their district board, or two rupees as chaukidari tax to their village unions, or income tax to the provincial government. Only a fraction of Bengal's population, about 2 percent, made it onto the 1920 voter rolls. Rates of enfranchisement were even lower for Bengal's Muslims at 1.6 percent, and lowest among rural Muslims in the jute-growing districts at 1.4 percent.[1] The voter rolls in the jute tracts' "rural Muhammadan constituencies" consisted almost entirely of jotedars and zamindars with sufficiently large landholdings to be assessed a high road cess or chaukidari tax and by mofussil professionals and businessmen who paid sufficient income or municipal taxes. However, this chapter argues that even though jute cultivators were not entitled to vote, the political category of the "rural Muslim" was critical to the making of electoral politics in the delta's jute tracts during the 1920s and 1930s.

Nationalists' disappointment with the Montford reforms did not stem from the limited franchise: Indian nationalists had by and large accepted the necessity of limiting the franchise. Rather, it was to do with the principle of "dyarchy," whereby real and substantive power over the state was reserved for unelected bureaucrats. Under the reforms, elected representatives were only given charge over so-called "developmental" institutions in provincial government: education, irrigation, industries, and so on. Control over the more powerful arms of the state—notably, law and order and finance—was retained for London-appointed colonial bureaucrats. Reforms had created toothless and powerless legislative councils, granting elected representatives only the ability to discuss, debate, and recommend government policy, not actually formulate and implement them. Despite these limitations, the Bengal Legislative Council emerged as a significant space in establishing the idioms and parameters of peasant-oriented state-craft in late-colonial Bengal.

In the same year that the colonial government introduced the Montford reforms, they extended the principle and practice of elections to local government bodies, thus transferring a modicum of control to elected executives and away from the subdivisional officers and district magistrates of the colonial bureaucracy. The Bengal Village Self-Government Act of 1919 established village unions that would raise chaukidari taxes and provide basic services—notably, medical dispensaries and road maintenance—within their locality. The government also extended elections to mofussil munic-ipalities and local boards, constituted at the subdivisional level. Increas-ingly, control over district boards was transferred to individuals indirectly elected by members of local boards. The franchise in these elections was much broader: in most cases, all male taxpayers, regardless of the amount of tax they paid, were entitled to vote. More significantly, the communal principle had not been extended to local elections, and the delta's Hindus and Muslims chose from a common slate of candidates. This chapter shows how elections to local government institutions during the 1920s and 1930s resulted in renewed contests over the boundaries between the intertwined categories of mofussil and the countryside, townsmen and peasants, and Hindus and Muslims.

The Government of India Act of 1935 substantially extended the franchise and redistributed constituencies between Hindus and Muslims, rural and urban areas, and eastern Bengal and the rest of the province. The tax require-ments for the franchise were lowered substantially: a minimum payment to district boards of half a rupee, instead of one rupee under the 1919 act; chaukidari tax of six annas (or 3/8th of a rupee) instead of two rupees; and a municipal tax of half a rupee instead of one and a half rupees. The relaxation of qualifications resulted in an increase in the franchise from 2 percent of Bengal's population to 12.5 percent. In contrast to the 1919 act, the rate of enfranchise-ment was slightly higher in rural Muslim constituencies in the jute tracts at 13 percent—partly due to the more even distribution of land and consequently the larger number of peasant taxpayers. The depression had, however, reduced enfranchisement rates to lower than expected levels, as many peasant house-holds had stopped paying chaukidari taxes: in experimental rolls of 1932,

14.8 percent were enfranchised, which was considerably higher than the final 13 percent in 1937. The act also redistributed constituencies in favor of rural Muslims. Out of a total 250 seats in the Legislative Assembly, 117 were reserved for Muslims. Of the 117 Muslim constituencies, 111 were rural, of which 57 were in the jute-growing districts. Thus the 1935 act increased the number and weight of rural Muslim peasant votes in the jute tracts, enabling the Krishak Praja Party's electoral triumph in 1937—the first elections held under the new act.

The first section of this chapter examines the emergence of the "rural Muslim" as a political category in rural election campaigns and in the Bengal Legislative Council following the 1919 Montagu-Chelmsford Reforms. The second section describes contests over the demarcation of mofussil towns and the countryside in the context of mofussil municipal government. The third section investigates the Hindu-Muslim riots in Pabna in 1926. Together, these three sections explore the electoral and representative politics that imbued the category of the "rural Muslim" with meaning and significance during the two decades preceding the KPP's electoral triumph of 1937. The fourth section examines the KPP's electoral victory in 1937, and the fifth and final section, the KPP's subsequent failure to deliver on its chief electoral pledge. The second half of the chapter describes the conditions and limits of state-centric peasant populism during the late colonial period.

The "Rural Muhammadan"

On the eve of the 1923 elections to the Legislative Council, the second held under the Montford reforms, Shah Abdul Hamid published a pamphlet titled *Shashon Shongskarey Gramyo Mussalman* (Rural Muslims in Government Reforms).[2] Hamid, a prolific writer and member of the mofussil Muslim intelligentsia, had written several tracts on rural Muslim peasant poverty.[3] In this particular pamphlet, written in the context of his campaign in the Mymensingh East (Muhammadan) Rural constituency, Hamid impresses on jute cultivators the importance and significance of the category of the "rural Muslim." His pamphlet tabulates the distribution of seats between Muslims and non-Muslims and between urban and rural areas created by the reforms, and emphasizes that rural Muslims for the first time have the opportunity to elect their own representatives to the legislature, the *lat majlis*. Hamid urged rural Muslims to take this "golden opportunity": "If we can work gradually in our own interests, present ourselves in a lawful manner in the Legislative

Council, then, bit by bit, we will be able to acquire our legitimate rights and, of course, we can reasonably hope that the various difficulties that have laid us low will be resolved."[4]

Directly addressing rural Muslims, in the tradition of agrarian Islamic texts, Hamid's pamphlet is devoted to defining the ideal rural Muslim candidate. For Hamid, as for mofussil Muslim intellectuals generally, Muslim and peasant were interchangeable categories: that is, to be a rural Muslim was to be a peasant and vice versa. As Hamid states: "when we say rural Muslim, we understand village Muslim peasant classes (*gramyo mussalman krishak shomproday*)."[5] Hamid repeatedly urges rural Muslim voters to choose a candidate from their own social and spatial community, that is, "those who are members of the rural peasant classes (*gramya krishak srenibhukto*) . . . because no one else can have a complete understanding of the legitimate grievances of rural Muslim peasants."[6] Hamid lists those who do not meet the standards of the rural Muslim candidate: zamindars, zamindari employees, townsmen, and city dwellers. It is possible, he admits, that certain professionals—doctors, lawyers, and barristers—could serve as rural Muslim candidates, though it was unlikely: "we are going to have to judge if they truly care for the poor farmers. It is unlikely, but some of them might."[7]

In locating the political category of the "Rural Muhammadan" enacted by colonial reforms in the delta's overlapping and intertwined categories of religion, class, and space, Hamid's emphasis is clearly on space. Hamid does state that ideal candidates must be true Muslims, "deen dar Mussalmans," though he does not specify how voters were to differentiate between true and false Muslims. Much of his pamphlet is devoted to emphasizing his own rurality and to celebrating the "simple rural life." Hamid opens with a claim to have found "shelter in *your* [the reader/voter's] peaceful, loving village society" after failing to make a home "in political society, religious society, the society of the wealthy, the society of the important, the society of the intelligent, and, last of all, the society that is the beloved of all—that of lawyers, advocates, barristers, and doctors. . . . So, I have found shelter for all these years in your peaceful, loving village society."[8] Hamid proceeds to a celebration of rurality that consists largely of a rejection of modern consumerism and urban sociality, in other words, rooted in the discourses of agrarian Islam described in the previous chapter: "The village hovel is our *rang mahal* (palace of color), the dim candle is our electric light, the winding narrow paths leading from one village to the next are our highways, and the village well, tank, pond, and lake are for us the pure tap water of the city." Hamid rejects "smart umbrellas, *babugiri* (babu-like or *bhadralok*) ways, sly thoughts, . . . beautiful mansions, dense dwellings, flirtatious smiles, . . . *babuyana shahebana* (the behavior of a *babu* or even a *sahib*), hats on black heads, and gates in front of empty homes."[9] The poem, the only one in all of Hamid's writing, reads very much like the agrarian Islamic poems described earlier:

> Let us have our coarse rice, farms bounded by aisles
> Let us have our plough stick, we do not want thin bamboo reeds
> Let us have the fish we catch, *koi* from an old *beel*
> Let us have our plough oxen, fresh yoghurt from our cows
> Let us have our white waist-cloth, and the white cap on our head
> We do not want hat-coat-boot, genuine English V.P.
> We do not want to be clever, we value our simple souls
> We know that cleverness results in ash, and that faith is the ultimate wealth.[10]

Hamid thus translates the category of the "Rural Muslim" created by colonial electoral reforms into meaningful and recognizable terms through the agrarian Islamic rejection of a consumerist metropolitanism in favor of an imagined and idealized simple rural life that was devoid of umbrellas, hat-coat-boots, electric lights, tapwater, mansions, flirtations, and fake cleverness. He used this language to depict himself as a simple villager and probably to lampoon some of his rival candidates. Syed Ali Nawab Chaudhuri, a prominent zamindar, was one such rival, who would serve as a minister during the 1920s. Portraits of Syed Ali Nawab Chaudhuri show him dressed in an urbane fashion—that is, in the "hat-coat-boot" that Hamid depicted as alien to the true rural Muslim.

TABLE 6.1. Voter Turnouts in Bengal, 1920–1937

	Overall turnout	Rural Muslim constituencies in East Bengal's jute tracts
1920	29.30%	24.30%
1923	39%	28.20%
1926	39.25%	37.50%
1929	26.10%	18.10%
1937	40.50%	42.10%

Compiled and computed from electoral returns in Government of Bengal, *Reports on the General Elections in Bengal*, Calcutta, 1920, 1923, 1926, 1929, and 1937.

Hamid received just 1,523 votes, 20 percent of the total number of votes cast. The hatted, coated, booted Nawab received 3,427 votes and was duly elected as one of the two representatives from Mymensingh East Rural Muhammadan.[11] Turnout was low in the 1923 elections: 20.4 percent of eligible voters in Hamid's constituency and 28.2 percent across the jute tracts' rural Muslim constituencies—far lower than the 39 percent turnout in all of Bengal (see table 6.1). Voter turnout was low throughout the Montford period: turnout never exceeded 50 percent of eligible voters in Bengal as a whole and turnout in the jute tracts' rural Muslim constituencies was lower than for the province. Turnout, however, may not be the most accurate indicator of the general interest in elections and voting. Both voters and nonvoters participated in campaign events and stump speeches. They participated in the festivities on polling days, in the schoolhouses and hastily erected corrugated iron sheds that served as polling booths. During the very first elections in 1920, the Khilafat boycott generated excitement that served to suppress voting figures—as "fake candidates" were nominated and Khilafat activists attempted to enforce a boycott in polling locations. In the 1923 elections, mofussil Muslims debated whether to support C. R. Das's Swarajist Party, which contested the elections on the pledge to make the Legislative Council and the system of dyarchy unworkable, or to support Muslim candidates campaigning to govern on behalf of rural Muslims—as Shah Abdul Hamid did. Tamizuddin Khan fell out with his influential father-in-law on this debate—Khan supported the Swarajists, his father-in-law opposed them, and the dispute was serious enough that the two men stopped speaking to each other for a while.[12] By 1926 many more mofussil Muslim elites decided to participate in elections, and turnout among rural Muslim voters reached its highest point under the Montagu-Chelmsford system.[13] Turnout was again depressed in the 1929 elections, falling even below the turnout for the Khilafat-boycotted 1920 elections. This sharp drop may have been related to rural Muslims' disappointment with the failures to legislate tenancy reforms in 1926. However, low voter turnout—even within the miniscule rate of enfranchisement—should not diminish the significance of elections and voting in the Bengal delta. Electoral and representative politics imbued the category of the "Rural Muhammadan" constituency, representative, and voter with social and political meaning and significance.

The category of the "Rural Muhammadan" was further fleshed out on the floor of the Legislative Council in Calcutta, as legislators tried to position themselves as representatives of the rural Muslim jute cultivator vis-à-vis state policies. These forms of positioning were most pronounced during legislative discussions on budgetary allocations. Representatives from the jute tracts—both Muslim and Hindu—pilloried budgetary allocations to metropolitan Calcutta, on the grounds that the metropolis was stealing the jute wealth generated by the hinterland peasantry to aggrandize the city. During budget discussions in 1927, Mohammad Sadeque, the member from Noakhali said:

> This year Rs. 1,50,000 have been budgeted for the Calcutta Improvement Trust. The funds for its operation are mainly derived from the terminus tax and jute cess, both of which come from the resources of the country. It is a matter of great wonder that the civilized government of the twentieth century should tax the jute growers of Bengal, who live in the swamps of Eastern Bengal wrecking with malaria, kala-azar and every form of epidemic, underfed, underclothed, scarcely able to find a glass of pure drinking water within 20 miles of their cottage, to rear palaces in Calcutta and to pave the streets of the city with dust-proof-tar-macadam.[14]

Competing claims to represent the "rural Muslim"—always interchangeable with peasant jute cultivator—resulted in shifting alliances on the floor of the Legislative Council, as rural Muslim legislators voted at times with rural non-Muslims and, at other times, with nonrural Muslims. In 1921 Indu Bhushan Dutt, a Hindu member from Tipperah, moved a resolution recommending "the Government to take steps to circulate in Bengali, to all the union boards, municipalities, and co-operative societies in Bengal, weekly statements of the price of jute, cotton, oilseeds and other country produce, prevailing in the foreign importing markets."[15] Shah Abdur Rauf of Rangpur spoke in support, seeing in the proposal a means of "protecting these illiterate people from being duped by middlemen, who make a large profit out of the labours of these poor agriculturists."[16] Haridhan Dutt, a member from Calcutta, opposed the bill on the grounds that the money used for circulating this information to illiterate cultivators would be better spent on educating them to read. However, he noted: "Coming here as a representative of this city [Calcutta], I am very loath to do anything or to take any step that might offend our mufassal friends."[17] The resolution was passed with a large margin, with Haridhan Dutt's "mufassal friends" voting en bloc against metropolitan representatives. Indu Bhushan Dutt was not surprised: "I am glad that I have got the support of the mufassal members; that was only natural."[18]

While it appeared "only natural" that mofussil members would agree on measures to redress the metropolitan dominance of the jute trade, the same members would split along religious lines when addressing relations of property and credit in agrarian production. As Partha Chatterjee has

argued, the most contentious and notable legislative discussion in the Montford Council was around reforms to agrarian tenancy laws in 1926.[19] During
the tenancy debates, mofussil Muslim members voted en bloc to enhance
peasant and sharecroppers tenancy rights vis-à-vis zamindars and were
consistently blocked by Hindu members. On amendment after amendment,
mofussil Muslim members like Tamizuddin Khan (Faridpur), Nurul Haq
Chaudhuri (Noakhali), Asimuddin Ahmed (Tipperah), Muhammad Ismail
(Mymensingh), Muazzam Ali Khan (Pabna), Kasiruddin Ahmed (Rangpur),
Nausher Ali (Jessore), Azizul Haque (Nadia), and Ekramul Haque (Murshi-
dabad) spoke in favor of enhancing peasants' and sharecroppers' rights. On
each amendment, they encountered a unified Hindu opposition that included
all the Hindu representatives from the jute tracts.[20] In his autobiography, Abul
Mansur Ahmed stated that the tenancy debates confirmed for the "rural Muslims" that they could not depend on Hindu politicians to deliver pro-peasant
policies. The acrimonious tenancy debates led eighteen Muslim members to
form a loose parliamentary group to champion tenancy rights, known as the
Bengal Praja Party, which subsequently became the Krishak Praja Party.

The political category of the "Rural Muhammadan" was enacted, embodied,
and imbued with meaning in election campaigns and on the floor of the
Legislative Assembly. Drawing on the languages of agrarian Islam and on
the spatial categories of hinterland, metropolis, and mofussil, certain Muslim
politicians attempted to fashion themselves as true representatives of the
"rural Muslim." Historians have argued that the principle of communal representation enshrined by the colonial state in the electoral process spurred the
growing acrimony between South Asia's Hindus and Muslims. However, the
categories of Muslim and Hindu voters and representatives were not defined
solely through antagonism toward each other. Instead, the rural Muslim as a
political category could and did inform moments of alliance with rural non-
Muslims or with nonrural Muslims on the floor of the Legislative Council.
The rural Muslim as a political category in electoral and representative politics
gained meaning and substance through shared discourses of what it meant
to be rural and Muslim. For Shah Abdul Hamid to be a rural Muslim meant
to be a peasant who rejected urban forms of life; for Mohammad Sadeque, it
meant to privilege the interests of "underfed, underclothed" peasants without
access to clean drinking water over the "palatial homes" and "dust-proof-tar-
macadam" that paved the streets of metropolitan Calcutta.

Local Elections

The communal principle was not extended to local government elections. At various times, mofussil Muslim elites demanded communal constituencies as a safeguard against more powerful Hindu elites. In 1923 the Faridpur District Muhammadan Association addressed a memorial to the governor: "Our experience in the District, Local, and Municipal Boards has also been extremely sad. The electors behind these self-governing institutions are in the grip of the zamindars and money-lenders, who are mostly Hindus, and consequently our election enterprises in the majority of cases end in utter disaster. We beg to suggest that the Local Self-Government Acts be amended immediately with a view to create separate electorates for the Mussalmans."[21] These demands notwithstanding, the growing economic and cultural clout of a section of mofussil and rural Muslims—discussed in the previous chapter—resulted in their gradually gaining control over some local government institutions. Further, the qualifications for elections to village unions, local boards, and mofussil municipal boards were much laxer—all taxpayers, regardless of the amount paid in taxes, were enfranchised.

Rural Muslims gained almost immediate control of the union boards, which were created by the Village Self-Government Act of 1919. Union boards were meant to introduce self-government at the village level, empowering locally elected chairmen of the board to raise taxes, maintain medical dispensaries, and maintain and improve basic infrastructure. The formation of union boards and the increase in chaukidari tax rates were a cause of peasant anger during the Khilafat movement, resulting in a broad boycott of these institutions across the jute tracts. However, after the Khilafat boycott came to an end in 1923, union boards were steadily expanded throughout the delta. At the end of 1923, only 706 union boards had been sanctioned in the eastern Bengal jute-growing districts, none had been sanctioned in Rangpur and Pabna, and of the 108 union boards sanctioned in Mymensingh only 30 had actually been formed. In 1926, during a short-lived jute boom, new union boards were established across the delta, and by the end of the year, there were, 2,217 union boards in the province.[22] Relatively wealthy rural Muslim peasants, who had diversified livelihoods away from purely agrarian pursuits, were largely in control of the union boards. Frank Bell, the British subdivisional officer in Tangail, reported that "the Union Boards were usually controlled by the richer and shrewder Moslem peasants."[23] For "richer and shrewder Moslem peasants," union boards offered a means to enhance their power within the hinterland and with respect to mofussil towns. The rise of the rich peasant was in stark contrast to the colonial expectation that "gentlemen"—"landlords, doctors, retired officials and other *gentlemen* whose qualifications enable them to manage the affairs of their unions"—would manage the union boards.[24]

However, while wealthy Muslim peasants were able to gain control over union boards, elections to mofussil municipalities were far more competitive, and led to debates over the proper demarcation of municipality and countryside and, hence, of townsmen and peasant and Hindu and Muslim. The influx of rural Muslim men into mofussil cities had changed both the demography and geography of mofussil towns. As newly arrived Muslim men threatened Hindu dominance over municipalities, associations of mofussil Hindus appealed for stricter spatial demarcation of towns and the countryside. In 1925 municipal taxpayers' associations in Jamalpur in Mymensingh and Brahmanbaria, Tipperah complained to the colonial government that the existing territorial boundaries of the municipality included large numbers of agriculturist voters who did not pay house and latrine taxes to the municipality. These taxpayers' associations were largely Hindu organizations and their complaint was against the inclusion of rural Muslims on the outskirts of the town in what they described as the "town proper." The Brahmanbaria town center, they complained, did not form a cohesive "ward," but was "parceled out and amalgamated with the villages which form the four existing wards, and consequently, *the town has lost its existence as it were*, and thus it has no representation on the Municipal Board."[25] Similarly, Shashi Mohan De, a Hindu lawyer in Jamalpur, complained about the spatial boundaries of the municipality: "the only really urban part [of Jamalpur] is the Ward No. I which stretches along the bank of the river, the rest of the municipal area being open country dotted with villages."[26]

These complaints about the loss of the town proper reflect not just the vagaries of territorially bounded municipalities and wards, but also Hindu fears of a loss of control over municipalities to Muslims and, also, the association of Muslim-dominated areas with the hinterland. It was not just Hindu townsmen who spoke in terms of a Hindu-dominated "town proper" and Muslim-dominated outskirts, so did colonial officials and even mofussil Muslim townsmen. In recommending against redrawing Jamalpur's municipal boundaries, the district magistrate of Mymensingh commented that a "village commissioner" of Jamalpur had expressed his "fears that if the municipal area were confined to the town proper there would be a practical disenfranchisement of Muhammadans."[27] The electoral competition between Hindus and Muslims for control over municipal boards morphed into disputes about the boundaries between mofussil municipalities and the hinterland and invoked a shared yet complex understanding of the overlapping and entangled spaces of town and countryside and Hindu and Muslim. Mofussil Hindus attempted to disentangle these spaces and to constitute the "town proper" as the legitimate municipality. However, the boundaries between the mostly Hindu town and a mostly Muslim countryside that had seemed clearer during the Swadeshi movement—when Muslim peasants from the countryside laid siege to Jamalpur town—had blurred during the post–World War I era of immiseration. Hindu Muslim violence in Pabna in 1926 demonstrates the complex ways in which the spaces of electoral politics interacted with the spaces of hinterland and mofussil and the languages of agrarian Islam.

Pabna, 1926

Historians of communal violence in the agrarian jute tracts have emphasized that violence between Hindus and Muslims always took the form of clashes between Muslim peasants and moneylenders, traders, and zamindars. However, as Partha Chatterjee rightly points out, Muslim peasants often spared Muslim rent-receivers and moneylenders in their attacks on the peasantry. Chatterjee argues that there was a "communal mode of peasant resistance," whereby the delta's "feudalistic" modes of production meant that peasants perceived social relations in religio-cultural rather than class terms.[28] Hence, Muslim peasants perceived Muslim talukdars and moneylenders as fellow peasants and directed their protests solely against Hindus. The economic bases of Hindu-Muslim violence in the 1920s need to be contextualized within a broader conception of the post–World War I peasant politics of immiseration than is permitted by the categories of "semi-feudal" or "proto-capitalist." With this in mind, I examine the Pabna riots of 1926.

After narrowly losing in the elections to the legislature from the Pabna Rural Muhammadan constituency in 1923, Wasimuddin Ahmed—a Muslim zamindar—turned his attention to the chairmanship of the Pabna District Board.[29] The candidates for the district board chairman in 1925 were Wasimuddin Ahmed and Ranjit Chandra Lahiry, a Hindu zamindar in the district. Ahmed was expected to win. Members of subdivision-level local boards elected the district chairman, and they were mostly Muslim. However, just before the elections, one of Lahiry's supporters obtained an injunction against the attendance of the Sirajganj Local Board on the grounds that its elections had been marred by irregularities. Wasimuddin Ahmed and his chief lieutenant, Abdul Hamid, persuaded the Sirajganj Local Board members to cast their votes despite the court's injunction. As a result, these Sirajganj members, Ahmed, and Hamid were charged with contempt of court, and the Sirajganj members were issued prison sentences. The colonial authorities voided the elections and appointed Wasimuddin Ahmed as chairman and Abdul Hamid as vice chairman by executive fiat.[30] They justified their decision on the grounds that the Sirajganj Local Board elections had been declared valid and, hence, Ahmed would have been elected by the Muslim majority in the local boards of Pabna district.

The disputed elections were followed by a period of simmering tension between Hindus and Muslims in Pabna town. On the morning of July 1, 1926, fragments of a smashed idol of a Hindu goddess were left on a public road near Sitlai house, the mofussil residence of Ranjit Lahiry. The town's Hindu community gathered there and, after a series of fiery speeches, decided on a procession through the town, carrying fragments of the idol to the Ganges to be immersed and reconsecrated. In later court proceedings, the towns' Muslims and government prosecutors alleged that the procession route was deliberately planned so as to pass in front of the towns' mosques while playing music—an act of provocation given episodes of Hindu-Muslim violence around the issue of music before mosques that had taken place throughout Bengal.

At around seven in the evening, at the time of the *Maghrib* or sunset prayer, the procession reached the Khalifapatti mosque—located in a predominantly Muslim neighborhood of tailors. When congregants within the mosque complained about the music, members of the procession attacked the tin-roofed, thatch-walled mosque, raining down bricks on the mosque roof and attempting to push down its walls. The bricks were taken from a nearby construction site—a new house that was being built to house some of Pabna's growing Muslim population. During the following week, most shops in the town remained closed and the streets were deserted. An uneasy calm prevailed over the town, punctuated with isolated attacks on individual Hindus by groups of Muslims. The Hindu and Muslim populations of the town were about equal and neither community mounted a full-on assault on the other.

The countryside, however, was soon engulfed in violence. In surrounding villages, assemblies of Muslim men attacked Hindu-owned shops and homes, focusing their anger not on Hindu bodies but on Hindu-owned commodities—boxes, bedding, clothing, utensils, umbrellas, grains, and fruits. In Bakshipur village, on July 4, 1926, a group of 100 to 125 Muslim men attacked Hindu houses, while the residents of these homes fled and hid. Returning to his house, Abhoy Sarkar found that "the Mahommedans not only broke his box, but his clothes were torn to pieces and his documents and paddy and rice were scattered about."[31] The judge presiding over the case against the accused noted: "The element of mischief seems to predominate in these wanton destruction of cooking utensils, the scattering of grain, tearing of clothes and bedding. The accused are not dacoits in the strict sense of the word. . . . They came more with the object of revenge than anything else and there is no evidence against the accused that they actually committed theft."[32] A similar attack took place against Hindu homes in Chandai, where "The mob entered each of the 21 houses in turn. . . . The accused not only plundered and went away with everything of value in these houses but smashed boxes, broke utensils, mixed up different kinds of grain and scattered it about."[33] In Ekdanta village, complainants alleged that "12 to 14 Mahomedans with *lathi*, scythe in their hands attacked them and beat them and took away their bundles containing clothes, their instruments of carpentry, cash, jack fruit and umbrellas."[34] By the time peace was restored through the deployment of armed police and the mass arrests of Muslim men, the Pabna district magistrate estimated that "29 shops and 158 houses [were] looted, goods worth Rs. 1,25,000 [were] carried away. *A greater value of property was damaged, but impossible to estimate.*"[35]

Was the focus of Muslim violence on Hindu-owned consumer goods— umbrellas, boxes, grains, fruits, bedding, tobacco, and the like—informed by an agrarian Islamic critique of consumerism? Was the non-Muslimness of Hindus signaled by their ownership of consumer commodities that impoverished Muslim peasants could no longer afford and, by the logic of agrarian Islam, would have to produce themselves instead of purchase at markets? The nature of the archive and the paucity of Muslim peasant voices do not permit a definitive answer to these questions. It is worth noting, however, that the destruction of Hindu-owned property exceeded the looting: as the British judge phrased it, "these men were not dacoits in the strict sense of the word." Muslim attacks on Hindu-owned property were not merely an attempt to obtain commodities that had become unaffordable through nonmarket means, that is, through the robbery of Hindu-owned property.

While the countryside staged attacks on Hindu belongings, the town was the setting for a different set of political contests—legal battles between the protagonists of the disputed district board elections to establish criminal culpability for the attack on the Khalifapatti mosque, which had been destroyed by the procession of Hindus. The prosecution launched a case accusing prominent members of the mofussil Hindu community of culpability: they had delivered "inflammatory speeches" inciting violence against Muslims and had deliberately planned a procession route that would pass in front of Pabna's mosques. At the mofussil level the case was assisted by Wasimuddin Ahmed and Abdul Hamid, who mobilized witnesses—one key prosecution witness worked in Abdul Hamid's brother's ganja shop and another was a private tutor to Hamid's son.[36] The district magistrate found the town's Hindu community guilty but that verdict was subsequently overturned by the sessions court and, in turn, the district magistrate's verdict was restored by the Calcutta High Court. For Bengali Muslim politicians, the sessions court's reversal of the district magistrate's verdict "testified to the downfall of the judiciary," and indicated that Hindus in different branches of the state were actively suppressing the Muslim community.[37] Thus Hindu-Muslim violence in Pabna took place against the backdrop of electoral competition between Hindu and Muslim mofussil elites. In the towns, mofussil Muslims mobilized social, professional, and family networks to build a legal case against Hindu elites for deliberately inciting violence. In the countryside, assemblies of Muslim peasant men gathered to attack Hindu homes and property, with a focus on destruction rather than theft and looting.

The Montford reforms and the extension of elections to local government institutions were very limited. The franchise was small, voter turnout was low, and the actual powers of elected representatives in the Calcutta Legislative Council and local government boards were highly restricted. However, despite these limitations, electoral and representative politics had transformed political life in the jute tracts during the 1920s and early 1930s. The political processes of campaigns, votes, local governance, and legislation gave new meaning and significance to the category of the "rural Muslim," leading to a reconceptualization of the borders between countryside and town, peasant and townsman, and Muslim and Hindu. The Krishak Praja Party's electoral triumph of 1937 needs to be understood against the transformations inaugurated by the introduction of electoral and representative politics into the delta's jute tracts after 1919. Further, the emergence of the KPP needs to be contextualized in the collapse in prices and credit markets during the depression decade of the 1930s.

Peasant Populism

The collapse in commodity prices and credit markets at the onset of the Great Depression in 1930 was met with concerted peasant protests. These were sometimes violent, as in Kishoreganj and Dacca, where groups of peasant men attacked Hindu moneylenders' homes and demanded that they turn over records of loans and debts. If the moneylenders refused, they were assaulted, their houses and belongings were destroyed and looted, and, occasionally, they were killed. Sugata Bose's study of peasant violence against moneylenders in Kishoreganj demonstrates that peasant collective action was spurred by moneylenders' refusal to advance emergency loans during a time of agrarian crisis.[38] However, a more sustained, widespread, and largely nonviolent movement accompanied these spectacular forms of collective action: the organization of mass peasant meetings, *krishak sabhas*, and the formation of peasant committees—*krishak samitis*. Krishak sabhas and samitis brought together the immiserated hinterland peasantry, mofussil and rural elites, and representatives of Rural Muhammadan constituencies in the Legislative Council.

During the first half of 1931, the colonial government began receiving reports of peasant meetings being organized in different parts of the jute tracts. The state perceived these meetings as "moderate in tone" and not "anti-government." Peasant anger was directed at zamindars and moneylenders, rather than the colonial state. Peasant attendees passed resolutions to stop payments of rent to zamindars and interest to moneylenders; they demanded reforms to tenancy laws and credit markets. Representatives of rural Muslim constituencies presided over many peasant meetings: A. K. Fazlul Haq, who would subsequently lead the KPP to electoral victory, established himself as a powerful orator and a peasant populist leader through his speeches at peasant conferences. Maulana Abdul Hamid Khan, also known as the Bhashani Char Maulana, organized numerous peasant meetings and gained a reputation for "inspiring an anti-Landlord 'No-Rent' campaign."[39]

Krishak samitis' membership was drawn from locally prominent Muslims, generally members or chairs of local government institutions or representatives to the Legislative Council. The colonial government had a deeply ambivalent attitude toward the krishak movement. They characterized the movement as a "no-rent campaign," and were concerned that it would result in the kind of violence against zamindars and moneylenders witnessed in Kishoreganj. However, when the government declared local krishak samitis to be unlawful, a delegation of rural Muhammadan legislators from East Bengal met with the

governor of Bengal and reassured him that they would pursue activities law-
fully, and the ban on peasant committees was withdrawn.[40] The colonial state
provided krishak samitis tacit support because they were a potential bulwark
against Gandhi's civil disobedience movement and the rising tide of revolutionary terrorism among Hindu bhadralok young men and women. Through
the early 1930s, the state alternated between punishing and patronizing the
krishak samitis. Colonial bureaucrats occasionally prosecuted leaders of the
krishak movement for "fomenting for the non-payment of rent" and at other
times themselves attended peasant conferences and took "an active part with
the object of guiding the cultivators on sound lines in the development of
their political ideas."[41] The colonial government seemed to believe that the
end of the economic depression would result in the cessation of the "no-rent
campaign." However, the depression did not end, and the krishak movement
continued to gain in prominence and popularity.

Peasant conferences and krishak samitis created new spatial configurations
of hinterland, mofussil, and metropolis. Krishak samitis brought together onto
a shared platform union board chairmen, that is, "richer and shrewder" rural
Muslims; members and chairmen of municipalities, local boards, and district
boards; mofussil Muslims who competed with mofussil Hindus for political
office; and representatives of rural Muslim constituencies in the Legislative
Council. Krishak conferences were organized in villages, rather than in mofussil towns, and brought together mofussil and metropolitan Bengali Muslim
political leaders on a hinterland platform. These new bodies of peasant organization, created out of the new spatial formations of the delta, provided the
organizational and institutional structure to the Krishak Praja Party and, also,
its peasant populist rhetoric during the 1937 election campaign.

The Government of India Act of 1935 substantially lowered the tax qualifications
for male voters: from 2 rupees to 3/8th of a rupee in chaukidari tax, from 1 rupee
to ½ rupee in district board tax, or from 1½ rupee to ½ rupee in municipal
taxes. Thus the act increased the number of voters from about 2 percent to about
12.5 percent of Bengal's population. Under the 1935 voter qualifications, the rate
of enfranchisement was slightly higher in rural Muslim constituencies in the
jute tracts than in the rest of the province (13 percent versus 12.5 percent), while
it had been lower under the Montford reforms (1.6 percent versus 2 percent).
Enfranchisement would have been even higher had it not been for the economic depression: many peasant households had stopped paying union board
taxes and, hence, fell off the voter rolls. Just as importantly, reforms altered the

distribution of legislative seats, increasing the number and proportion of rural Muslims constituencies. Out of a total of 250 seats in the Legislative Assembly, 117 were reserved for Muslims, 111 were rural, and 57 were in the jute-growing districts. Thus the "Rural Muhammadan" constituencies of the jute tracts were critical in the battle to capture power in the provincial government.

In 1936 the colonial government announced that it would be hold-ing elections within a year and sparked a leadership contest in the various political groupings that had emerged out of the shifting alliances of the Legislative Council. The main group of legislators from Rural Muhammadan constituencies—the Nikhil Bangla Praja Samiti—split in two after A. K. Fazlul Haq failed in his bid to capture the leadership of the coalition. Haq and a group of representatives from Rural Muslim constituencies primarily from East Bengal's jute tracts broke away to form the Krishak Praja Party. Fazlul Haq was elected as the KPP leader at a peasant conference or krishak sabha in Mymensingh.[42] The KPP's organizational structure consisted of the krishak samitis that had been established throughout the jute tracts. Their candidates were drawn from the local leadership of krishak samitis and the samitis func-tioned as the KPP's political offices in the mofussil. Their campaign relied on the krishak sabhas that had become commonplace in the delta, mass peasant meetings where KPP candidates and leaders outlined their plans and programs for pro-peasant legislative and executive action. The KPP's fourteen-point program promised the abolition of zamindari, the strengthening of peasant proprietors' property rights, a greater share of the produce to sharecrop-pers, debt forgiveness for peasants, free primary education, the provision of healthcare, clearing water hyacinth (an invasive weed), and the eradication of malaria. The defining slogans of the campaign were "Abolish Zamindari Without Compensation," "Land Belongs to the Tiller," and—the slogan most popularly associated with the KPP's 1936 campaign—"Rice and *Dal* for Every-one." Throughout the campaign and fiery speeches promising pro-peasant government that would redress agrarian immiseration, Fazlul Haq styled him-self as the champion of the Bengal peasantry.

In rural Muslim constituencies, the KPP's major rival was the Muslim League. The League was an all-India political party that claimed to represent *all* South Asian Muslims. The League had initially courted the KPP in an attempt to form a broad alliance of Muslim parties. Their courtship, however, was clumsy. Haq responded angrily when the League excluded KPP mem-bers from leadership positions, stating that such behavior was typical of the zamindar-dominated League. He termed the KPP's exclusion "a fresh and deliberate attempt to insult the KPP and to make them feel that as Krishaks and Projas they must submit here as elsewhere to what the Nawabs and Zamindars may choose to decide on their behalf."[43] Throughout the election campaign, the KPP consistently depicted the League as the party of zamindars, an accusation supported by the large number of Muslim zamindars nominated by the League. For its part, the League campaigned on the cause of Muslim unity against the Hindu-dominated Congress. The League accused members of the KPP of being stooges of the Hindu Congress and of undermining Muslim unity. A Muslim League–aligned newspaper warned: "Muslim voters Beware! Do you want Congressmen to rule Bengal? If not send Fazlul Haq to the wall, smash up the PP."[44] K.G.M. Faroqui, a prominent zamindar, followed the League's electoral strategy to the letter in his campaign against Habibur Rahman Chaudhuri, the candidate from the Tipperah Krishak Samiti—which conducted a very similar campaign to the KPP's—in the Tipperah North Muhammadan constituency. Faroqui's campaign circulated pamphlets and rumors that Chaudhuri was a Congress stooge and a vote against the Muslim League was a sin.

Faroqui's campaign printed and distributed a pamphlet titled *Maulana Saheber Ashal Katha* (The True Words of the Maulana), written in the form of a conversation between a *maulana*—a Muslim religious leader—and an ordinary voter. The maulana saheb informs the voter, Pancha's father: "It is my duty to keep you informed not only in order to save Islam, but also ourselves, our descendants and neighbours from hell fire." The maulana describes Chaudhuri and the Krishak movement as a Hindu conspiracy: "the Hindus held a meeting with Ashraf Mia . . . and then with some *khaddar* wearing members of Ashraf Mia's party they founded an association and named it the Krishak Proja Samiti . . . in order to destroy the faith of the Muslims and the claims of that community and to cut the throats of their Muslim brethren." "Ashraf Mia" refers to Ashrafuddin Chaudhury, a prominent leader of the Tipperah Krishak Samiti, and "the Hindus" probably refers to Kamini Kumar Datta, a Hindu lawyer in Comilla town and the main organizer and financier of the party. The pamphlet claimed that renowned maulanas across India had issued a fatwa that the members of the Krishak Samiti were "enemies of Islam" and that those who voted for them would "fare badly in this world and the next." The maulana asked Pancha's father to vote for Faroqui as "he is one of the real Muslims of the Muslim party."[45]

The League's strategy of painting the KPP as the party of Congress stooges failed. The KPP's pro-peasant platform was always recognizably a Muslim platform; as Shah Abdul Hamid had argued more than a decade earlier, in the context of a very different election, in the Bengal delta's jute tracts the categories of the rural Muslim and the peasant were interchangeable. The KPP's peasant populist message generated considerable enthusiasm among both the enfranchised and unenfranchised in the rural Muslim constituencies of the jute tracts. For the first time in Bengal's electoral history, voter turnout in rural Muslim constituencies in the jute tracts exceeded the turnout in the province as a whole (see table 6.1). This voter enthusiasm was partly due to the introduction of symbols. To overcome the problem of voter illiteracy, candidates were assigned symbols—for example, a palanquin or an umbrella—and voters would indicate their choice by choosing their preferred candidate's symbol. A colonial official wrote: "canvassing by symbol is easier, and more effective than canvassing by name. It was common for party supporters and canvassers to arrange for choruses or party calls by symbols outside polling booths."[46] Campaigning was intense: supporters of candidates painted their candidate's symbols on their foreheads and campaigns arranged for motorcars to bus voters to the voting stations. Importantly, voter enthusiasm was also related to the KPP's success in crafting a peasant populist campaign, in translating the language of agrarian Islam into a manifesto for pro-peasant government action. The KPP was able to convince enfranchised jute cultivators that it would successfully utilize state power to reverse agrarian immiseration.

The League's argument that members of the KPP were anti-Muslim stooges of the Hindu Congress was not persuasive in the jute tracts, where to be pro-peasant necessarily implied being pro-Muslim. In the entire province, including Calcutta and the non-jute-growing west, the KPP received 31.8 percent of rural Muslim votes against the Muslim League's 27.1 percent. Margins were considerably greater in the KPP's stronghold of eastern Bengal. In a much-publicized contest, Haq challenged the Muslim League leader and scion of the Dacca Nawab family, Nazimuddin Ahmed, to a contest in a constituency of his choice. Nazimuddin chose to contest Patuakhali North, where his family held zamindari estates. Haq trounced Nazimuddin by a margin of 17 percent. KPP politicians scored similarly impressive victories throughout the jute tracts' rural Muslim constituencies: Rajibuddin Tarafdar winning by a margin of 24 percent in Bogra, Abu Hossain Sarkar by 15 percent in Rangpur, and Abdul Majid by 14 percent in Mymensingh.[47] An important exception to this was in Faridpur, where the League's candidate Tamizuddin Khan trounced his KPP rival by a margin of 22 percent.[48]

As neither the Indian National Congress nor the Muslim League had a clear majority, it fell to the KPP's leader, A. K. Fazlul Haq, to cobble together a coalition. After the Congress rebuffed Fazlul Haq, he turned to the Muslim League. The fierce and bitter electoral campaign was put aside, and the KPP and the League agreed to form a cabinet with Haq as premier. However, the Muslim League, much to the chagrin of the KPP's rank and file membership, held the bulk of the ministerships. In the very first budgetary session, KPP members stood one by one to condemn the coalition government's budget and Ataur Rahman announced plaintively: "Although I am sitting physically behind the Government benches, my heart is on the other side to fight with the Ministry over the question of the budget."[49] The KPP's organizational structure disintegrated over the following years and, by the 1940s, the Muslim League had absorbed the KPP's membership in the jute tracts. In the 1946 elections, the KPP was virtually wiped out and the Muslim League swept the jute tract's rural Muslim constituencies. The KPP's failures, however, lay not in Haq's less-than-astute coalition politics but in the limited ability of a government to influence jute prices. For market-entangled jute cultivators, the KPP's inability to control prices meant that they could not fulfill their election promise of "Rice and Dal for Everyone"—the campaign pledge that came to epitomize the KPP's unfulfilled promise of a peasant populist government.

Jute Prices

A. K. Fazlul Haq's coalition government successfully implemented pro-peasant legislation reforming credit markets and tenancy laws. The government established debt conciliation boards throughout the delta, which renegotiated peasant debts under highly favorable terms. Also, their amendments to tenancy law in 1939 strengthened the position of the occupancy ryot—the peasant with more secure rights to the land they tilled—empowering them to sell their lands outright and to make improvements to their arable land. The coalition, however, stopped short of abolishing zamindari and did not strengthen the position of sharecroppers and under-tenants. In effect, the KPP–Muslim League coalition's reforms strengthened the economic position of relatively prosperous occupancy ryots—the primary support base of the Krishak Praja Party—many of whom extended their moneylending operations and augmented their landholdings during the depression decade.[50]

The coalition, however, was unable to effectively influence commodity prices. During their first two years in power, the coalition government did not attempt to intervene in commodity markets despite concerted criticism from its own members. Humayun Kabir, a prominent member of the Krishak Praja Party, criticized the coalition government's budget for its lack of a jute policy. He said: "With regard to jute, I do not find any provisions for remedial measures for the agriculturists."[51] Kabir proposed a long list of measures to raise jute prices: legislating a minimum price, researching alternative uses of fiber to raise demand, providing state credit to cultivators to enable them to hold back fibers from sale, eliminating middlemen from the trade, and regulating futures markets. However, the coalition required the votes of European capitalist interests in the Legislative Assembly to remain in power, effectively stymying their ability to intervene in jute markets. The prominent jute magnate Edward Benthall gloated privately: "What a wonderful position we have with the Government. In fact, if we work things rightly I believe they would adopt any policy we liked to press on them."[52]

However, the persistently low prices of fiber forced elected representatives to focus on jute markets, despite continuing resistance from European capitalist interests. Their attempts to raise jute prices ran into concerted opposition from an organized cartel of Calcutta jute manufacturers who, by the 1940s, were consuming well over half of the delta's jute crop. The cartel, represented by the Indian Jute Mills Association (IJMA), was tacitly aided and abetted by British bureaucrats in Calcutta and Delhi. The inability of a peasant populist state to intervene in commodity markets had tragic consequences for the jute tracts' peasant inhabitants. In 1943, when rice prices rose far more rapidly than jute prices, the poorest and most marginal jute-cultivating peasant households starved. The impossible task of controlling jute prices spelled the end of state-centric peasant populism for market-entangled jute cultivators.

In August 1939 jute prices took a tumble just as cultivators prepared to harvest their fiber. The coalition government issued a press communiqué declaring its intentions to implement a compulsory scheme restricting jute cultivation, to investigate measures to regulate futures markets, and to "stabilize jute prices." This was soon followed by an ordinance that set minimum prices for raw jute in futures markets at 36 rupees per bale. The minimum prices established in futures markets were accompanied by intense publicity about government efforts in the hinterland, as various associations urged cultivators to hold on to their stock of fiber until the government's policies took effect. In Elashin in Mymensingh, "cultivators [were] advised to hold on to stocks and not to sell under 7 Rs. local, otherwise they might be penalized by Government." In Chandpur: "picketing [was] resorted to at various *hauts* [*hats*] by Moslem Associations" to prevent cultivators from selling their jute. In Goalunda: "all the Bengali newspapers had printed in large letters that the Government had brought into force an Ordinance forbidding the sale or purchase of 'kutcha' jute below Rs. 36 per bale." Fazlul Haq's considerable reputation as a champion of the delta's peasantry was utilized in such publicity efforts. A pamphlet published by the Public Institute in Choumohani, Noakhali stated: "the Chief Minister, Hon. Mr. A.K. Fazlul Huque is trying to increase the price of jute and has requested the cultivators not to sell their jute at a reduced rate, as the price of jute will go higher. So, it is evident that the price of jute must go higher."[53]

Just a month after the government began its intensive effort to raise jute prices, Britain declared war on Germany. Jute prices rose sharply in anticipation of the allied war requirement of jute sacks and tents. Concerned about the rising cost of their raw material, members of the Indian Jute Mills Association organized to fix fiber prices. The IJMA mills consumed close to 70 percent of the delta's jute and thus could function effectively as a cartel. The government shifted its focus from raising prices through futures market interventions and awareness campaigns among jute cultivators toward attempting to break the IJMA's price agreement. H. S. Suhrawardy, the commerce and labor minister, wrote a strongly worded letter to IJMA, describing the standstill in jute markets as a "a tug-of-war between a highly organized group of purchasers with infinite resources, and an unorganized group of sellers whose daily requirements compel them to part with their jute at any price they can get."[54] The IJMA ended their price agreement in November 1939, at which point prices promptly doubled. By November, however, cultivators had sold their jute and the mills had filled their warehouses with fiber.

During the early years of the war, the government issued a steady stream of press communiqués stating their intentions to intervene in jute markets. Futures markets, already rocked by uncertainties over the extent of Britain's war requirements of jute, were buffeted by frequent and contradictory press announcements. Prices fluctuated wildly. Rumors circulated that government ministers were profiting heavily from the futures markets. Nalinaksha Sanyal, chief whip of the Congress, accused government ministers on the floor of the Legislative Assembly, openly hinting that the commerce minister, Suhrawardy, was a prime beneficiary.[55] Sanyal's public accusation was widely reported in the press, and was the "the chief topic of week" in Calcutta's business and political circles.[56]

In 1940 it became clear that Britain's war requirements of jute would not be as heavy as expected. The tank blitzes and aerial bombardment that characterized World War II required far less in the way of jute sacks than the trench warfare of World War I. In January 1940 the government decided to delay the delivery date for their orders of jute fabrics and, consequently, prices tumbled in futures markets. The government closed down futures markets and turned, instead, toward a scheme of restricting jute cultivation by requiring individual cultivators to obtain licenses to sow jute. IJMA members vociferously denounced all restriction schemes during a time of war, informing the KPP–Muslim League coalition that they "consider[ed] it a shocking state of affairs that political ambition should cloud the issue of war requirements."[57]

This scheme was not, however, easily implemented. The government required a comprehensive census of jute cultivators and their acreage of fiber so as to set limits for each and every peasant household. They also needed to create an administrative structure through which licenses could be issued and enforced throughout the hinterland. Perhaps in the hope that the mere intent to restrict cultivation would raise prices, the government issued communiqués and made statements announcing that restriction would be enforced. These statements were not taken seriously. When the 1940 sowing season commenced, the government was forced to announce that restriction would be delayed until the following year. Jute markets in the meantime continued their steady downward slide and, in May 1940, when news that Germany had overrun Western Europe reached Calcutta, the slide turned into a tumble. Desperate, the government offered another scheme—to buy up all existing stocks of the previous crop of jute. The provincial government, however, lacked the finances to influence prices through purchases in the open market. They approached the central government in Delhi for a loan to conduct this scheme, and were promptly rebuffed.

Rumors began to circulate that the government would establish minimum prices for jute. The IJMA mills approached the Haq ministry with an offer, to stave off a state-determined minimum price. They were concerned that the government was "genuinely anxious about the position from the economic point of view of the cultivator," was "unlikely to think that discretion is the better part of valour," and was "not always prepared to concede to reason."[58] In July of 1940 the IJMA agreed to a minimum price that would hold until December. However, the IJMA simply held off making any purchases, as they had sufficient stocks of jute to last them until December. Farmers and hinterland traders, on the other hand, were desperate to sell at any price and prices continued to fall in hinterland markets despite the minimum prices set by the mills. In October 1940 the IJMA unilaterally abrogated the minimum price agreement.

The low prices of the 1940 jute season and the failures of the agreement with the IJMA brought another round of recrimination on the Legislative Council floor—especially from dissident KPP members. Jalaluddin Hashemy of the KPP and Nalinakshya Sanyal of the Congress jointly moved a resolution in the Legislative Assembly criticizing the government for its agreement with the IJMA. Hashemy spoke in the strongest possible terms: "I am pained to say that the Government do not know their own mind. Either they have no well-thought of and scientific plan . . . or they are doing it to help the IJMA. . . . The deparament concerned is either fool or knave or both—I cannot use a stronger term."[59] Sanyal repeated his allegations of ministerial corruption, naming a futures market trader who he alleged was close to certain ministers and was manipulating markets in support of their private speculations.

For the 1941 jute season, the compulsory restriction scheme was in place. A census of jute cultivators had been conducted and an administrative mechanism for setting quotas for individual jute growers had been established. The jute acreage of 1941 was set at one-third of the previous year's acreage and jute prices finally rose at the opening of the 1941 jute season—perhaps for the first time since the brief boom in jute prices back in 1926. For the first time in its tenure, the peasant populist government could claim some success in providing a better jute price for cultivators. In a pamphlet distributed throughout the jute tracts, titled *Instructions to Jute Growers*, the government "proclaim[ed] with very great pleasure that their hopeful efforts and cooperation of jute cultivators and their law abidedness had not been in vain. At present it may be safely expected that . . . Government efforts to maintain permanently high price of Jute for jute cultivators will be successful."[60]

The government could not, however, savor its success. Relationships between A. K. Fazlul Haq and the Muslim League's all-India leader, M. A. Jinnah, deteriorated to the point that Haq was ejected from the League. With the progressive defection of KPP members to the opposition, the League was virtually propping up Fazlul Haq's cabinet singlehandedly. After the League withdrew from government, Haq managed to cobble together a new coalition cabinet drawing from a range of political platforms—not least, the communalist Hindu Mahasabha and its leader Shyamaprasad Mukherjee. The Shyama-Haq ministry lasted from December 1941 to March 1943, when the British governor dismissed it on grounds of incompetence. During its brief tenure, the Shyama-Haq ministry similarly failed to overcome the IJMA cartel. When jute prices began tumbling in March 1942, the provincial government made a belated effort to revise the compulsory acreage of jute downward, hoping a yet smaller crop would cause prices to rise. This did not work: by mid-May, mofussil jute agencies were estimating a crop of more than the stipulated acreage. The Scottish manager of one of the larger jute manufacturing companies reported with glee: "The crop has . . . got an excellent start and . . . there ought to be plenty of jute next season."[61] Prices fell sharply at the beginning of the 1942 season. Under attack in the Legislative Assembly for failing to prevent the fall in prices, Haq admitted to missing his old rival and former commerce minister, H. S. Suhrawardy: "he really turned out to be a jute expert and it was really pleasant to find that even those who were in the market or who were experts in the Government of India could not cross swords with my friend, Mr. Suhrawardy, without admitting that he knows practically all that is necessary to know for dealing with the problem of jute."[62]

Predictably, jute prices rose in November, after desperate cultivators had sold off their stocks of fiber and mills had already filled their warehouses. At the same time, however, rice prices began to rise—much higher and faster than the price of fiber. Speculators responded to Japan's occupation of the Burmese rice tracts and colonial governments' requisitions of rice for military and urban requirements by driving up rice prices rapidly. Between November 1942 and March 1943, rice prices increased by 250 percent, while jute prices increased by between 80 percent and 150 percent—depending on quality— during the same period (see chapter 4). The rapid rise in rice prices put subsistence beyond the reach of most of the delta's inhabitants and three to four million people died of hunger in 1943 and 1944. By the time famine struck, a new government, headed by Khwaja Nizamuddin of the Muslim League—the same Nizamuddin who had been defeated in the Patuakhali North constituency by Fazlul Haq—took over the reins of provincial power. Fazlul Haq protested that his government had been dismissed because of his unwillingness to follow colonial policies of food procurement for urban and military requirements, which seems plausible given the Nizamuddin government's quiet cooperation with colonial wartime policies.

During 1943 and 1944, as rice prices rose beyond the affordability of everyone, the inhabitants of the jute tracts starved by the millions. Estimates for mortality from starvation and starvation-related disease range between three and four million. Amartya Sen has demonstrated that prevailing wages for landless workers and earnings in a variety of occupations—fishermen, barbers,

tailors, and so forth—were insufficient to procure enough rice to stave off starvation. Paul Greenough has shown that mortality was highest among women
and the elderly, and that peasant households made heart-wrenching decisions
about which family members should starve and who should be kept alive.
Greenough argues that households chose to keep younger men alive as they
would be critical to rebuilding the agrarian economy after famine. Millions
of starving men and women made their way toward metropolitan Calcutta,
in hopes of sustenance. Zainul Abedin's charcoal sketches of skeletal starving bodies picking through garbage alongside street dogs and crows depicted
the horrors of famine witnessed by metropolitan Bengalis. Famously, the
colonial state refused to officially recognize the famine that was apparent to
everyone—to do so would necessitate that the government mobilize relief
measures. Preoccupied with the war effort, the British Empire refused to be
distracted by the millions of dying Bengalis.

Culpability for the famine should not be laid at the door of the elected
representatives of the people, whether the Fazlul Haq or Nizamuddin
administrations. The elected government was unable to counter the IJMA's
cartel-like machinations in manipulating prices and real power always resided
with unelected bureaucrats in the central government in Delhi. The close relationship between colonial bureaucrats and colonial businessmen was made
apparent by the appointment of G. M. Garrie, jute mill manager and prominent IJMA member, as acting adviser on jute supplies to the Government
of India. Garrie's main task was to ensure the supply of manufactured jute
goods to Britain's primary war ally, the United States. The US government had
placed a large order for jute fabric, to be delivered at below a maximum price.
The IJMA mills complained that they could not meet the US maximum price
given the prevailing prices of their main raw material.[63] With the blessings of
the colonial state, at a time when the worsening terms of trade between fiber
and grain were causing massive starvation, the jute manufacturers' cartel fixed
a lower price for peasant produce. Even as they starved the delta by rigging
jute markets, the IJMA made a token gesture at charity: they contributed five
rupees per loom for the "relief of distress in Bengal."[64]

The KPP's inability to influence commodity prices meant that they were
unable to deliver on the promise of their peasant populist electoral campaign.
As early as 1940 Fazlul Haq's ministry was attacked for failing to fulfill its
promise of "Rice and Dal for Everyone." Haq disavowed the popular slogan:
"What I said in the manifesto was this: 'the problem of *dal bhat* is the problem

to-day.' That does not mean I have got *dal bhat* in my house . . . which any-body can come and eat. . . . If there was anyone who believed that I would give *dal bhat* to five crores of people he must be a fool. Not only that, he must be living in a fool's paradise."[65] Fazlul Haq's reputation as the champion of the peasantry was ruined. As a Congress legislator gleefully announced on the assembly floor: "a large section of the people in Bengal have lost their confidence in Mr. A.K. Fazlul Haq. He knows it, I know it, and everybody knows it. . . . The people who once adored Maulvi A.K. Fazlul Haq . . . have now lost their confidence in him."[66] Famine exposed in the starkest possible manner the KPP's utter inability to fulfill its signature campaign pledge of two square meals a day for everyone. In the next round of elections in 1946, the KPP was wiped out as a political force from the Bengal delta's jute tracts.

Conclusion

The introduction of electoral and representative politics in the jute tracts cre-ated a new political category—the "Rural Muhammadan." This category was imbued with meaning through discourses of agrarian Islam and the spatial rearrangements of hinterland, mofussil, and metropolis that characterized the peasant politics of immiseration. This meaning was solidified in election cam-paigns, in the act of voting, speeches, debates, and alliances on the floor of the legislature, and in debates over the spatial boundaries between mofussil towns and the rural hinterland. The interaction between the categories and spaces of electoral politics, discourses of agrarian Islam, and the relations of hinterland and mofussil informed communal riots between Muslims and Hindus in the jute tracts.

The prolonged depression of the 1930s gave rise to new forms of peasant political associations and activities—the peasant conferences and committees that united rural Muhammadans across the hinterland and mofussil. It also provided the context for the rise of a potent political force in the jute tracts—the peasant populist Krishak Praja Party, which promised legislative and executive action that would restore the viability of market-entangled peasant lives and livelihoods. The electoral victory of the Krishak Praja Party's peasant populism over the Muslim League's appeals to religious community should be understood through a broader frame of the peasant politics of immiseration.

However, the elected representatives of the jute growers were unable to fulfill their campaign promises. Attempts to affect jute prices ran into an orga-nized cartel of metropolitan jute manufacturers in Calcutta, who were aided and abetted behind the scenes by the unelected bureaucrats who retained real power within the colonial state. In a bitter speech after his dismissal on the ostensible grounds of incompetence, Fazlul Haq stated: "The Ministers have been given a mockery of authority, and the steel frame of the Imperial Services still remains intact, dominating the entire administration and casting somber shadows over the activities of Ministers."[67] Their efforts to cajole and bully the IJMA mills into offering better prices were doomed to fail, as the IJMA played their game of duplicity with confidence, always aware that real power lay with sympathetic colonial bureaucrats in Delhi rather than the popularly elected representatives of jute cultivators in Calcutta.

The KPP's inability to influence commodity prices spelled the end of state-centric peasant populism. The effects and memories of famine loomed over peasant politics after 1944. Peasant faith in the possibility of a pro-peasant government that could effect change through legislative and executive action gave way to a utopian ideal of Pakistan, an imagined future devoid of injustice, immorality, and hunger. In the 1946 elections, jute cultivators voted in overwhelming numbers for the Muslim League, which conducted the elections as a referendum on the Pakistan cause. The next chapter investigates the emergence of the idea of Pakistan as peasant utopia in the 1940s. The chapter also examines how the utopian vision was extinguished by the Pakistani state after independence and partition. As it attempted to cope with the dislocations of partition that severed the hinterland from its metropolis and to harness fiber as a revenue-generating national resource, the postcolonial state became a source of harassment and violence for the delta's jute-cultivating peasantry.

7

Pakistan and Partition

PEASANT UTOPIA AND DISILLUSION

IN 1946, barely a decade after its electoral triumphs of 1937, the Krishak Praja Party was wiped out as a political force in the Bengal delta. The Muslim League scored decisive victories over their KPP rivals, especially in the rural Muslim constituencies in jute-growing distrits, the KPP's former heartland. The League received 83.7 percent of Muslim votes in Bengal as a whole and performed even better in the jute tracts, where it received 87 percent of the vote. On the other hand, the KPP received just 2 percent of votes in jute-growing districts. The Muslim League had campaigned in elections throughout British India on a Pakistan platform, transforming the elections into a virtual referendum on the Pakistan cause. The all-India Muslim League leadership left the idea of Pakistan sufficiently vague and capacious for local branches of the party to define and specify Pakistan through their election campaigns.[1] In Bengal's jute tracts, the League and its candidates presented Pakistan as a utopian peasant society: Pakistan was a place and time characterized by freedom, truth, justice, and morality; and free from sin, corruption, exploitation, greed, scarcity, and hunger. As the League's overwhelming electoral success underscores, the delta's jute cultivators were persuaded that they could realize this peasant utopia—all they had to do was vote for the Muslim League and the Pakistan cause.

During the depression decade of the 1930s, the delta's jute cultivators had voted for state-centric and legislative solutions to immiseration; in the post-famine election of 1946, they turned to the utopian promise of Pakistan. The League's Pakistan campaign utilized many of the same slogans, idioms, and tropes as the KPP's peasant populist campaign ten years earlier, repeating popular slogans like "The Land Belongs to the Tiller" and "Abolish Zamindari."[2]

168

The erstwhile KPP stalwart, Abul Mansur Ahmed described the Pakistan movement as a continuation of the *krishak praja* movement that underpinned the KPP's political organization: "today the Muslim League is the carrier and conductor [*dharok o bahok*] of the *krishak praja* movement . . . [and] the *Praja* movement has been fully realized in the Pakistan movement."[3] The Pakistan campaign, however, was crucially different from peasant populism: while the KPP promised pro-peasant state action, the League campaigned on the poetry of utopia. Pakistan was the "land of eternal Eid," where "speech and food were pure," where the nightingale calls the *azaan* and the flowers say their *namaaz* after doing their ablutions with the morning dew.[4]

Prior to the 1946 election campaign, debates and discussions on Pakistan were restricted to Calcutta and Dacca's Muslim literary and political milieus. The Muslim League did not have any official branches outside Calcutta, though the family home of the Dacca nawab, the Ahsan Manzil, functioned as an unofficial second office in Dacca. Prior to the elections, the idea of Pakistan was popularized by a Calcutta-headquartered Muslim Bengali cultural and literary organization: the East Pakistan Renaissance Society, founded in 1942. The Renaissance Society established a second center in Dacca and offices in several mofussil towns, but was most active in Calcutta. Members of the Muslim League and the Renaissance Society discussed and debated Pakistan in terms of culture and territory: the cultural distinctiveness of Muslim Bengal that necessitated forming a separate nation-state from Hindu Bengal, and the potential and appropriate territorial extent of that nation-state. Discussions of Pakistan in terms of cultural distinctiveness or territorial extent in metropolitan Muslim literary circles did not generate interest among the delta's jute-cultivating peasantry. However, rural Muslim voters would subsequently respond enthusiastically to the League's election campaign in the winter of 1945–46, during which the League's candidates consistently described Pakistan as the promise of an ideal Muslim peasant society that would be characterized by justice, truth, morality, and the absence of sin, corruption, exploitation, and hunger.

Pakistan was realized through the partition of Bengal. On August 14 and 15, 1947, just as cultivators were bringing their jute crop into market, the postcolonial nation-states of Pakistan and India came into existence. A four-thousand-kilometer line carved out the Bengal delta and incorporated it into the territory of Pakistan. Partition and independence had separated the jute tracts from their industrial and commercial center; East Pakistan was a hinterland without a metropolis. The decision to partition Bengal was greeted with dismay by Muslim League leaders who could not imagine that the territory of the impoverished and famine-racked jute tracts shorn of metropolitan Calcutta and western Bengal's mineral resources could constitute a viable nation-state. In support of a last minute scheme to create a United Independent Bengal, spearheaded by the Bengal Muslim League's leaders—H. S. Suhrawardy and Abul Hashim, M. A. Jinnah stated: "What is the use of Bengal without Calcutta; they had much better to remain united and independent. I am sure they would be on friendly terms with us."[5]

With partition and independence, the promise of Pakistan as peasant utopia ran up against the imperatives of postcolonial state formation: the necessity of creating a national economy that produced sufficient revenue and resources to sustain the institutions and pageantry appropriate to a modern state. For post-partition Pakistan, which had received a raw deal in the "spoils of parti-tion," this task of creating a territorial and sovereign national economy appeared particularly daunting.[6] Jute became critical to the statist project of fashioning a national economy. Fiber was the leading source of state revenue and foreign exchange. It was of strategic importance in Pakistan's emerging rivalry with India—East Pakistan's jute farmers produced 70 percent of the world's jute and India's jute mills consumed 70 percent of East Pakistan's jute. However, in order to derive revenue, foreign exchange, and strategic advantage from fiber, the postcolonial state had to monitor, regulate, and police the production and circulation of fiber within and across the jute tracts. That is, the state had to establish its sovereignty over fiber.

Toward this end, the Pakistani state established customs offices, regulated currency exchanges, monitored the "national loyalties" of jute traders and merchants, and kick-started a jute baling and milling industry. Simultane-ously, the state criminalized economic activities—such as smuggling, black-marketeering, and tax evasion—that subverted the statist project of extracting revenue, resources, and strategic advantage from fiber. Jute cultivators and traders were subjected to intense state surveillance; they were liable to being criminalized, and to being subjected to draconian punishment. Ahmed Kamal has described how the peasant utopian vision of Pakistan was rapidly extin-guished by the Pakistani state embarking on a campaign of violence against sections of the peasantry: brutally enforcing state policies of food supply and distribution and water management on its peasant population and violently punishing peasant attempts to evade state policies.[7] The history of jute in post-partition Pakistan accords with Ahmed Kamal's narrative of centralizing bureaucratic policies, the criminalization of peasant avoidance and evasion of such policies, and the inhumane treatment of said criminals. Instead of the promised utopia of freedom, emancipation, justice, and morality, East Pakistan's peasant households experienced statist harassment, oppression, and violence. This chapter adds another dimension to this larger narrative, demonstrating how the state's efforts to monitor, regulate, and police fiber turned, in Ahmed Kamal's brilliant phrase, "the state against the nation"—that is, the bureaucratic structures of government against the utopian vision contained in the idea of Pakistan.

The contradiction between postcolonial state formation and peasant utopian aspirations is exemplified, as Ahmed Kamal demonstrates, in an encounter between Ataur Rahman Khan, a young Muslim politician who would later become chief minister of East Pakistan, and an elderly villager, soon after independence in August 1947. The elderly man asked the young politician: "Now that Pakistan has been achieved, should there still be police, courts, and kutcheries, soldiers and sentries, jails and lockups?" Khan replied, "Why not? How could you protect the state without these institutions?" The old man sighed and responded "then what kind of Pakistan have we got? Change the name please. You will name it Pakistan yet allow sins and corruptions to exist."[8]

The first section of this chapter explores the formulation of the idea of Pakistan as peasant utopia during the League's 1946 election campaign. The following sections describe how peasant aspirations for Pakistan gave way, after partition and independence in 1947, to extreme disillusionment. The second section examines the Pakistani state's attempts to harness jute as a national resource by establishing bureaucratic institutions and processes to monitor, regulate, tax, and police flows of fiber across newly drawn partition lines. The final two sections of the chapter investigate this dynamic of harassment, evasion, and violence in state and society relations in postcolonial East Pakistan: first, with respect to petty traders and the state's efforts to criminalize and punish certain forms of trade as jute smuggling and, second, with respect to jute cultivators and the state's efforts to impose a tax on jute production.

Peasant Utopia

Prior to the 1946 elections, the idea of Pakistan in Bengal was limited to Muslim literary milieus in Calcutta. In Calcutta, the East Pakistan Renaissance Society and the journal *Mohammadi* provided literary and cultural forums to discuss and develop a Muslim Bengali idea of Pakistan during the early 1940s. The speakers and writers at the society envisioned Pakistan in cultural, economic, and territorial terms.[9] In a landmark speech to the society's annual meeting in 1944, Abul Mansur Ahmad, whose involvement in the Khilafat movement was discussed earlier, characterized Pakistan as a space of "cultural autonomy"—*tamadduni azadi*. Ahmed suggested that Pakistan would provide the autonomous space needed for a "renaissance" in the distinctive Bengali Muslim culture. These cultural imaginings were accompanied by territorial imaginings. Mujibur Rehman Khan wrote a pamphlet in 1942 discussing the appropriate territorial limits of "Eastern Pakistan." Khan's proposal focused on securing an expansive territory that would provide for a viable and prosperous nation-state. His state encompassed the entire province of Bengal and large portions of Assam, and was far larger than East Pakistan's final territorial inheritance of solely the jute tracts.[10] However, these discussions in metropolitan Muslim literary milieus during the early 1940s did not make much of an impression among rural Muslim voters in the delta's jute tracts. The election campaign during the winter of 1945–46 popularized the idea of Pakistan among rural Muslims and redefined Pakistan as peasant utopia.

In March 1945, to mark the fifth anniversary of the Lahore Resolution, the Muslim League organized Pakistan Day celebrations throughout Bengal.[11] The League's events were "thinly attended," and the colonial state received "no indication from the districts that the celebrations were on any large scale."[12] Even as the Muslim League failed to generate enthusiasm around the Pakistan movement, peasant meetings focused on agrarian issues such as jute prices, tenancy laws, and shortages of cloth, kerosene oil, and rice drew large crowds. In March 1945 crowds of more than three thousand peasant men attended meetings organized by the Communist-affiliated All-India Kisan Sabha in Jamalpur, Kishoreganj, Faridpur, and Bogra.[13] In less than a year, however, the Pakistan cause moved from the fringes of the delta's politics to its very heart, and Pakistan came to represent a promised utopia for the vast majority of the delta's jute-cultivating Muslim peasantry.

The Muslim League's "left-faction"—under the leadership of H. S. Suhrawardy and Abul Hashim—spearheaded the Pakistan campaign and, in the process, sidelined the party's traditional zamindar faction. Hashim and Suhrawardy carefully and deliberately constructed a party organization and campaign message that reflected the peasant politics of immiseration. When Abul Hashim was elected general secretary in 1943, the League had no offices in the province of Bengal outside Calcutta.[14] During 1944 and 1945 Hashim toured the entire province, visiting every part of Bengal: "not only district and sub-divisional headquarters but also important places in rural Bengal."[15]

In each of these locations, Hashim established local offices, absorbing krishak sabhas, former KPP members, and a new generation of idealistic young Muslim men into the Muslim League in the process. In his autobiography, Hashim fondly reminisces on the hours he spent in discussion with idealistic mofussil Muslim men.[16] After elections were announced in September 1945, Hashim and Suhrawardy gained control of the Muslim League's Parliamentary Board in an acrimonious intraparty election. Through the board, Hashim and Suhrawardy hand-selected the League's candidates to contest the elections, vetting potential candidates to screen out zamindars and pro-zamindari individuals. The two men even handpicked the slogans that would define the League's campaign: "Land belongs to the plough," "Abolish Zamindari without compensation," and "End interest payments to moneylenders."[17]

In its campaign through the hinterland, the Bengal Muslim League's candidates did not dwell on the cultural aspirations of Bengali Muslims nor on the territorial limits of the proposed state—topics that had hitherto dominated discussion in the Eastern Pakistan Renaissance Society and in the pages of the *Mohammadi*. Instead, they characterized Pakistan as a place of freedom, emancipation, and justice, free of hunger and scarcity. Suhrawardy spelled out the promise of Pakistan in a campaign speech: "[Pakistan] will mean raising the standards of living for the poor, the oppressed and the neglected; more food, wealth, resources, work, better living conditions and more joy and happiness for the common people; opportunities for all and the establishment of a reign of truth and justice, of tolerance and fair play."[18]

The utopian ideal of Pakistan combined an aspiration for a moral and ethical society with that of a society free of hunger and starvation. For "the ordinary Muslim peasant," Ahmed Kamal has argued, Pakistan was both the promise of "a new moral community, where an ethics of reciprocity and justice would dominate social life" and, also, of a "land where the poor peasants' dream of 'two square meals a day' would come true."[19] The poetry of peasant utopian Pakistan equally emphasizes moral and ethical life and food, as in the following boyan written in postcolonial Pakistan:

Always speak the truth
In the land of Pakistan
Everything is pure in Pakistan,
Food and speech, all aspects of life.
Falsehood and bad deeds
Must be shunned.[20]

The configuration of Pakistan as peasant utopia took place in the context of a post-famine peasant society. The *Millat*, the League's newsletter, carried numerous articles on Bengal's post-famine peasant society.[21] In many articles advocating abolishing zamindari, tackling the debt crisis, guaranteeing food security, and bolstering jute prices, the *Millat*'s writers evoked the horrors of famine. An October 1946 article "Bengal, Granary of the Past, Yet people Starve to Death" urging for concerted measures to grow more food stated: "The famine has ripped apart and emptied our political, social and economic lives (*rashtriyo, shamaji, o arthanaitik jibon*). Three years later, we still feel the effects of the famine with every step."[22] Famine was also evoked in arguing for the "absolute necessity" of abolishing zamindari: "it is clear that the 1943 famine would not have taken this terrible form if zamindari law did not prevail over this country."[23]

Proposals to abolish landlordism and debt and to raise jute prices and guarantee food security were hardly original in the Bengal delta. These were the very proposals that the Krishak Praja Party had floated a decade back. On the eve of the elections, Abul Mansur Ahmed—who had earlier described Pakistan as the promise of cultural autonomy—wrote: "the Muslim League is the carrier and conductor of the *krishak praja* movement . . . [and] the *Praja* movement has been fully realized in the Pakistan movement."[24] Indeed, in characterizing Pakistan as peasant utopia, the League had absorbed the Krishak Praja Party's idioms and slogans, institutions and organizational structure, and erstwhile supporters. However, unlike the KPP's peasant populist campaign, Pakistan was not a manifesto of legislative reforms and executive action. It was instead a promised future: "Pakistan *will be* the ordinary people's state, where zamindars and the rich will have no place." Pakistan was not a program of policies but an aspiration: "the Pakistan demand is a symbol of Muslim mass aspiration (*gono-akangkha*)."[25] This symbol of aspiration could even be generously extended to all of India's "oppressed masses": "Pakistan's message is of the right to self-determination (*atmo-niyontron*); it may have been uttered by Muslims, but it is the demand of all of India's oppressed people's (*nirjatito jati*). It is true that Bengal's *praja* movement was started solely by Muslims, but the movement is that of all of Bengal's oppressed masses."[26]

Unstated in Abul Mansur Ahmed's editorial but explicit throughout the League's campaign was perhaps the most remarkable aspect of this promise: that the peasant utopia of Pakistan could be achieved by the simple task of voting. The Bengal delta's Muslim jute cultivators responded to the Muslim

League's campaign in overwhelming numbers. The League secured 87 percent of the rural Muslim vote in Bengal's jute tracts. Muslim League candidates inflicted heavy defeats on incumbent legislators from the KPP: the KPP incumbent from Tipperah Central received just 900 against 23,800 votes for the League candidate; the KPP incumbent in Tipperah West received 890 votes against 19,200 for the League candidate; and in Bogra North, the KPP incumbent received 510 votes against 19,700 for the League.

The Muslim League's ability to contain the utopian politics of Pakistan within an electoral contest is actually remarkable. This was utterly unlike the peasant pursuit of utopian swaraj during the Khilafat movement of 1921–22 (chapter 3), where peasants willfully and forcefully disobeyed, resisted, and boycotted the colonial state and its agents. In 1946 utopian politics focused on the polls—on the act of going and voting for the Muslim League in the polling booth. The peasant politics of utopia did, however, spill out of the polling booth after the elections, manifesting in violence against Hindus in parts of Tipperah and Noakhali in October 1946. The following description of the Noakhali riots of 1946 by a colonial official is worth quoting in full:

> The 'modus operandi' appears to have been for a mob of Muslims to surround a Hindu village and offer protection if the latter would embrace Islam. Many thousands of Hindus, to avoid extinction, capitulated while panic seized others who bolted before they were approached. The method of conversion has been, in the main, not forcible. In some cases Hindus have been made to eat the flesh of their own cattle but usually the Mahommedans have eaten that themselves and have been content if the Hindus have donned "the cap," very large numbers of which, bearing the legend "Pakistan Zindabad" have appeared mysteriously as required; or substituted lungi for dhoti. There appears also to be a large supply of the former.[27]

The riots were instigated by a former member of the Legislative Assembly, Golam Sarwar, who had been soundly defeated in the 1946 election by the Muslim League candidate, Fazlul Karim.[28] The "Mahommedan mob" consisted of a number of demobilized soldiers and local Muslims who joined in attacking their neighbors. Further, the attacks were preplanned, as the sudden appearance of large numbers of lungis and caps in the cloth-starved province suggests. "Conversion" thus consisted of donning specifically Muslim articles of clothing: that is, of forcing Hindus to adopt the distinctive material cultures of Bengali peasant Muslims that had been crafted through consumption during the pre–World War I era of prosperity.

The idea of Pakistan that peasants had voted for and, in postelection Noakhali and Tipperah, had violently attacked the Hindu community to achieve, did not entail or envision the partition of Bengal. As partition emerged as the likeliest outcome, articles and editorials in the *Millat* took on a strident note criticizing the British and Congress partition movement—the *Banga-bhanga andolon*. In May 1947 the *Millat* ran an editorial characterizing partition as an imperialist-capitalist and upper-caste Hindu plot to maintain ownership over Calcutta's wealth, which had been built up through two centuries of exploitation of the jute-cultivating peasantry.[29] On June 4, 1947, when Lord Mountbatten presented partition as a take-it-or-leave-it scheme for the Muslim League, the *Millat* ran an editorial titled "Crippled (*Pongu*) Pakistan." "According to the British government's announcement, Bengal will be partitioned (*dikhondito*)," the editorial announced, "and of this partitioned Bengal, the wealthiest, most advanced, and resource-rich portion will be snatched away from Bengali Muslim hands and given to a few self-interested friends of the British." The partition plan, the *Millat*'s editors alleged, was intended to "squeeze Bengal's Muslims into one corner of Bengal and to crush them to death." The "crippled (*pongu*) Pakistan" would be an economic disaster with a bleak future; partition was a "fearsome cloud over the lives of Bengali Muslims."[30]

Abul Hashim, the architect of the League's Pakistan campaign in the delta, greeted Mountbatten's partition plan with dismay. He stated to the *Millat* that he had accepted partition not out of "satisfaction and hope but out of fear and helplessness." He feared that the state would not be able to achieve the promised peasant utopia: "Eastern Pakistan will be mainly reliant on jute. This is probably the most densely populated region in the entire world. . . . At anytime, artificial jute might be invented and, if that happens, it will be a disaster for jute cultivation. . . . In this situation, Eastern Pakistan will probably develop as a good market for American manufactured goods. America might give us loans and we will have to buy American cigarettes and other goods to repay those loans."[31] Notably, Hashim chose the agrarian Islamic critique of the consumption of American-made cigarettes to explain his fears for the post-partition state.

National Resource

The East Pakistan Renaissance Society had floated a territorially expansive vision of an East Pakistan that included not only the entirety of Bengal, but also Assam: "East Pakistan must include Assam to be financially and economically strong."[32] Colonial officials and academics wrote disparagingly about the future of an East Pakistan that excluded Calcutta. In a conference of provincial governors, it was stated that "economically [East Bengal] could not survive as all the coal mines, the minerals and the factories are in western Bengal, so are the jute processing mills with two exceptions."[33] In 1943 O.H.K. Spate, a geographer at the London School of Economics, wrote gloomily about the economic prospects of "Bangistan" composed solely of the delta's jute tracts: "If partition left this metropolis [Calcutta] out of Bangistan, the economic situation of the remnant state would not be enviable—a small territory suffering from severe agrarian overcrowding, cut off from the sources of power and raw materials on which Bengal's industries have flourished, and by the very communal hypothesis to which it owed its existence unable to seek relief in emigration."[34] In supporting the short-lived United Independent Bengal scheme promoted by Hashim and Suhrawardy, Jinnah stated: "If Bengal remains united . . . I should be delighted. What is the use of Bengal without Calcutta; they had much better to remain united and independent."[35]

These fears were put aside at the moment of independence. On August 14, 1947, Pakistan was celebrated with joy and fanfare throughout the delta's jute tracts. In the new provincial capital of Dacca, gates were erected, buildings decorated, processions brought out, and flags of the new nation raised. Celebrations also took place in mofussil towns such as Barisal, Sylhet, and Rajshahi and in rural parts of Mymensingh and Tipperah.[36] Probhash Chandra Lahiry, a Congress politician in Rajshahi and participant in the celebrations, in 1964 remembered that "every face of the vast population . . . [showed] signs of a radiant glow of fulfillment of a long cherished desire of winning freedom."[37] The bureaucrats charged with running the newly created state were conscious of their challenges, but were also optimistic. O.H.K. Spate wrote in January 1948: "Morally, to judge from many conversations with young Muslim officials flocking into Western Pakistan there is a good spirit among them—a realization of the enormous difficulties, the shortages of resources and of technical cadres, but a determination to tackle them resolutely."[38] Bureaucrats in the capital of Karachi announced a program of rapid industrialization and economic modernization, in order to bring "improvements in the standard of life of the people . . . by harnessing, to the maximum extent possible, the forces and treasures of nature in the service of people by providing gainful and legitimate employment and by assuring freedom from want, equality of opportunity, and a more equitable distribution of wealth."[39] Their plans and ambitions focused on jute, on harnessing fiber toward programs of nation-state formation. Jute was Pakistan's "golden fibre," the national resource that would finance the making of a modern nation-state.

Jute was thus transformed from a colonial commodity into a national resource, from the basis of colonial exploitation through the exchange of fiber for cigarettes to the means of national development by generating revenue and resources for the state. The hinterland's severance from its former metropolis came to be seen as a boon to the post-partition nation-state. In publicity and propaganda pamphlets, the Pakistani state celebrated East Bengal's "virtual monopoly" over jute, and "practical monopoly" over "finer varieties of jute." Partition harmed the metropolis more than it did the hinterland: "the emergence of Pakistan as a separate sovereign state has substantially altered the position of India. . . . While Pakistan has emerged with 80 percent of the world's jute and 100 percent of the best varieties of the fibre, India has only about 18 to 20 percent of the jute fibre which is quite insufficient to feed her mills which number more than a hundred."[40] Partition liberated the hinterland from the metropolitan capital: "Her jute market has now shaken off her age long dependence on Calcutta and is at present linked with the world market of jute independent of her earlier intermediaries in Calcutta."[41]

Pakistan's national economy was critically dependent on primary commodity exports: jute, cotton, tea, and hides and skins. Export duties on primary commodities contributed the lion's share of state revenue and, even more significantly, brought in foreign currency. The postcolonial state-building project relied on earnings of foreign currency to finance imports of capital goods, military stores, and consumer goods. Pakistan benefited from high global commodity prices in the years following 1947, particularly during the Korean War commodity boom of 1950–51.[42] The high prices of its chief commodity exports enabled Pakistan to maintain a favorable balance of trade position and to import capital goods for industrialization, arms and munitions for the armed forces, and consumer goods for a burgeoning urban middle class. A government pamphlet celebrating the fifth anniversary of the Pakistani state noted: "a favourable balance of trade position . . . has, of course, been a cornerstone of Pakistan's economy."[43]

The commerce minister, Fazlur Rahman, underscored Pakistan's reliance on jute and cotton in a broadcast on Radio Pakistan in February 1952:

Immediately after partition it was realized that Pakistan's internal economy as well as the external financial position will depend almost entirely upon the two major cash crops of jute and cotton. All our defense stores, capital equipment, materials required for industrial consumption and essential consumer goods had to be paid for out of our earnings of foreign exchange from the exports of jute and cotton. . . . The export duties on jute and cotton . . . constitute the single biggest source of internal revenue of the Central and Provincial Governments. In fact the entire fabric of Pakistan's economy is woven with these two fibres.[44]

In weaving the "fabric of Pakistan's economy" from jute fibers, the Pakistan state sought to transform jute from a colonial commodity subject to the speculations of colonial capital into a national resource producing revenue and foreign exchange for the state. Toward this end, the Pakistani state had to create the bureaucratic structures necessary to monitor, regulate, and police circulations of jute through its territory—in other words, it had to assert its territorial sovereignty over the commodity. In order to do so, the postcolonial state had to create—more or less from scratch, given the dislocations of partition—customs offices, regulatory institutions, procedures of inspection and documentation, and systems of penalties and punishments.

The postcolonial transformation of colonial commodity into national resource took place gradually, over the first few years of independence and partition. Partition did not initially disrupt the circulation of jute between peasant farms and metropolitan Calcutta. In their haste to depart India, the British Empire did not work out a trade agreement between the partitioned nation-states and, instead, independent Pakistan and India decided on a "standstill agreement," agreeing to let trade continue as before. In the months following partition, jute prices barely registered a blip and more jute was transported to metropolitan Calcutta than in the previous pre-partition year. This situation, however, would not last.

On October 13, 1947, after two months of unobstructed flows of jute between East Bengal and Calcutta, officials of the Government of Pakistan wrote to their counterparts in India complaining that they were not receiving their legitimate share of the export duty on jute.[45] They pointed out the injustice that "India is likely to receive over 90 percent of the jute revenue, although only 27 percent of the jute is grown in that Dominion."[46] They proposed that Pakistan should receive "at least 75 percent of the export duty on 5.9 million bales" as its legitimate share. Officials of the Government of India prevaricated in their response, arguing that any agreement on jute would have to wait for a comprehensive trade and payments agreement. They stated that it would "scarcely be fair to question its equity isolating any particular source of revenue . . . in regard to which one party may feel that it had any special claim."[47]

The newly created Pakistani government desperately needed revenue, and was not willing to forego the export duty earned from fiber. On November 13, 1947, Liaqat Ali Khan, the prime minister of Pakistan, wrote directly to Jawaharlal Nehru announcing that, "in the interests of their revenue my Government now feel compelled most reluctantly to charge export duty on jute leaving borders of East Bengal both by sea and land." This was a momentous announcement: for the first time since its creation, Pakistan was to enforce its sovereignty upon flows of commodities across partition lines.

The Pakistani government hurriedly established customs posts and checkpoints and appointed customs officers in thirteen key jute-trading towns, located on rail and steamer routes connecting the delta to Calcutta (see map 3). The Central Board of Revenue in Karachi announced that "customs on raw jute exported from the Dominion of Pakistan by land" would be collected at river ports like Chandpur, Narayanjganj, Sirajganj, Munshiganj, Dacca, and railway towns like Sarishabari, Hajiganj, Bera, and Ishwardi. In these towns, the state constructed customs offices, appointed customs officials, and distributed the forms, receipts, and other paperwork involved in customs collections. None of these towns were located on the physical border, which was yet to be officially demarcated. The government found it easier to police jute bulked on steamer flats and railway wagons in jute-trading towns, rather than smaller quantities loaded on country boats and ox carts along its borders.

In September 1948 India and Pakistan signed their first trade and payments agreement. The two governments specified their requirements of essential commodities from each other. India wanted 5.5 million bales of raw jute and 900,000 bales of raw cotton from Pakistan; Pakistan wanted 3.4 million tons of coal, 400,000 bales of cotton cloth and yarn, and 50,000 tons of jute manufactures from India. This trade would take place at "free" or market prices, between private merchants and traders. The two governments agreed, in principle, to free trade: "both Dominions should try to reduce the number of commodities which when moving from one Dominion to the other shall be subject to an import or export duty."[48] They agreed that Pakistani and Indian rupees should be of equal value, and payments up to 150 million rupees should be settled in local currencies—saving scarce foreign currency for trade with the wider world. The official agreement to free trade between the postpartition states was not, however, implemented in practice. Pakistan imposed duties on exports of jute and cotton fiber to India and India on exports of manufactured jute and cotton cloth to Pakistan. Commodities traded exclusively across Bengal's partition lines were also subjected to duties: Pakistan on exports of fish and bamboo to India and India on imports of raw tobacco.[49]

India and Pakistan also pursued plans to disentangle their economies: in the language of the state, to reduce their "economic dependence" on each other. For the Bengal delta, this meant disentangling the hinterland from its metropolis. The Pakistani state attempted to build trade and manufacturing facilities within the hinterland to displace flows of jute to Calcutta. The state allocated scarce foreign currency and subsidized loans to favored businessmen, particularly the Adamjee and Ispahani families, established Calcutta jute traders and prominent donors to the Muslim League in the years preceding partition. In the first months after partition, the Ispahanis had established three large warehouses in Chittagong—which were, according to a Dundee jute businessman, "of immense trading value"—and had imported secondhand machinery from Dundee to start a 500-loom jute mill, also in Chittagong. The Ispahanis were dwarfed by the ambitions of the Adamjees, who announced plans to build a 3,000-loom jute mill near Narayanganj. The Adamjee Mills would become the largest jute mill in the world, displacing the Ludlow Jute Mills in Massachusetts. By February 1952 the Adamjees had installed 2,000 looms, of which 1,200 were in production—it was, in the words of a Dundee businessman, "a tremendous project."[50] For East Pakistan, the Adamjee Jute Mills were a symbol of the successful partnership between the state and favored capitalists in creating a modern and industrial economy in the agrarian delta.[51]

On the other hand, the Indian government focused on increasing jute cultivation within its borders: India's output of raw jute increased from 1.6 million bales in 1946–47, to 2 million in 1947–48 and 2.8 million in 1948–49.[52] The provincial governments of Assam, West Bengal, Bihar, and Orissa distributed jute seeds and provided advice and technical assistance to cultivators. India also constructed the Assam Link railway, a single-track narrow-gauge railway line connecting Calcutta with jute and tea tracts in Cooch Behar, Assam, and Tripura without passing through Pakistan.

In September 1949, barely a year after the two governments had concluded their trade agreement, all official trade between Pakistan and India came to an abrupt and prolonged halt. The Pakistani and Indian rupees were pegged to the British pound sterling. When Britain devalued its pound, India followed suit but Pakistan did not. Hence, the exchange rate stood at 144 Indian rupees for a 100 Pakistani rupees. India refused to honor the new Pakistani rupee and official Indo-Pak trade came to a sudden standstill. Official trade resumed in April 1950, when the two governments signed a new and much more limited trade agreement. The devaluation crisis and trade stoppage of 1949 and 1950, rather than the political partition of 1947, rent asunder the formerly united economic space of British India.

In the aftermath of the crisis, both India and Pakistan stepped up efforts to reduce their dependence on each other. As India increased domestic jute cultivation and Pakistan expanded manufacturing capacity, the two economies began to compete with each other for international markets for jute manufactures. The two governments openly discriminated against each other and engaged in frequent economic warfare. The Pakistan government imposed a license duty payable solely on exports of jute fiber to India and imposed higher export duties on exports of kutcha bales, which were only sold to the Calcutta mills. India, for its part, imposed a surcharge on exports of coal to energy-starved Pakistan. When the Indian trade delegation accused their Pakistani counterparts of discrimination in raw jute exports in July 1952, the Pakistani delegates countered that, "this was, in fact, not an act of discrimination, but merely a matter of their commercial policy calculated to help the sale of raw jute. . . . India, having progressed towards self-sufficiency in raw jute, could only consume a small part of the raw jute which Pakistan had to sell. Therefore, Pakistan had no option but to offer jute to India's competitors at cheaper prices so that the latter could stand in competition with India in the American market."[53]

The trade stoppage of 1949–50 also witnessed an intensified effort by the Pakistani government to police the national loyalties of traders and corporations engaged in the jute trade. The Marwari and Hindu traders who dominated Bengal's hinterland jute trade were particularly subject to state suspicion. In July 1949 an editorial in the *Dawn*, the Karachi-based official mouthpiece of the Pakistan government, blamed the fall of jute prices on "Indian Big Business." They pointed the finger of blame at "big Marwari business interests in Dacca and other places who, acting as the agents of jute manufacturers in India, are engaged in speculation in jute crops in order to force down prices." The *Dawn* urged the government to tackle the issue "with prompt and energetic action." "Tendering advice to the Big Business in India," the *Dawn* opined, "is as futile as preaching the gospel to an angry bison."[54]

The East Bengal legislature passed the "Jute Dealers' Registration Act." Ostensibly meant to standardize weights and measures and prevent illegal exactions in hinterland markets, the central feature of the act was to make it compulsory for all jute dealers to be registered. The act became a means of controlling the national loyalties of jute dealers, as merchants and corporations whose Pakistani loyalties were suspect—mainly because they were Hindu—were frequently denied licenses or had their licenses canceled.[55] Marwari firms were also denied access to state facilities and contracts. During the devaluation crisis, in an attempt to shore up jute prices, the National Bank of Pakistan provided credit on easy terms to dealers to purchase fiber. Only registered firms were eligible for state credit and only three Marwari firms in all of Bengal made the list.[56]

Following the devaluation crisis of 1949–50, the Pakistani state intensified its surveillance of the jute trade. From the state's perspective, it became even more important to police flows of jute across national borders and to punish traders who were trying to evade state surveillance. The state's desperation resulted in a dynamic of harassment, evasion, and punishment that came to characterize state and society relations in the postcolonial Pakistani jute industry. This was not limited to those whose national loyalties were considered suspicious—that is, to Hindus and Hindu-owned businesses. In 1954 the Pakistan Jute Association (PJA) complained that steamers carrying jute from Narayanganj to Calcutta had to pass through numerous customs or police checks and, at each point, the shipment was stopped and inspected and traders were harassed.[57] Jute shippers' exports were monitored through a complex system of documentation and inspections that the PJA described as "cumbersome, complicated and time-consuming."[58] In 1954 the president of the Pakistan Jute Association complained: "the export control procedure for jute which has been allowed to just grow since partition without a systematic overhaul, has become so unwieldy as to render it almost unworkable." He detailed the delays and difficulties involved in exporting jute through official channels:

> The procedure for obtaining State Bank permission to export through EPC forms, and obtaining export licenses from the Jute Board has become lengthy and unwieldy, it is still difficult to get the State Bank to allow remittances to buyers to their legitimate claims. The Customs Department . . . are delaying consignments where there is the slightest reason. All these difficulties are . . . having an effect on consumers of jute causing confusion and uncertainty not only within Pakistan but also in the trade and industry all over the world.[59]

State harassment was coupled with jute traders' evasion and avoidance. They falsified paperwork: "under-invoicing" and "under-grading" were rife in jute exports. Firms underreported the value of exports in official documents, claiming smaller quantities or a poorer quality of fiber than the actual consignment. Traders then collected the difference between the officially reported value and actually received value for themselves, thus denying the state its share of revenue. The state responded with punishment. In November 1954 the government canceled the licenses of thirteen firms, stating in a press release that "they were forced to take this measure owing to the alarming proportions that malpractices in the jute trade, such as under-invoicing, under-grading and registration of bogus contracts were assuming, resulting in loss of foreign exchange to the State and making it increasingly difficult for reputable shippers to carry on normal trade."[60]

Even such punitive measures did not put an end to the practices of under-invoicing and grade manipulation. Avoidance, evasion, and corruption were so widespread as to be considered commonplace. In May 1955 the Calcutta Jute Brokers and Dealers Association wrote to ask the Indian government *not* to protest Pakistani trade policy, because "if the Pakistani authorities rigorously enforced their rules about currency exchange and correct grading, India would have to pay more for Pakistani jute than she has done in the past."[61] They added, "if one takes the prices current in Pakistan, adds the cost of transport, insurance, export duty, etc. and converts into Indian currency at the Pakistani rate of exchange, it is obvious that Pakistani jute cannot be sold in India at the prices at which it is sold, unless there is under-grading or exchange manipulation or some such irregularity."[62] In effect, Indian jute importers were asking their government not to push the Pakistani government to relax its regulations on jute exports to India because Pakistani jute exporters were effectively abrogating those regulations thus making them meaningless.

The Pakistani state's failures in implementing its laws did not, however, diminish the dynamic of harassment, evasion, and avoidance that characterized postcolonial state and society relations in Pakistan's jute economy. This dynamic was not restricted to merchants with means in the export trade; it also extended down to petty traders and cultivators. When the Jute Dealers Registration Act was floored in the Legislative Assembly, Mir Ahmed Ali, a legislator from a rural, jute-growing constituency, asked that the act exclude farias and beparis—petty jute traders who often combined cultivation with small trade. He said, "If the Act does not exclude those who do business with less money, who buy and sell less than 100 maunds of jute, these people will be oppressed (*zuloom*). I am saying these few words so that these poor people are not made to suffer and the police don't go after them. . . . Please remember Pakistan is a country of the poor."[63] Farias, beparis, and cultivators were also subject to bureaucratic harassment and they were just as adept at evading and avoiding the postcolonial state as more substantial capitalists at the top of the commodity chain. They were, however, subject to far more extreme forms of state violence than wealthy and well-connected merchants.

Smugglers

When the devaluation of September 1949 put a stop to official trade between India and Pakistan, smuggling flourished. British trade interests estimated that 600,000 bales of jute were smuggled out of Pakistan in the first six months of the trade stoppage—that is, 600,000 bales were transported across partition lines to India without paying any duties and exchanging currencies on the black market.[64] During the 1950s and the 1960s, the IJMA and PJA regularly estimated the amount of jute smuggled out of Pakistan into India: estimates ranged between 300,000 and 900,000 bales annually. Smuggling was a threat to Pakistan's national economy and jute smugglers were enemies of the state. Not only were jute smugglers denying the state much-needed revenue and resources, they were aiding and abetting the enemy: India.

Smuggling was, however, almost impossible to control. While the Pakistani state had hurriedly established customs posts and checkpoints along major railways and steamer routes connecting the delta to its former metropolis in Calcutta, it found it much more difficult to police the numerous country roads and waterways that crisscrossed East Pakistan's twisting and undemarcated borders. In the northeastern borders of Sylhet and Assam, jute was smuggled on country boats into India, where it was relabeled as Indian-produced jute, before being transported to Calcutta. P. Das Gupta, the Government of India's trade commissioner in Dacca, stated in a report in December 1949: "On the Sylhet border, it would be quite true to say, that jute is smuggled into Assam and rebooked to Calcutta in bond through Pakistan."[65] In the southwest, the borders of Jessore and Khulna close to Calcutta, "have gained some notoriety for smuggling to India."[66] The rhythms of smuggling were closely related to the weather. During the monsoons, smugglers along the northern borders, where the Brahmaputra and Meghna river systems crossed partition lines, used boats to cross the flooded borders. On the other hand, in the southwest region, smuggling increased during the drier winter months, as waters receded and rural roads became usable by ox carts. On December 8, 1949, the Indian government reported that smuggling "was expected to increase in a few weeks time with the drying up of the roadways which were at present impassable. It was estimated that 2 to 3 lakhs bales in all would move into India by this means."[67]

Smuggling was financed by black-market currency transactions. The over-valued Pakistani rupee had resulted in a substantial unofficial market, where the Pakistan rupee traded at much lower values. Within a month of devalua-tion a "free market on a strictly cash basis in Indian and Pakistani currency had sprung up in Calcutta at rates varying from Rs. 100 to Rs. 115 (Indian) to Rs. 100 (Pakistan)."[68] Rates for "Hundi transactions"—promisory notes—varied from Rs. 105 to Rs. 115 Indian to Rs. 100 Pakistan. This was against an official rate of Rs. 144 Indian to Rs. 100 Pakistani. Currency black markets sprang up all along the East Pakistan–India border in order to finance the illicit trade between the regions: the value of the Pakistani rupee increased as one moved further away from the border into East Pakistan.

For the Pakistani government, jute smuggling resulted not just in reduced revenue to the state but also weakened its bargaining position vis-à-vis India, in trying to force the Indian state to recognize the higher value of the Pakistani rupee. India, on the other hand, did its best to encourage—or at least not prevent—smuggling. The Indian collector of land customs stated in November 1949: "The only [Government of India] restriction in regard to jute smuggled into the Indian Union was insistence on the execution of a bond from the parties that sales would be made only to duly licensed purchasers. . . . [We] were inclined to the view that no restrictions of any kind should be placed on the flow of jute across the border from Pakistan into India."[69]

The Pakistani government, on the other hand, attempted to put an end to smuggling during the devaluation crisis. They intensified the surveillance of jute-laden steamer flats and railway wagons: in November 1949 steamer com-panies claimed that between 700,000 and 800,000 maunds of raw jute loaded onto flats were being held up in Khulna's river port. The Pakistani govern-ment refused to release flats without proof that payments for the jute, includ-ing export duties, had been made in Pakistani rupees at official exchange rates. The steamer companies complained that it was difficult to provide these documents as the seized jute was made up of small consignments purchased in small trading towns scattered throughout the delta.[70] The procedure was considered to be so "complex and difficult" that the Pakistani government never actually received a written request for the release of jute, though the IJMA sent several representatives to meet with Pakistani authorities.[71]

The government also seized consignments of "India to India" jute—that is, jute from Assam, Tripura, or Cooch Behar—traveling through its territory. On December 22, 1949, the Indian government was informed that "24 flats loaded with 345,116 mds (or 69,023 bales) of 'India to India' jute were being held in Khulna by the Pakistan authorities. It was also reported that Pakistan proposed to appoint a jute expert for inspecting every consignment with a view to determining whether the jute was of Indian or Pakistan origin."[72] The steamer companies responded by stopping loading jute for Calcutta in river ports in Assam. Jute was stuck in the Indian state of Tipperah, unable to find transport through Pakistan. Pakistan's barriers to the transit trade led to a rapid buildup of raw jute in Tipperah and "some parties had found it worth their while to shift jute by air from Tipperah State to Calcutta."[73]

While the Pakistani state found it easy to police jute bulked on railway wagons and steamer flats in market towns, they found it much more difficult to police the nation's largely undemarcated borders. The government attempted to control sales and movements of jute in border regions by instituting a border security force—the East Pakistan Rifles, reconstituted from the colonial Eastern Frontier Rifles. The strengthening of its border force constituted a significant portion of the province of East Bengal's budget, eating up the province's strained resources.[74] In 1951 the EPR seized three jute-laden country boats at the Assam/Mymensingh border, near Kaliarchar thana.[75] Later that year, the officer in charge of the Fulbari police station, at the Rangpur–Cooch Behar border, prevented a number of jute-laden ox carts from going to India. The Indian government alleged that about six thousand maunds of jute from an Indian enclave in East Pakistan could not be transported "on account of harassment caused at the Rangpur border to the cartmen carrying jute by the East Bengal Police of the Fulbari police station."[76]

In November 1949 the Pakistani government appointed agents to buy up all the jute within ten miles of Pakistan's international boundary to prevent smuggling: the state's favored capitalists, the Ispahanis, received the bulk of the contract. In subsequent years, the government intensified these controls. In 1953 the provincial government of East Bengal assumed the power to ban jute cultivation outright in parts of East Bengal for "improved quality, to prevent smuggling, and to bring more money to cultivators."[77] In 1954 the government issued orders banning the movement of jute within five miles of the border, with only the Jute Board authorized to arrange for purchases of jute. Such measures were experienced as oppression and harassment by the delta's citizenry. In October 1954, Probhash Chandra Lahiry, the Congress member from Rajshahi, complained that jute could not move "to the bazaars of the interior of the country" as the Jute Board had not, as yet, arranged for purchases of jute from those areas.[78]

These measures, however, were not sufficient to put an end to smuggling, and the increasingly desperate state adopted more draconian measures. In February 1952 the civilian government called in the army—with shoot-to-kill orders—to put a stop to smuggling. This measure was justified on the grounds of national security, the economic and existential threat posed by India. In a speech in February 1952, Fazlur Rahman, Pakistan's commerce minister, argued that, "instead of coming to an agreement with us, India is banking on smuggling jute from Pakistan. . . . This therefore has thrown a challenge to the integrity of our people and the efficiency of our administration. . . . The issue is made one of national prestige and honour."[79] The India Pakistan British Association catalogued the draconian anti-smuggling measures taken by the Pakistani state in 1952:

> The Government are certainly taking determined steps to stop the smuggling of jute which has undermined the strength of their bargaining power with India. During the past two years, smuggled jute has done much to keep some of the Indian mills going. The Army has been called in to help deal with smugglers and orders are practically on a "shoot at sight" basis. The National Bank of Pakistan has advanced Rs 50 lakhs to the cooperative societies in East Pakistan and these societies, and some private firms, are to buy up all jute within five miles of the frontier. After six weeks, even possession of jute within the five-mile belt will be an offence.[80]

Even army intervention could not stop smuggling. The government of Pakistan called in the army once again to prevent smuggling in late 1957—the military's anti-smuggling mission was appropriately titled "Operation Close Door." Defending the decision to call in the army, then prime minister of the East Pakistan provincial government, Ataur Rahman Khan, said, "I considered it [smuggling] to be a war. It was one of the greatest menaces trying to strangulate East Pakistan."[81] The military's anti-smuggling drive led to accusations on the floor of the East Pakistan Legislative Assembly of "indignities, harassment, physical assault inflicted upon licensed businessmen and traders and citizens holding responsible positions."[82] Fazlul Quader Chowdhury defended the army in the assembly, pointing to its success in preventing smuggling—the army had seized fifty thousand maunds or ten thousand bales of jute during the operation. Ten thousand bales, however, was only a fraction of the several hundred thousand bales smuggled to India annually.

Cultivators

This dynamic of harassment, evasion, and punishment extended further down the jute commodity chain, down to the primary producers. In 1948, in a desperate attempt to raise revenue, the cash-strapped provincial government of East Bengal announced a tax of one rupee per acre on jute cultivation. The provincial government had inherited the task of regulating the acreage of jute by issuing licenses to individual jute cultivators. The peasant populist Krishak Praja Party had undertaken the task of regulating acreage through licenses as a means of raising jute prices during the closing years of the depression. For the resource-starved post-partition provincial government, this duty was to prove onerous and expensive.

The provincial government estimated in 1948 that over 5 million licenses were to be issued at a total cost of 5.6 million rupees. The Finance Ministry proposed that "the cultivators may perhaps pay a portion of the cost of the Jute Staff maintained for their benefit."[83] The ministry estimated that a license fee of 4 annas per quarter acre of land sown with jute would provide the government with about 2 million rupees. The provincial government of East Bengal decided to implement the Finance Ministry's proposal through an ordinance, bypassing the need for debate and discussion in the legislature.[84] On February 26, 1948, the government promulgated an ordinance stating that "no grower of jute . . . shall be granted a license unless he applies in writing to the licensing officer . . . and that no such appliance shall be entertained unless it bears a court-fee stamp calculated at [four annas for every quarter acre of jute]."[85] Just over six months after independence and partition, the postcolonial state of Pakistan had imposed a tax on jute cultivation.

The ordinance was renewed in 1949 and extended to Sylhet district, formerly a part of Assam where jute cultivation had been unregulated prior to partition. In February 1950, after two years of collecting license fees, a bill was finally introduced on the floor of the Legislative Assembly. Tofazzal Ali, agriculture minister of the provincial government, introduced the bill, stating that it was "in the interests of the national economy that the cultivators should also pay a portion of the cost [of regulating acreage] in the shape of a jute license fee."[86] Tofazzal Ali did not think that the fee was excessive: "I, for one, hailing from a rural area of this province, having been in constant touch with the jute growers, make bold to submit that this fee will not be a burden on the growers to an extent that they will find difficult to bear."[87]

The jute license fee proved an extremely difficult tax to collect, and government collections regularly fell far below expectations. The director of agriculture wrote in September 1949 that "it now appears that a large sum on that account [of the Jute License fee] for both years [1948 and 1949] still remains unrealized. In majority of cases this was due to the intentional defaults of the growers." In 1950 the Jute Regulation Department listed the reasons why "the collection of license fees have been so far very unsatisfactory in most of the districts": the "exodus" of Hindu growers and Hindu government employees, "economic distress among the people," the "scarcity of Pakistani small coins in Mufassal areas," and the nondisposal of prosecution cases against cultivators for not paying fees in the previous two years.

The collection of the license fee was a burdensome task. The distribution of five million licenses required a lot of paper and paper was scarce in East Bengal. In January 1949 S. Abdullah, the director of agriculture in East Bengal, wrote that there would be delays in issuing licenses because "there is almost no chance of getting from the Government Press the Jute Regulation forms sent for printing."[88] Further, the administrative hierarchy of the new government was weak. In April 1949 the chairman of the Goalmari Jute Committee wrote to the Jute Regulation Department of the Government of East Bengal, stating that they had collected up to 60 percent of the license fee and asked if the government would extend the allotted time period for collections. The telegram stated that "partial collection . . . will create serious disturbances."[89] The Jute Department wrote back somewhat irritably that the period had been extended until June and there should be no confusion about full collection.

The main problem with the collection of license fees was, however, that cultivators simply evaded and avoided them—that they "intentionally" or "willfully" defaulted on payments. The Jute Department felt that this was due to "some parties . . . making anti-propaganda against collection of jute license fees which as a result is badly suffering in certain areas."[90] "Anti-propaganda" was met with "counter-propaganda." In April 1949 the Directorate of Agriculture requested 150 rupees to print and distribute leaflets in jute tracts in rural Bengal "to make counter-propaganda"—100 rupees for Mymensingh and 50 rupees for other parts of Bengal. The following year, the department requested 965 rupees for distribution of pamphlets throughout the delta. The pamphlet distributed in Mymensingh stated, "It is regrettable that in some places Pakistan's bitter enemies (*ghorotor shotru*) are misinforming simple believing peasants (*shorol, bishwashi chashigon*), who are hesitating to pay the license fee."[91]

The pamphlets also announced punishments for cultivators who sowed jute without paying license fees, warning that failure to pay the fee in time would result in six months' imprisonment or a 350 rupee fine. In the summer of 1949 the department prosecuted cultivators across the jute tracts for not paying the fee. The government, however, was concerned that strict punishments would result in agrarian unrest. In August 1949, when touring the jute-growing subdivision of Gaibandha in Rangpur, "certain people complained" to the provincial minister of relief "that cases have been instituted against cultivators who did not pay 'jute license fee', and in some cases the court has fined the accused. The local grievance is that it is a hardship on the part of the cultivators."[92] To prevent these grievances from boiling over into agrarian unrest, the government proposed that prosecutions would be withdrawn "in cases . . . in which the persons prosecuted pay up the license fee and apologise."[93] The Jute Department tasked with collecting license fees, however, felt that lenience would only encourage evasion. The director of agriculture wrote that the withdrawal of prosecution cases would "likely result in serious consequences and regulation of jute cultivation would become meaningless and collection of license fees would in course of time be impossible. . . . Once this is given out that the growers can get out of prosecution only by paying the license fee it would be impossible to control such a large number of them."[94]

In an effort to put more pressure on cultivators to pay license fees, the Directorate of Agriculture requested permission to prosecute cultivators under the Public Demands Recovery Act. Under this act, the department would be able to confiscate the cultivators' property as punishment for nonpayment of license fees. They "hoped that the mere fact of the grant of permission . . . would have a salutary effect on growers and it may not be necessary to have recourse to that procedure in large scale."[95] In the end, the government chose not to confiscate property, though the debate underlined the repressive tendencies of the postcolonial state as it set about realizing revenue from jute. Notably, peasant households did not simply submit to government policies— farias and beparis continued to smuggle jute and jute cultivators continued to withhold taxes. The government responded with draconian laws—six months' imprisonment and/or a 350 rupee fine for nonpayment of taxes and shoot-on-sight orders for the smuggler sneaking a boatload or ox cart of jute across the border. These draconian measures were implemented sporadically and unevenly, which further encouraged evasion. As Ahmed Kamal has demonstrated, this dynamic of surveillance, evasion, and violence put an end to the peasant utopian vision of Pakistan.

Conclusion

Jute informed both peasant aspirations for Pakistan prior to 1947 and peasant disillusionment with Pakistan after 1947. Through the 1946 election campaign, the Bengal delta's jute cultivators came to see Pakistan as a Muslim peasant utopia—a promised time and a place characterized by justice, truth, morality, and freedom, and devoid of corruption, sin, exploitation, and hunger. In formulating Pakistan as peasant utopia, the Muslim League absorbed the idioms, institutions, and even the personnel of the Krishak Praja Party. However, while the KPP had campaigned on legislative and statist solutions to agrarian immiseration, the League campaigned on the poetics of utopia. Famine had discredited the KPP's statist solutions to agrarian immiseration and, moreover, famine had heightened the appeal of a peasant utopian Pakistan. Remarkably—with the important exception of violent attacks on Hindus in Noakhali and Tipperah after the 1946 elections—the Muslim peasant utopian politics of Pakistan was contained within electoral processes.

Peasant disappointment with Pakistan arose out of the postcolonial state project of transforming jute from a colonial commodity into a national resource producing revenue, foreign exchange, and strategic advantage for the state. The project of harnessing fiber to the national economy required the state to monitor, regulate, and police circulations of fiber across the Bengal delta's newly and arbitrarily drawn partition lines. The Pakistani government's first attempt to enforce these partition lines took place in November 1947, through an effort to assess an export duty on jute fibers traveling from the delta to Calcutta.

The devaluation crisis of 1949 brought an end to the possibility of free and open trade between the two post-partition states. India and Pakistan now engaged in open and hostile economic rivalry. The delta's former metropolis of Calcutta was now, in the state's imagination, enemy territory and flows of jute along well-grooved lines between the deltaic hinterland and metropolitan Calcutta were subjected to extreme forms of surveillance. Attempts to evade surveillance were criminalized as smuggling and black marketeering. The postcolonial state did not see smugglers and black-marketers as average criminals, but as enemies of the state who, in the words of an East Pakistani chief minister, were engaged in "war" with Pakistan. Thus the Pakistani state's project of transforming jute into a national resource resulted in extreme forms of state violence against its own citizenry, as the army was deployed on East Pakistan's border to shoot and kill suspected smugglers on sight.

The efforts to transform the colonial commodity into a national resource created a particular dynamic in state and society relations around the jute economy, up and down the commodity chain. The state implemented measures to regulate, inspect, police, and tax the production and circulation of jute; jute cultivators and traders devised strategies to evade the state; and the state implemented draconian measures to punish jute cultivators and traders for their evasions. For jute cultivators, this dynamic of harassment, evasion, and punishment took place in the form of a license fee on jute cultivation; laws that restricted the trade of jute near borderlands; and, subsequently, laws that banned jute cultivation from borderlands outright. Wealthier jute cultivators who combined cultivation with petty trading faced even more regulations— they were required to register as jute dealers, their ox carts and boats could be seized upon suspicion of smuggling, and, in the most extreme case, they could be shot on sight if suspected of smuggling. The state's extreme measures never worked: smuggling continued unabated and the government was unable to realize license fees from most cultivators. Yet failure only prompted the state to implement ever harsher punishment against those who thwarted its ambitions.

Far from the agent of peasant economic emancipation, the postcolonial Pakistani state was a source of harassment and oppression, an entity to be avoided and evaded. Ahmed Kamal has argued that in East Pakistan, during the years following independence and partition, the "state" turned against the "nation," brutally suppressing peasant movements over sharecroppers' rights, water management, and food distribution.[96] This violent oppression of its agrarian citizenry, Kamal contends, extinguished the aspiration of Pakistan as peasant utopia, leading to the resounding electoral defeat of the Muslim League in 1954.[97] Complementing Kamal's argument, this chapter has charted the dynamics of harassment and evasion that resulted from the state's efforts to assert sovereignty over fiber. Jute cultivators' disillusionment with Pakistan arose out of the government's frequently violent efforts to monitor, regulate, and tax the cultivation and trade of jute.

Conclusion

TODAY, JUTE is no longer significant to economic life in the Bengal delta. Not only has global jute production reduced significantly, but the delta has lost its monopoly over jute cultivation.[1] A far smaller proportion of the delta's population relies on jute for their livelihoods and jute occupies much less of the delta's farmland than it did in the colonial period.[2] Green revolution technologies and the extension of groundwater irrigation have led to a boom in rice cultivation and, for the first time since the turn of the century, the Bengal delta can claim to be rice self-sufficient in years of good harvests.[3] The cultivation of winter vegetables and spices for commercial sale has increased: traditional rabi crops—like pulses, oilseeds, spices, and vegetables—now have a combined acreage that is threefold that of jute.[4] The delta's peasant households are also experimenting with and expanding the production of relatively new commercial plants: notably, maize, bananas, and potatoes. Even more significantly, the agricultural sector has diminished in significance in the delta's economic life—less than half of the delta's official labor force is engaged in agriculture and agriculture contributes roughly 20 percent of the delta's gross domestic product, a share that is declining every year.[5]

The declining importance of fiber to economic and material life in the delta has, however, been accompanied by the heightened significance of jute in the national discourse of Bangladesh, the nation-state incorporating the Bengal delta that became independent from East Pakistan in 1971. In Bangladesh, the decline of jute is a staple topic of public and private conversation. While conducting archival research there, I was often asked by friends and family members whether my research would help in reviving the jute industry—if I was going to "bring jute back." This desire to "bring jute back" is an oft-repeated slogan for politicians, academics, policy makers, and newspaper editorialists in the region. Newspapers run editorials headlined "Revival of Golden Fibre" or "Lost Glory of Jute Needs to Be Revived,"[6] and the Bangladeshi state has sponsored initiatives promoting jute handicrafts and decoding the jute genome, and policies mandating the use of jute bags for packaging. How do we square the declining significance of jute in people's material lives with its continued relevance to the nation-state's intellectual life?

Jute, I have argued in this book, transformed peasant economic life in the delta during the nineteenth and twentieth centuries. The cultivation of fiber changed peasant men and women's rhythms of work and leisure, homes, clothing, and diets, practices of domesticity and sociality, and ideas of religiosity and Islam. Critically, jute created new patterns of risk and vulnerability, especially as peasant households came to rely on sales of jute to procure subsistence from markets. Second, I have argued that the circulation of fiber through the delta created new spaces of capital, namely, the mofussil towns where fiber was stored, bulked, and assorted en route from peasant homes to metropolitan Calcutta. Mofussil towns emerged as important spaces of peasant political engagement—as jute-cultivating families visited towns to buy and sell commodities, register property, contest lawsuits, and attend English language schools. The mofussil also emerged as a critical site in the production and circulation of different kinds of ideas—in the form of gossip, rumors, public speeches, and printed texts—that challenged the ideologies of both the colonial state and metropolitan nationalists. Third, transformations in economic life and the newly constituted mofussil spaces gave rise to new forms of peasant politics in the decades before independence and partition which sometimes manifested in collective action against the agents of capital and the state and at other times in individual acts of petitioning and voting. This book demonstrates that the social and political history of the Bengal delta cannot be properly understood without accounting for the ways in which fiber connected the delta's inhabitants to global capital. It is thus not surprising that jute was, from the beginning, entwined with the nationalist discourse of Bangladesh; after all, the territory and peoples that make up the contemporary nation-state were in a sense constituted by the production and circulation of fiber.

The idea of jute in the Bengal delta has persevered beyond the actual significance of the fiber in the everyday economic life of the Bengal delta's inhabitants. This nostalgia for jute can be traced back to Bangladesh's struggle for independence. A core aspiration of Bangladeshi statehood was that jute would finally fulfill its promise of delivering a higher standard of living and economic development to jute cultivators rather than delivering profits to foreign capital, whether British or Pakistani. The independent Bangladeshi state, the new nation was promised, would manage the jute industry not for the benefit of foreign capitalists but for the benefit of the delta's jute cultivators.

With the creation of Bangladesh in 1971, a government belonging exclusively to the delta and its inhabitants took control over the deltaic jute tracts. Toward this end, the post-1971 state nationalized jute mills and fixed the prices at which these state-owned mills would purchase fiber. Nationalization, however, failed to deliver on its promise: in 1974 famine revisited the delta's jute tracts. As in the 1943–44 famine, starvation in 1974 was market driven: a sharp rise in the price of rice had placed basic subsistence beyond the reach of peasant labor that relied on market exchanges to procure rice.

Following the assassination of Sheikh Mujibur Rahman, Bangladesh's founding father and first president, in August 1975, the Bangladeshi state abandoned nationalization as its economic model. During the late 1970s and the 1980s, successive military regimes in Bangladesh pursued development through crony capitalism, as state institutions worked closely with favored capitalists to develop industrial and commercial enterprises. After 1990 the Bangladeshi state firmly embarked on a policy of neoliberalism: deregulating the economy, opening up borders to finance and trade, and privatizing state-owned enterprises. For many Bangladeshis, the closure of the Adamjee Jute Mills in 2002 signaled the final deathblow to the jute industry. Today, Bangladeshis blame the demise of jute on different agencies and factors, depending on their political and ideological leanings. For some, the state's mismanagement and corruption are to blame for the demise of state-owned jute mills and the fiber. For others, the World Bank and agents of neo-imperialist capitalism effected the death of Bangladesh's jute industry to open up the country for the exploitation of global neoliberal capital. A leading Bangladeshi economist asked: "Is it only the Adamjee that has gone into history or is it a trend of this economy to become a land of supermarkets destroying potential manufacturing enterprises?"[7] When the World Bank recently canceled an infrastructure loan to Bangladesh on grounds of corruption, the prime minister launched a "blistering attack on the World Bank," stating that "the country's jute industries . . . had been destroyed through accepting the global lender's prescriptions."[8]

The frequently expressed nostalgia for jute in contemporary Bangladesh is not merely an echo of the past that reverberates in the present. The desire to bring jute back is also a critique of contemporary local formations of neoliberal global capital in the Bengal delta. In contrast to the ready-made garments sector and overseas migrant labor, jute nostalgists imagine fiber as a completely indigenous export commodity. The labor to produce jute—to cultivate fiber and to convert fiber to fabric—was entirely contained within the territorial boundaries of the nation-state. Bangladesh's position as the

second-largest exporter of clothing, on the other hand, depends on imports
of raw cotton, cotton fiber, buttons, and zippers and the delta's comparative
advantage is in its ready supply of cheap labor rather than in its soil and water.
Jute nostalgia also serves as a critique of the retreat of the state from the economy. In contrast to the unregulated garments industry of today, jute nostalgists
refer to the statist modernization of the 1950s, when the postcolonial Pakistani
government fostered and promoted the cultivation and manufacture of fiber
and fabric. Jute nostalgia serves as a critique of deregulation, footloose finance,
flexible supply chains, just-in-time delivery mechanisms, and precarious and
casual wage labor that characterize the contemporary neoliberal global capital.

Jute nostalgia in the twenty-first century is similar to Swadeshi discourses
of the early twentieth century, particularly Swadeshi depictions of an imagined
past economy where Bengal's peasant households produced commodities for
themselves and their communities instead of for export into global markets.
Whether or not such an autarkic economy ever existed in the Bengal delta is
besides the point; the invention and imagination of a precolonial, nonconsum-
erist economy provided a powerful critique of a colonial economy based on the
exchange of peasant produce for manufactured consumer goods. Similarly, nostalgia for jute in contemporary Bengal imagines a completely indigenous export
commodity—cultivated on the soil of the delta, processed into fiber and fabric
by the delta's manufacturers—as a critique of the readymade garments sector.

However, in reimagining the history of jute, Bengal's jute nostalgists—much
like the Swadeshi activists of the twentieth century—do not acknowledge the
economic lives of peasant producers. The discourse of jute nostalgia is framed,
much as Swadeshi discourses were, around abstract economic concepts like
per capita income, balance of payments, and foreign exchange earnings. The
Swadeshi movement failed by its inability to understand jute-cultivating peasants' desires and pleasures—and they were blinded partially by their inability
to recognize that rural marketplaces, hats and melas, were spaces of pleasurable
consumption where peasants treated themselves to occasional luxuries. Similarly, the postcolonial Pakistani project of state formation floundered because
it attempted to impose territorial and political sovereignty over jute, failing
to recognize peasant concepts of market morality. Finally, today, discourses
on reviving the jute industry do not acknowledge the economic realities of
contemporary Bangladesh—the new kinds of economic lives that have been
structured around new forms of labor, production, and consumption.

To return to the question that was posed to me repeatedly in Bangladesh:
no, this book is not intended to help revive the jute industry. Instead, my

ambition is to provide a language to describe local histories of global capital *as they exist*, rather than as they are imagined by utopian nationalist projects. To the jute nostalgists of the contemporary delta, I would suggest a deeper engagement with the economic lives of garment workers and overseas laborers. During the late nineteenth and early twentieth centuries, jute transformed the rhythms of work and leisure and abundance and scarcity of peasant households. The question for contemporary times is this: How does the increasing importance of nonagricultural sources of income transform seasonal patterns of labor and vulnerability? Jute production resulted in the consumption of new kinds of consumer commodities—Manchester cloth, kerosene lamps, metal utensils, corrugated iron roofing, schooling, legal services, and the like—that changed peasant practices of domesticity and sociality. How is the replacement of corrugated iron with bricks and cement, of kerosene lamps with electric lighting, lungis with trousers and saris with Arabian-style *niqabs* transforming peasant dress and dwellings in contemporary Bangladesh? The circulation of peasant-produced jute and peasant-consumed commodities underpinned the growth of mofussil towns in the Bengal delta during the nineteenth century. The spaces of capital in the Bengal delta today seem to be very different. The garment industry, however, is concentrated in Dhaka, which is currently the undisputed metropolis of Bangladesh. Electrification and the spread of refrigerators, on the other hand, have created a boom in rural marketplaces, with temporary hats becoming permanent marketplaces in many villages. The immiseration of the jute cultivating peasantry led to the emergence of new agrarian forms of Islam, based on a market morality and the ethical practice of market-based livelihoods. How does the Bengal delta's current position in global circuits of commodities and capital shape its practice and discourses of Islam?

Even as it serves as a critique of the Bengal delta's contemporary experience of global capital, jute nostalgia willfully ignores what this book presents as the means through which the local history of global capital is realized: the economic lives of commodity producers and consumers, the spaces through which commodities and capital circulate, and the local politics of global capital that arise out of interactions between individual lives, ways of self-fashioning, and the opportunities and risks opened up by a global economy. Critiques of neoliberal global capital are certainly necessary in contemporary Bangladesh and across postcolonial Asia and Africa. However, such critiques must not fall back on an uncritical nostalgia for the primary commodities that they once produced for former imperial metropolises.

ABBREVIATIONS

BL   British Library, London

BLA   Bengal Legislative Assembly

BLC   Bengal Legislative Council

BPBEC   Bengal Provincial Banking Enquiry Committee

DUA   Dundee University Archives, Dundee

EBLA   East Bengal Legislative Assembly

ECC   Economic Committee of the Cabinet

EPLA   East Pakistan Legislative Assembly

GOB   Government of Bengal

GOEB   Government of East Bengal

GOI   Government of India

IOR   India Office Records, London

IPBA   India Pakistan Burma Association

NAB   National Archives of Bangladesh, Dhaka

NAI   National Archives of India, New Delhi, Delhi

SSR   Survey and Settlement Report

NOTES

Introduction

1. Jute's monopoly in global packaging gradually eroded after the mid-twentieth century, with the rise of synthetic fibers, cardboard cartons, and, most significantly, the aluminum container. The aluminum shipping container was first used in Newark, New Jersey, in 1956 and is now as ubiquitous as jute used to be in global shipping. Marc Levinson, *The Box: How the Shipping Container Made the World Smaller and the World Economy Bigger*, Princeton: Princeton University Press, 2006.

2. The jute-growing districts of the Bengal delta—Mymensingh, Rangpur, Faridpur, Dacca, Tipperah, Pabna, and Bogra—consistently produced more than 80 percent of the world's jute from the mid-nineteenth to the mid-twentieth century. Its share of global production fell after partition and the creation of Pakistan in 1947, though it remained around 50 percent until the 1970s. After 1947 jute cultivation began in neighboring regions—the postcolonial Indian states of Assam, Bihar, Tripura, and Orissa—as well as in Brazil, China, Thailand, and Vietnam. Today, the Bengal delta, the nation-state of Bangladesh, produces around 25 percent of the world's jute.

3. Tara Sethia, "The Rise of the Jute Manufacturing Industry in Colonial India: A Global Perspective," *Journal of World History*, 7(1), Spring 1996, p. 82. In addition to Dundee and Calcutta, there were significant jute manufacturing industries in Germany, France, Belgium, Austria-Hungary, Italy, and the United States. A.Z.M. Iftikhar-ul-Awal, *The Industrial Development of Bengal, 1900–1939*, New Delhi: Vikas Publishing House, 1982, p. 165.

4. The acreage figures here and in the remainder of the book are unreliable and imprecise. The colonial state started collecting statistics on jute acreage in 1888, but their numbers were notoriously unreliable and were the subject of frequent and scathing criticism from jute traders and manufacturers who desired reliable statistics as to the estimated crop. M. W. Ali estimated that 50,000 acres were sown with jute in 1850, in Ali, *Jute in the Agrarian History of Bengal, 1870–1914*, Rajshahi, 1998. The second figure of 3.9 million acres is from Department of Statistics, *Estimates of Area and Yield of Principal Crops in India, 1914–15*, Calcutta: Superintendent Government Printing Press, 1915, p. 11.

5. *Report on the Administration of the Custom Department in the Bengal Presidency for the Year 1874–5 and 1909–10*, Calcutta: Printed at the Bengal Secretariat Press.

6. The figures for Ghanaian cocoa are from Beverly Grier, "Underdevelopment, Modes of Production, and the State in Colonial Ghana," *African Studies Review*, 24(1), 1981, p. 32; for Senegalese peanuts, Bernard Moitt, "Slavery and Emancipation in Senegal's Peanut Basin: The Nineteenth and Twentieth Centuries," *International Journal of African Historical Studies*, 22(1),

1989, p. 27; for Philippines' abaca, Norman Owen, *Prosperity without Progress: Manila Hemp and Material Life in the Colonial Philippines*, Berkeley: University of California Press, p. 79; for Malayan rubber, P. J. Drake, "The Economic Development of British Malaya to 1914: An Essay in Historiography with Some Questions for Historians," *Journal of Southeast Asian Studies*, 10(2), September 1979, p. 285; for Burmese rice, Michael Adas, *The Burma Delta: Economic Development and Social Change on an Asian Rice Frontier*, Madison: University of Wisconsin Press, 1974, p. 58; and for Indian cotton, Peter Harnetty, "Cotton Exports and Indian Agriculture, 1861–1870," *Economic History Review*, 24(3), August 1971, p. 414.

7. Sven Beckert traces the constitution of this global countryside through a single commodity—cotton—and the global dispersal of cotton cultivation during and after the emancipation of slaves on the cotton plantations of the American South. His focus on cotton distorts the larger narrative of the making of a global countryside: first, it suggests a too-simple transition from slave labor on plantations to peasant labor on smallholdings, and second, it overemphasizes the power and capacity of European empires and capitalists to coerce peasant households into commodity production. Sven Beckert, *Empire of Cotton: A Global History*, New York: Vintage Books, 2015; see particularly chap. 10, pp. 274–311.

8. During the nineteenth century, major European newspapers carried regular columns on prices of colonial produce, which tabulated prevailing quantities, qualities, and prices of jute, cotton, sugar, coffee, tea, cocoa, hemp, etc., available in major markets. The quote on cocoa prices is from the "London Produce Market," *Manchester Guardian*, June 3, 1874, p. 7.

9. Laxman Satya emphasizes the significance of railways and the development of Khamgaon as a cotton depot in the spread of cotton cultivation in Berar. See Satya, *Cotton and Famine in Berar, 1850–1900*, New Delhi: Manohar, 1977.

10. Beckert, *Empire of Cotton*, pp. 278–79. Beckert's argument about the reconstruction of capital through cotton was also made in an earlier article, "Emancipation and Empire: Reconstructing the Worldwide Web of Cotton Production in the Age of the American Civil War," *American Historical Review*, 109(5): 1405–38.

11. Sugata Bose, *Peasant Labour and Colonial Capital*, Cambridge: Cambridge University Press, 1993.

12. For rice in Burma, see Michael Adas, *The Burma Delta: Economic Development and Social Change on an Asian Rice Frontier*, Madison: University of Wisconsin Press, 1974. For cocoa in Ghana, see Polly Hill, *The Migrant Cocoa-Farmers of Southern Ghana: A Study in Rural Capitalism*, Cambridge: Cambridge University Press, 1963. For peanuts in Senegal, see George E. Brooks, "Peanuts and Colonialism: Consequences of the Commercialization of Peanuts in West Africa, 1830–70," *Journal of African History*, 16(1), 1975, pp. 29–54. For rubber in Borneo, see Michael Dove, *The Banana Tree at the Gate: A History of Marginal Peoples and Global Markets in Borneo*, New Haven, CT: Yale University Press, 2011. For hemp in the Philippines, see Norman Owen, *Prosperity without Progress: Manila Hemp and Material Culture in the Colonial Philippines*, Berkeley: University of California Press, 1984.

13. Cheikh Anta Babou, *Fighting the Greater Jihad: Amadu Bamba and the Founding of the Muridiyya of Senegal, 1853–1913*, Athens: Ohio University Press, 2007.

14. In 1910 all Malaya's rubber exports were produced on large-scale plantations. By 1922 40 percent of exports were produced by peasants on their smallholdings. Drake, "Economic Development of British Malaya," p. 285.

15. Adas, *Burma Delta*, pp. 24, 41.

16. Cheikh Anta Babou, *Fighting the Greater Jihad: Amadu Bamba and the Founding of the Muridiyya of Senegal, 1853–1913*, Athens: Ohio University Press, 2007. I want to thank my colleague Mauro Nobili for bringing my attention to the Murudiyya and their connection to peanut cultivation in colonial Senegal.

17. C. A. Bayly, *The Birth of the Modern World, 1780–1914*, Oxford: Blackwell, 2004, p. 11.

18. For rubber cultivators' dreams in Borneo, see Michael Dove, "Rice-Eating Rubber and People-Eating Governments: Peasant versus State Critiques of Rubber Development in Colonial Borneo," *Ethnohistory*, 43(1), Winter 1996, pp. 33–63. For rubber cultivators' rebellions against the Raja of Sarawak, see Vinson H. Sutlive, *Tin Jugah of Sarawak: Colonialism and Iban Response*, Kuala Lampur: Penerbit Fajar Bakti, 1992, pp. 85–86. For the Saya San rebellion in Burma, see Robert L. Solomon, "Saya San and the Burmese Rebellion," *Modern Asian Studies*, 3(3), 1969, pp. 209–23. For jute cultivators' attacks on moneylenders in Kishoreganj, Bengal, see Sugata Bose, "The Roots of 'Communal' Violence in Rural Bengal: A Study of the Kishoreganj Riots, 1930," *Modern Asian Studies*, 16(3), 1982, pp. 463–91. For the cocoa holdups in Ghana, see Gareth Austin, "Capitalists and Chiefs in the Cocoa Hold-Ups in South Asante, 1927–1938," *International Journal of African Historical Studies*, 21(2), 1988, pp. 63–95.

19. J. C. Jack, *The Economic Life of a Bengal District: A Study*, Oxford: Clarendon Press, 1916, p. 2.

20. Dipesh Chakrabarty, *Provincializing Europe: Postcolonial Thought and Historical Difference*, Princeton, NJ: Princeton University Press, 2002, p. 19.

21. David Harvey, *Limits to Capital*, New York: Verso Books, 2007.

22. William Cronon's history of Chicago and the American Midwest provides a model for understanding how processes of commodification structure the relationship of hinterland and metropolis. *Nature's Metropolis: Chicago and the Great West*, New York: W. W. Norton, 1991.

23. Strictly speaking, as the *Hobson-Jobson* describes it, the mofussil was a relational term; from the perspective of Calcutta, the delta's small towns were the mofussil, but from those small towns themselves, the surrounding countryside was the mofussil. The *Hobson-Jobson* definition of the mofussil is "The provinces—the country stations and districts, as contra-distinguished from 'the Presidency'; or, relatively rural localities of district as contra-distinguished from the sudder or chief station, which is the residence of the district authorities." Henry Yule and A. C. Burnell, *Hobson-Jobson: A Glossary of Colloquial Anglo-Indian Words and Phrases and of Kindred Terms, Etymological, Historical, Geographical and Discursive*, London: J. Murray, 1903, p. 570.

24. An important exception, which the book deals with in more detail, are instances of violence against Hindus in parts of the jute tracts at the end of 1946.

25. The 1871 census counted the population of the jute-growing districts at 10,800,463. The census provided no reliable estimates of the breakdown of population by occupation, though colonial officials' impressions were that between 80 and 90 percent of the delta's population was engaged in agriculture. Of the total population (6,846,941), 63.4 percent were Muslim; a much higher proportion of cultivators were Muslim. The significant non-Muslim cultivating castes were the Namasudras (known by the derogatory category of Chandal in 1871, who made up 6.0 percent of the total population), Rajbansis (who were concentrated in Rangpur, where they were 18.5 percent of the population as against 2.9 percent of the entire jute tracts' population), and Kaibartas (2.2 percent of the total population).

26. British observers frequently noted the absence of English-style villages, with a noticeable village center. However, the weekly and twice-weekly rural markets—hats—performed many of the same roles as the English village center.

27. Sugata Bose, *Agrarian Bengal: Economy, Social Structure, and Politics, 1919–1947*, Cambridge: Cambridge University Press, 1986, chap. 1.

28. Richard Eaton, *The Rise of Islam in the Bengal Frontier, 1204–1760*, Berkeley: University of California Press, 1993, describes the early settlement of the frontier, particularly the incentives provided by the Mughal state to settle the frontier. Iftekhar Iqbal, *The Bengal Delta: Ecology, State, and Social Change*, Basingstoke: Palgrave Macmillan, 2010, discusses the continued settlement of the frontier in the nineteenth century, and colonial policies to encourage such settlement. Sugata Bose, *Agrarian Bengal*, argues that the delta's agrarian limits were reached by the early twentieth century.

29. Andrew Sartori, *Liberalism in Empire: An Alternative History*, Berkeley: University of California Press, 2014.

30. Histories of agrarian colonial Bengal often proceed from the assumption that the Permanent Settlement of 1793 was a foundational moment. For a detailed history of its implementation, see Sirajul Islam, *The Permanent Settlement in Bengal: A Study of Its Operation, 1790–1819*, Dhaka: Bangla Akademi 1979. For an intellectual history of the various land policies debated by East India Company officials in the early days of the Company Raj, see Ranajit Guha, *A Rule of Property for Bengal: An Essay on the Idea of the Permanent Settlement*, Durham, NC: Duke University Press, 1963.

31. See Iqbal, *Bengal Delta*, chap. 1, for how zamindars found it difficult to exert authority over the shifting ecology of the delta. See John Wilson, "'A Thousand Countries to Go': Peasants and Rulers in Late Eighteenth Century Bengal," *Past and Present*, 189, 2005, 81–109, for a case study of how peasants in Rangpur would "vote with their feet," leaving zamindari estates if they felt their exactions were too onerous.

32. Rajat Datta, *Society, Economy, and the Market: Commercialization in Rural Bengal, c. 1760–1800*, New Delhi: Manohar, 2000.

33. Eaton, *Rise of Islam*, chap. 3.

34. See Asim Roy, *The Islamic Syncretistic Tradition in Bengal*, Princeton, NJ: Princeton University Press, esp. chaps. 5 and 6, for Muslim Vaishnavism and for the significance of devotionalism to Sufi saints and their shrines.

35. Muin-ud-din Ahmed Khan, *History of the Faraizi Movement in Bengal, 1818–1906*, Karachi: Asiatic Society of Pakistan, 1965.

36. Ahmed Kamal, *State against the Nation: The Decline of the Muslim League in Pre-Independence Bangladesh, 1947–1954*, Dhaka: University Press, 2009.

Chapter 1

1. M. W. Ali estimated that 50,000 acres were sown with jute in 1850, in *Jute in the Agrarian History of Bengal, 1870–1914*, Rajshahi, 1998. The second figure of 3.9 million acres is from Department of Statistics, *Estimates of Area and Yield of Principal Crops in India, 1914–15*, Calcutta: Superintendent Government Printing Press, 1915, p. 11.

2. *Report on the Administration of the Custom Department in the Bengal Presidency for the Year 1874–5*, Calcutta: Printed at the Bengal Secretariat Press, 1875, p. 4.

3. *Report on the Administration of the Custom Department in the Bengal Presidency for the Year 1909–10*, Calcutta: Printed at the Bengal Secretariat Press, 1910. p. 3.

4. N. C. Chaudhuri, *Jute in Bengal*, Calcutta: Printed by J. N. Bose, 1921, pp. 210–11.

5. Computed from Department of Statistics, *Estimates of Area and Yield of Principal Crops in India, 1914–15*, Calcutta: Superintendent Government Printing Press, 1915, p. 11.

6. "Resolution," 4th February 1873, GoB, Agri Dept, NAB.

7. Sugata Bose, *Peasant Labour and Colonial Capital*, Cambridge: Cambridge University Press, 1993.

8. Omkar Goswami, *Industry, Trade and Peasant Society: The Jute Economy of Eastern Bengal*, New Delhi: Oxford University Press, 1991.

9. Hemm Chunder Kerr, *Report on the Cultivation of, and Trade in Jute, in Bengal*, London, 1874, p. 18.

10. Chaudhuri, *Jute in Bengal*, pp. 210–11.

11. Acreage figures are from Government of India, *Agricultural Statistics of India, 1900–01 to 1904–05*. Calcutta: Office of the Superintendent of Government Printing, 1906.

12. Supply of jute seed to the Queensland Acclimatization Society, Revenue and Agriculture, Fibers and Silk, 9/13, Part B, January 1874, NAI.

13. In a government resolution to investigate the cultivation and trade of jute, George Campbell, the lieutenant governor of Bengal, noted: "The Americans are actively prosecuting the experimental growth of the plant in various parts of their country." "Resolution," 4th February, 1876, GoB, Agri Dept, Agri Branch, List 14, Bundle 4, NAB.

14. S. Waterhouse, *Report on Jute Culture and the Importance of the Industry*, Department of Agriculture: Special Report, Washington, DC, Government Printing Office, 1883, p. 14.

15. J. C. Jack, *The Economic Life of a Bengal District: A Study*, Oxford: Clarendon Press, 1916, p. 2.

16. J. C. Jack was not referring to the much broader distinction of soil between the moribund delta of western Bengal and the active delta of eastern Bengal—the distinction between red clay or *khiyar* and the black clay or *pali mati* of the east. There were no khiyar lands in Faridpur, and red clay in the east was only found in the Madhupur jungles of Dacca and Mymensingh, and in parts of north Bengal. Jute was not grown at all in these khiyar lands.

17. Government of Bengal, *Agricultural Statistics of Bengal*, Calcutta, 1901, pp. 6–13.

18. Government of Bengal, *Report of the Banking Enquiry Committee*, Calcutta, 1930, p. 27.

19. Estimated from Government of Bengal, Department of Land Records and Agriculture, *Season and Crop Reports of Bengal*, 1901–2 to 1904/5, Calcutta, 1902 to 1905.

20. W. W. Hunter, *A Statistical Account of Bengal*, London: Trubner, 1876, Mymensingh, vol. 5, p. 423.

21. Hunter, *Statistical Account*, Mymensingh, vol. 5, p. 420.

22. Excerpted in the report of the Chittagong Commissioner, 2nd September 1872, in D. J. McNeile, Secretary, Government of Bengal, 4th February 1873, GoB, Agri Dept, Agri Branch, List 14, Bundle 4, NAB.

23. Hunter, *Statistical Account*, Mymensingh, vol. 5, p. 421.

24. Several witnesses before the Indigo Commission of 1860 claimed that cultivators were reluctant to sow their lands with indigo because greater profits could be made from jute,

safflower, and rice cultivation. *Report of the Indigo Commission, 1860*, ed. Pulin Das, Darjeeling: University of North Bengal, 1992, pp. 91–92 and p. 160.

25. Kerr, *Report on Jute*, p. 18.

26. Hunter, *Statistical Account*, Tippera, vol. 6, p. 398. I will write in more detail about the rising demand for fish as a consequence of the "improved condition of the people" in chapter 2.

27. Kerr probably overestimates the alienation of rice lands: if fully two-thirds of jute land were former rice lands, rice and jute exports could not have simultaneously extended during this period. Kerr, *Report on Jute*, p. 49.

28. Kerr, *Report on Jute*, p. 50.

29. Sambhu Chandra Mookerjee, *Travels and Voyages between Calcutta and Independent Tipperah*, Calcutta, 1887, pp. 255–56.

30. Memorandum on the Material Conditions of the Lower Orders in Bengal, 1891–92, p. 13, Agri Dept, Proc B, List 14, Bundle 13, NAB.

31. Sugata Bose has argued that the Tenancy Act of 1885, which I address in greater detail in chapter 2, spelled the end of the rent and revenue offensive in the Bengal delta and its subsequent replacement by high-interest loans as the major mechanism of surplus extraction.

32. "Ore amar shadher paat! / Tumi chheye achho Bangala muluk, bangala desher math. / Je deshe jekhane jai, shethhay tomar dekhtey pai / Grame Grame office [afis] tomar, paray paray hat." Islam Robi, Sirajganj, 18 Bhadro, 1321, or September 2, 1914.

33. Dwijdas Datta, *Pat ba nalita*, Calcutta, 1911, p. 1. Kurukshetra was the scene of the final battle between the Pandavas and the Kauravas in the Mahabharata. The reference to having to eat jute would become a popular trope in folk literature on jute; see chapter 5.

34. Michael Adas, *The Burma Delta: Economic Development and Social Change on an Asian Rice Frontier, 1852–1941*, Madison: University of Wisconsin Press, 2011.

35. Jack, *Economic Life*, p. 85.

36. F. A. Sachse, Settlement Officer, Mymensingh to Revenue Dept, Government of Bengal, 21st February 1914, GoB, Proc A, Agri Dept, Agri Branch, List 14, Bundle 28, NAB.

37. See David Glasner and Thomas F. Cooley, "Crisis of 1873," in *Business Cycles and Depressions: An Encyclopedia*, New York: Garland, 1997, pp. 132–33.

38. Kerr, *Report on Jute*, p. 62.

39. H. Anstruther and H. C. Kerr, Jute Commissioners to Secy, GoB, Statistical Dept, 10th May 1873, GoB, Proc A, Agri Dept, Agri Branch, List 14, Bundle 4, NAB.

40. Hunter, *Statistical Account*, Tippera, vol. 6, p. 391.

41. "Commercial Epitome," *Economist*, 31(1534), January 18, 1873, p. 18.

42. The Collector of Bogra reported in 1872: "The cultivators of jute, however, have suffered a check during the year under review, from the fall in its market price; and the greatly increased sale of non-judicial two-anna stamps seems to indicate that the rayats in many cases have preferred borrowing to reducing their expenditure." Hunter, *Statistical Account*, Bogra, vol. 8, p. 206.

43. B. B. Chaudhuri, "Commercial Agriculture: 1859–85," *Indian Economic and Social History Review*, 7(2), 1970, p. 244.

44. R. M. Waller, Commissioner of Chittagong Division to Government of Bengal (GoB), Revenue Dept., 19th May 1894, Agri Dept, Agri Branch, List 14, Bundle 14, NAB.

45. R. M. Waller, Commissioner of Chittagong Division to GoB, Revenue Dept., 21 June 1894, in ibid.

46. L. Birley, District Magistrate, Dacca, to Commissioner of Dacca, 5th October 1914, in "Depression in Jute Trade on Account of the Outbreak of War in Europe," February 1915, GoB, Proc A, Agri Dept, Agri Branch, List 14, Bundle 29, NAB.

47. Note dated 15th August 1914, in ibid.

48. L. Birley, District Magistrate, Dacca, to Commissioner of Dacca, 5th October 1914, in ibid.

49. Ibid.

50. Ibid.

51. Shah Abdul Hamid, *Krishak Bilap*, Bandulia, 1328 b.e. (1921). The title translates as "extinction of the peasantry," the main theme of this pamphlet. His two previous publications, mentioned in the foreword to *Krishak Bilap* are titled *Prajakahini* (Stories of Prajas) and *Shashon-shongskarey Gramya Mussalman* (Rural Muslims in Political Reforms).

52. Hamid, *Krishak Bilap*, pp. 9–10.

53. Ibid, p. 11.

Chapter 2

1. Sambhu Chandra Mookerjee, *Travels and Voyages between Calcutta and Independent Tipperah*, Calcutta, 1887, p. 10.

2. Memorandum on the Material Conditions of the Lower Orders in Bengal, 1891, GoB, Agri Dept, List 14, Bundle 20, NAB.

3. K. C. Dey to GoB, Revenue Dept., 4th February 1914, in GoB, Agric Dept, August 1914, in ibid.

4. Kaminikumar Chakrabarty, *Krishak*, Sherpur, published by Sree Tamijuddin Ahmed, 1893, p. 38.

5. Among many other poets from eastern Bengal, Abed Ali Mian, from Mymensingh, wrote extensively on the inedibility of the fiber, contrasting it with the taste of home-grown rice. Abed Ali Mian, *Kali Chitra*, Rangpur: Alamnagar Lokaranjan Press, 1323 b.e. (1917).

6. Dipesh Chakrabarty, *Habitations of Modernity: Essays in the Wake of Subaltern Studies*, Chicago: Chicago University Press, 2002.

7. Andrew Sartori, *Liberalism in Empire: An Alternative History*, Berkeley: University of California Press, 2012.

8. Chapter 3 discusses the growth of these market towns during the late nineteenth century in more detail.

9. J. C. Jack, *The Economic Life of a Bengal District: A Study*, Oxford: Clarendon Press, 1916, p. 47.

10. Hunter, *Statistical Account*, Dinajpur, vol. 7, p. 387.

11. F. A. Sachse, *Bengal District Gazetteers: Mymensingh*, Calcutta: Bengal Secretariat Book Depot, 1917, p. 89.

12. Hunter, *Statistical Account*, Bogra, vol. 8, p. 206.

13. Hunter, *Statistical Account*, Dinajpur, vol. 8, pp. 387–88.

14. Sugata Bose, in *Agrarian Bengal*, has established that credit and interest rather than land and rent were the primary mechanism for expropriating peasant surplus. Iftekhar Iqbal,

in *Bengal Delta*, has shown how the delta's ecology prevented the application of the permanent settlement over large tracts of farmlands.

15. Sartori, *Liberalism in Empire*, pp. 29–30.

16. David Washbrook, "Law, State and Agrarian Society in Colonial India," *Modern Asian Studies*, 15(3), 1981.

17. John Wilson. "'A Thousand Countries to Go To': Peasants and Rulers in Eighteenth Century Bengal," Past and Present, 189, 2005, pp. 81–109.

18. K. K. Sengupta, *Pabna Disturbances and the Politics of Rent, 1873–1885*, New Delhi: People's Publishing House, 1974, p. 75.

19. The relatively small district of Pabna had the most land sown with jute in 1872–73 according to government estimates. Hemm Chunder Kerr, *Report on the Cultivation of, and Trade in Jute, in Bengal*, London, 1874.

20. With the exception of Bakarganj and—to a lesser degree—Faridpur, all the affected districts had significant jute acreage. All the jute-growing districts of the delta, except for Rangpur, experienced the antirent movement. Also, agrarian leagues did not emerge in non-jute-growing districts of western Bengal.

21. Sengupta, *Pabna Disturbances*, pp. 45–46.

22. Sengupta, *Pabna Disturbances*, p. 13.

23. Sengupta, *Pabna Disturbances*, p. 91.

24. From the Commissioner of Chittagong to the Revenue Department, GoB, July 29, 1875, in *Proposed Amendment of the Rent Law in Bengal*, Dept of Rev, Agri and Comm, Land Revenue and Settlements, February 1879, Nos. 11–29, File 21, 1879, NAI.

25. "Minute," Lieutenant Governor of Bengal, August 21, 1875, in *Rent Disputes between Landlords and Their Tenants in Bengali*, Dept of Rev, Agri and Comm, Land Revenue and Settlements, Pros No. 3–5, February 1876, NAI.

26. Petition by zemindars and other landholders of Bengal and Behar against the Tenancy Bill, Rev and Agri, Revenue, File N. 21, Part B, December 1883, NAI.

27. Sugata Bose, *Peasant Labour and Colonial Capital*, Cambridge: Cambridge University Press, 1993.

28. Hunter, *Statistical Account*, Tippera, vol. 6, p. 387. The charge of "laziness" as an outcome of prosperity is obviously false. As chapter 1 demonstrated, cultivators worked considerably harder to produce additional cash with which to finance consumption.

29. Hunter, *Statistical Account*, Mymensingh, vol. 5, p. 418.

30. Quoted in Hunter, *Statistical Account*, Noakhali, vol. 6, p. 289.

31. Expenditure per head on clothing in eastern districts in 1877–78 was one rupee, 4 annas, and 7 paisas against one rupee, three annas, and 6 paisas in central, and 14 annas and 3 paisas in western districts. In the jute districts of Pabna and Faridpur, expenditure on European piecegoods exceeded two rupees per head.

32. Calculated from *Reports on the Rail-Borne Traffic of Bengal during the Years 1884–85 to 1891–2*, Calcutta: Printed at the Bengal Secretariat Press, 1886 to 1893.

33. Between 1906–7 and 1911–12, imports of cloth into the Rajshahi, Dacca, and Tipperah blocks increased at a barely noticeable 1.5 percent annually. Compiled from Government of Eastern Bengal and Assam, *Reports on the Trade Carried by Rail and River in the Province of Eastern Bengal and Assam during the Years 1906–1907 to 1910–11*, Shillong, 1907–11.

34. J. C. Jack estimated that a family living in "comfort" in Faridpur spent £1.67 on clothing out of a total budget of £16.67 and a family living in "extreme indigence" spent £0.67 on clothing out of a total annual expenditure of £6.67. Jack, *Economic Life*, p. 71. F. A. Sachse presented the budget of a wealthy family of sixteen members in Mymensingh who spent 140 rupees on clothing out of an annual budget of 1,400 rupees. Sachse, *Mymensingh District Gazetteer*, p. 72.

35. The *Tippera District Gazetteer* noted: "Their [Muslim] dress, the *lungi* and the muslin cap, and speech distinguish them from the Hindus." J. E. Webster, *Bengal District Gazetteers: Tippera*, Calcutta, 1910, p. 29. Similar comments were made of the distinctive Muslim peasant dress in other parts of the jute tracts. The *Dacca District Gazetteer* stated: "Muhammadans in place of a *dhuti* wear a *lungi* or petticoat of coloured cloth reaching to the ankles and a fez or cap." B. C. Allen, *Eastern Bengal District Gazetteers: Dacca*, Allahabad: Pioneer Press, 1912, p. 87.

36. Quoted in Muin-ud-Din Ahmed Khan, *History of the Faraizi Movement in Bengal*, p. 132.

37. Allen, *Dacca District Gazetteer*, p. 87.

38. Mookerjee, *Travels and Voyages*, p. 10.

39. Webster, *Tippera District Gazetteer*, p. 43.

40. Hunter, *Statistical Account*, Bogra, vol. 8, p. 205.

41. *Reports on the Administration of the Customs Department in the Bengal Presidency for the Year 1893–94*, Calcutta: Printed at the Bengal Secretariat Press, 1894, p. lxiii.

42. Abul Hai, *Adarsha Krishak*, Mymensingh: Mymensingh Zilla Bhandar Press, 1920, p. 43.

43. Allen, *Dacca District Gazetteer*, p. 87.

44. Allen, *Dacca District Gazetteer*, pp. 86–87.

45. Sachse, *Mymensingh District Gazetteer*, pp. 67–68.

46. Jack, *Economic Life*, p. 27.

47. Hunter, *Statistical Account*, Noakhali, vol. 6, p. 290.

48. "Bolo bhai, nailyar shaman krishi nai / Nailya bepari, satkhanda bari / Joanshaiya thuni diya banchhe choari," quoted in Bose, *Agrarian Bengal*, p. 80.

49. B. C. Prance, *Final Report on the Survey and Settlement Operations in the Riparian Area of District Tippera Conducted with the Faridpur District Settlement, 1909 to 1915*, Calcutta: Bengal Secretariat Book Depot, 1916, p. 4, emphasis added.

50. Maulvi Mokhtar Ahmed Siddiqi, *Sirajganjer Itihas*, Sirajganj, B.E. 1322 (1915–16), p. 53, emphasis added.

51. Gobindo Chandra Das, "Paater Gaan," *Islam Robi*, Bhadro, 1321 (September 1914), reprinted in Siddiqi, *Sirajganjer Itihas*, p. 88.

52. Hunter, *Statistical Account*, Bogra, vol. 8, p. 206.

53. Allen, *Dacca District Gazetteer*, pp. 86–87.

54. Jack, *Economic Life*, p. 29.

55. J. C. Jack estimated that a "family in comfort" in Faridpur spent 2 shillings and 8 pence annually on kerosene oil and a family living in "extreme indigence" spent 6 pence. Jack, *Economic Life*, p. 71. Further, a wealthy peasant family in Mymensingh purchased five tins of kerosene oil each year, at 2¼ rupees a tin during the 1910s. Sachse, *Mymensingh District Gazetteer*, p. 72.

56. Memorandum on the Material Conditions of the Lower Orders in Bengal, 1891, GoB, Agri Dept, List 14, Bundle 20, NAB.

57. Allen, *Dacca District Gazetteer*, pp. 86–87.

58. Sachse, *Mymensingh District Gazetteer*, p. 79.

59. Nira Wickremasinghe, *Metallic Modern: Everyday Machines in Colonial Sri Lanka*, New York: Berghahn Books, 2014.

60. Webster, *Tippera District Gazetteer*, p. 44.

61. Hunter, *Statistical Account*, Rangpur, vol. 7, p. 226.

62. Webster, *Tippera District Gazetteer*, p. 31.

63. Sidney Mintz brilliantly traces the rising importance of sugar to English working-class diets in *Sweetness and Power: The Place of Sugar in Modern History*, New York: Penguin, 1986.

64. Hunter, *Statistical Account*, Noakhali, vol. 6, p. 291.

65. Ibid., p. 78.

66. Webster, *Tippera District Gazetteer*, p. 44.

67. The *Mymensingh District Gazetteer* reported that wealthier peasant households were consuming higher-quality tobacco grown in Rangpur, rather than the "locally-grown weed." Sachse, *Mymensingh District Gazetteer*, p. 31.

68. Jack, *Economic Life*, pp. 47–48. Also, the jackfruit is nothing like a large melon.

69. Hunter, *Statistical Account*, Tippera, vol. 5, p. 398.

70. Siddiqi, *Sirajganjer Itihas*, p. 25.

71. Dadabhai Naoroji, *Poverty and Un-British Rule in India*, London: S. Sonnenschein, 1901.

72. R. C. Dutt, *The Economic History of India*, vols. 1 and 2, London: Kegan Paul, Trench Trubner, 1902 and 1904.

73. Memorandum on the Material Conditions of the Lower Orders in Bengal (1892), GoB, Proc A, Agri Dept, Agri Branch, List 14, Bundle 12, NAB.

74. Chandrashekhar Kar, *Shekal-ekal*, Calcutta, 1918, p. 7.

75. Ray Nikhilnath, *Sonar Bangla*, Calcutta, 1906, p. 132, emphases added.

76. Manu Goswami discusses the significance of Friedrich List to Swadeshi economic thought in "From Swadeshi to Swaraj: Nation, Economy, Territory in Colonial South Asia, 1870 to 1907," *Comparative Studies in Society and History*, 40(4), 1998, pp. 609–36.

77. Statement of the Inspector General of Police, December 1, 1905, in *State of Affairs in Eastern Bengal and Assam and Bengal in connection with the partition and the swadeshi movement*, Home, Public, Part A, Nos. 169–186, June 1906.

78. See the numerous reports from the various districts in ibid.

79. According to the inspector general of police, the movement "was given a fillip by Judgish Chundra Roy, a pleader, who in a meeting at Pabna made the claim that English sugar was purified with the blood and bones of cows." Ibid.

80. From P. C. Lyon, Chief Secy, G of EB&A to Secy, Home Dept, GoI, February 21, 1906, ibid.

81. From P. C. Lyon, Chief Secy, G of EB&A to Secy, Home Dept, GoI, February 21, 1906, ibid.

82. "Sumit Sarkar, *The Swadeshi Movement in Bengal, 1903–1908*, Bangalore: Permanent Black, 2010.

83. From R. W. Carlyle, Chief Secy, G of EB&A to Secy, Home Dept, GoI, January 25, 1906, ibid.

84. From P. C. Lyon, Chief Secy, G of EB&A to Secy, Home Dept, GoI, February 21, 1906, ibid.

85. Copy of Mr. B. C. Allen's diary, dated 21st April, 1907, in *Hindu-Muhammadan Riots in Mymensingh District in Eastern Bengal and Assam*, Proc A, Home Dept, Political, Nos. 6–16, July 1907, NAI. For a description of the Nangalband fair, including the legend of its origins, see F. D. Bradley-Birt, *The Romance of an Eastern Capital*, London: Smith, Elder, 1906, pp. 297–304.

86. From the *Amrita Bazaar Patrika*, 25th February 1907; reprinted in *Riots at Comilla and Certain Other Places in Tippera District*, Home, Public, Part A, Nos. 159–171, May 1907.

87. Ibid.

88. D. H. Wares, SDO, Brahmanbaria to Collector, Tipperah, 25th March 1907, in ibid.

89. Ibid.

90. Ibid.

91. D. H. Lees, District Magistrate, Tipperah, to Commissioner, Chittagong, in ibid.

92. Reprinted in ibid.

93. Ibid.

94. Confidential Report of R. Nathan, Commissioner of Dacca, 24th April 1907, in ibid.

95. "Enclosure III," in ibid.

96. "Enclosure II: Tour Diary, 22nd to 23rd April, 1907," in ibid.

97. *State of Affairs in Eastern Bengal and Assam and Bengal in connection with the partition and the swadeshi movement*, Home, Public, Part A, Nos. 169–186, June 1906, NAI.

98. Govt of Bengal to the Home Department, Govt of India, 21st January 1918, *Report of the Cases of Looting of Hats in Bengal, Bihar, Orissa and Assam*, Home, Public, Part B, Nos. 184–205, NAI.

99. Govt of Bihar and Orissa to Home Department, Govt of India, 22nd January 1918 and Govt of Assam to Govt of India, 1st February 1918, in ibid.

100. Govt of Bengal to Govt of India, 14th December 1917, in ibid.

101. Govt of Assam to Govt of India, 1st February 1918. Also, Govt of Bengal to Govt of India, 1st February 1918 and Govt of Bihar and Assam to Govt of India, 22nd January 1918, in ibid.

102. Ibid.

103. Govt of Bengal to Govt of India, 1st February 1918, in ibid.

Chapter 3

1. Strictly speaking, as the Hobson-Jobson describes it, the mofussil was a relational term; from the perspective of Calcutta, the delta's small towns were the mofussil, but from those small towns themselves, the surrounding countryside was the mofussil. The Hobson-Jobson definition of the mofussil is "The provinces—the country stations and districts, as contra-distinguished from 'the Presidency'; or, relatively rural localities of district as contra-distinguished from the sudder or chief station, which is the residence of the district authorities." p. 570.

2. Government of India, *Census of India*, 1901, part 6, part 1, pp. 31–33.

3. Government of Bengal, *Reports on the Internal Trade of Bengal*, 1877–80.

4. "Letter from Dr. Peck," *Missionary Magazine*, 34(6), June 1854, p. 164.

5. W. W. Hunter et al., *Imperial Gazetteer of India*, vol. 12, Oxford: Clarendon Press, 1908, p. 279. In 1908, after numerous shifts, Goalundo was located seven miles from its original 1865 location. Further, enormous sums were expended in dredging the Padma near the rail terminus, in an effort to prevent the rivers from displacing excessively.

6. *Reports on the Internal Trade of Bengal for the Year 1876–77*, Calcutta: Government of Bengal, 1877, p. 69. In 1872–73, George Burnett reported that there were two ways to send jute from Sirajganj to Calcutta: "the steamers of the Eastern Bengal Railway, and the rail itself from Goalundo to Calcutta, at six annas per maund, while by native boats it costs three to four annas per maund, but occupies thirty to forty days in transit." George Burnett, *The Jute-Growing Districts and Markets of India with Notes of a Tour, 1872–73* (reprinted from the *Dundee Advertiser*), Dundee, 1873, p. 15.

7. Hemm Chunder Kerr, *Report on the Cultivation of, and Trade in Jute, in Bengal*, London, 1873, p. 59.

8. *Report on the Internal Trade of Bengal for the Year 1879–80*, Calcutta, 1880, p. 63.

9. Hunter et al., *Imperial Gazetteer of India*, vol. 11, p. 367.

10. Hunter et al., *Imperial Gazetteer of India*, vol. 23, p. 17.

11. Hunter et al., *Imperial Gazetteer of India*, vol. 23, p. 373.

12. Hunter et al., *Imperial Gazetteer of India*, vol. 19, p. 301.

13. *Census of India*, 1901, vol. 6, part 1, p. 19.

14. Rumer Godden's 1946 novel *The River*, and Jean Renoir's 1951 film based on it, depicts the social life of a British family in Narayanganj, whose income earner is employed at a jute press.

15. Hunter et al., *Imperial Gazetteer of India*, vol. 18, p. 301.

16. Roy's request for one seat for the Indian commercial community on the municipal board was refused. BLC, vol. XX, no. 3, 1926, p. 112.

17. *Census of India*, 1901, vol. 6, part 1, p. 79. Chandpur was not officially recognized as a town and the census figures did not include the urban population.

18. Quoted in "Assam-Bengal Railway," *Herapath's Railway Journal*, vol. 60, September 9, 1898, p. 935.

19. Quoted in ibid.

20. Hunter et al., *Imperial Gazetteer of India*, vol. 23, p. 384.

21. BLC, vol. III, 1921, p. 321.

22. Webster, *Tippera District Gazetteer*, p. 55. In 1947, after partition, the only hydraulic baling presses in the newly created territory of East Pakistan were in Narayanganj and Chandpur.

23. *Census of India*, 1901, vol. 6, part 1, p. 31.

24. Hunter et al., *Imperial Gazetteer of India*, vol. 23, p. 384.

25. From Narayanganj Chamber of Commerce to Commissioner, Dacca Division, 6th July 1916, in GoB, Agri Dept, September 1916, Proc A, Agri Dept, Agri Branch, List 14, Bundle 30, NAB.

26. "The Jute Trade in Bengal," *Capital*, 6th May 1915, reprinted in GoB, Agri Dept, September 1916, NAB.

27. Burnett, *Jute-Growing Districts*, p. 10.

28. Thomas A. Timberg, *The Marwaris: From Traders to Industrialists*, Delhi: Vikas, 1978, p. 57.

29. In 1915 they were paid twenty-five to thirty rupees per month, according to an article in the *Capital*. "The Jute Trade in Bengal," *Capital*, 6th May 1915, reprinted in GoB, Agri Dept, September 1916, NAB.

30. "A Note by Registrar, Co-operative Societies, Bengal, on Marketing of Agriculture Produce," in *Agriculture and Industries*, Agriculture, March 1927, List 14, Bundle 24, NAB.

31. Collector of Jalpaiguri to Divisional Commissioner, Rajshahi, 20th June 1916, in Agri Dept, Agri Branch, Proc A, List 14, Bundle 30, NAB.

32. Narayanganj Chamber of Commerce to Commissioner, Dacca, 6th July1916, ibid.

33. J. M. Mitra, Registrar, Co-op Societies, Bengal, to Rev. Dept, GoB, 19th July 1916, ibid.

34. N. C. Chaudhuri, *Jute in Bengal*, p. 77.

35. Burnett, *Jute-Growing Districts*, pp. 8–9.

36. "The Jute Trade in Bengal," *Capital*, 6th May 1915, reprinted in GoB, Agri Dept, September 1916, NAB.

37. *Report on the State of Police in the Lower Provinces*, 1882, Calcutta, 1883, p. 4.

38. In 1907 Akhaura was made into a union, the lowest unit of local government. Akhaura Union was more of a village than a small-town institution—its membership was drawn from surrounding villages and the board had no permanent structures in the town. *Report on the Administration of Eastern Bengal and Assam, 1906–07*, Shillong: Eastern Bengal and Assam Secretariat Press, 1908, p. 35.

39. Hunter et al., *Imperial Gazetteer of India*, vol. 12, p. 279.

40. *Report of the Indian Police Commission*, London: 1905, p. 11.

41. David Washbrook, "Law, State and Agrarian Society in Colonial India," *Modern Asian Studies*, 15(3), 1981, p. 677.

42. *Report on the State of the Police in the Lower Provinces of Bengal*, 1882, Calcutta: Bengal Secretariat Press, 1883, p. 6.

43. *Report on the State of the Police in the Lower Provinces of Bengal*, 1884, Calcutta: Bengal Secretariat Press, 1885, pp. 4–5.

44. Crime on Navigable Waterways," Com & Ind, Com & Trade, 10/11, Part B, November 1906, NAI.

45. Messrs. David and Company used a motorboat costing over 100,000 rupees to distribute cash among its out-agencies. P. C. Bramley, District Superintendent of Police (Benares), 1st September 1905, "Crime on Navigable Waterways," Com & Ind, Com & Trade, 10/11, Part B, November 1906, NAI.

46. In 1911 the post-partition government of Eastern Bengal and Assam created a special river police force to patrol the major waterways of Bengal—the highways of the Jamuna, Padma, and Meghna and also smaller rivers like the Gorai, Dhaleswari, Surma, Buriganga, Titas, and Gumti that served as the delta's trade routes. *Constitution of a "general police district" to be controlled by the Eastern Bengal and Assam river police*, Home, Police-A, 181–182, March 1912, NAI. The river police were, however, unsatisfactory and river dacoities continued unabated—between 1912 and 1920, only about twenty-two cases of river dacoities were, on average, annually reported to the river police. BLC, vol. III, 1921, p. 223.

47. E. C. Ryland, October 15, 1906, "Crime on Navigable Waterways," Com & Ind, Com & Trade, 10/11, Part B, November 1906, NAI.

48. Burnett, *Jute-Growing Districts*, p. 16.

49. Ibid., pp. 16–17.

50. From the India Office in London to the Governor General of India in Council, 26/11/1874, *Report drawn up by the Vice-Counsel at Dunkirk on the Jute Trade of that place*, Revenue and Agriculture, Fibres and Silk, January, 1875, Nos. 1/3.

51. "Crop Reports: Notes and Orders, 20th January, 1894, Agricultural Bundle, April 1894, NAB.

52. Report on the extension of Jute Cultivation in India by Mr. R. S. Finlow, Jute Specialist to the Government of Eastern Bengal and Assam, Revenue and Agriculture, Agriculture, January 1907, Proc. A, Agri Dept, Agri Branch, List 14, Bundle 22.

53. The Dundee Chamber of Commerce, the European Jute Association, the American Trade Consul in India, and the Indian Jute Mills Association, in addition to individual businessmen, particularly Marcus Koch in Calcutta, wrote a series of letters to the government urging special measures to increase the cultivation of jute.

54. Peter Robb, "Law and Agrarian Society in India: The Case of Bihar and the Nineteenth Century Tenancy Debate," *Modern Asian Studies*, 22(2), 1988, pp. 319–54.

55. Campbell's note, January 23, 1872, Agriculture Department, GoB, Proc A, Agri Dept, Agri Branch, List 14, Bundle 4, NAB.

56. A. Abercrombie, Commissioner of Dacca, to General Department, GoB, 8th February 1873, Agriculture Department, GoB, Proc A, Agri Dept, Agri Branch, List 14, Bundle 4, NAB.

57. D. R. Lyall, Collector of Dacca, to Commissioner of Dacca, 4th February, 1873, Agriculture Department, GoB, Proc A, Agri Dept, Agri Branch, List 14, Bundle 4, NAB.

58. H.J.S. Cotton, Asst Secy to GoB, to Commissioner of Dacca, 13th February 1873, Agriculture Department, GoB, Proc A, Agri Dept, Agri Branch, List 14, Bundle 4, NAB.

59. The Famine Commission and the much-celebrated Famine Code were the colonial government's response to the devastating famines of the late 1870s and early 1880s in southern and western India. These famines had led to the dominant theme of Indian nationalist thought in the late nineteenth century—the poverty debate. In the nationalist framing of the debate, the very legitimacy of empire rested on the question: Had British rule impoverished India?

60. GoB to GoI, proposing the establishment of an Agriculture Dept in Bengal, 1st June 1883; in Agriculture Department, May 1885, GoB, Proc A, Agri Dept, Agri Branch, List 14, Bundle 9, NAB.

61. Ibid.

62. C. S. Bayley, Under-Secy, GoI, to Secy, GoB, 9th June 1886, GoB, Proc A, Agri Dept, Agri Branch, List 14, Bundle 9, NAB.

63. P. Nolan, Offg Secy to GoB, to Rev and Agri Dept, GoI, 1st December 1886, GoB, Proc A, Agri Dept, Agri Branch, List 14, Bundle 9, NAB.

64. "Notes and Orders," T.W.R., 14th February, 1894, GoB, Agri Dept, Agri Branch, List 14, Bundle 14, NAB.

65. Forecasts issued by the Government of Bengal of the jute crop of 1903, Revenue and Agriculture, Agriculture, 10–13, Part A, 1904, NAI.

66. Dundee Chamber of Commerce to Dept of Rev & Agri, GoI, October 19th, 1903, ibid.

67. Proceedings of a meeting held on the 28th November to discuss various questions affecting the jute trade, Agriculture Dept, GoB, March, 1914, Proc. A, Agri Dept, List 14, Bundle 27, NAB.

68. E.C. Buck, Secy to GoI, to Secy, Rev & Agri Dept, GoB, 15th July 1885, Proc A, Agri Dept, Agri Branch, List 14, Bundle 9, NAB.

69. Creation of the post of a specialist in jute and indigo for the Bengal Agriculture Department and the appointment to it of Mr. R.S. Finlow, Revenue and Agriculture, Agriculture, 1–5, Part A, August 1905, NAI.

70. US Department of Commerce and Labor, *Monthly Consular and Trade Reports*, May 1907, p. 209.

71. H. M. Haywood, Secretary, IJMA, to Secy, Rev Dept., GoB, 25th September 1913, Proc. A, Agri Dept, Agri Branch, List 14, Bundle 27, NAB.

72. Report on the extension of Jute Cultivation in India by Mr. R.S. Finlow, Jute specialist to the Government of Eastern Bengal and Assam, Revenue and Agriculture, Agriculture, 14–16, Part A, January 1907, NAI.

73. Ibid.

74. "Suggestions made by Robert S. Finlow, Fibre Expert, for increasing the output of Jute from India," 20th January 1914, Agriculture Department, June 1914, Proc A, Agri Dept, Agri Branch, List 14, Bundle 28, NAB.

75. The details of jute sales and the government's agreement with the London Jute Association are from a speech in the Legislative Council by Azizul Huque in March 1930. Huque accuses the department of acting in the interests of foreign capital to increase jute output and lower its price. BLC, vol. XXXIV, no. 3, 1930, pp. 558–59.

76. The idea that Chittagong was a natural outlet for the delta's produce had been floated since the 1870s, and was premised on the north-to-south flow of the Brahmaputra and the Meghna, and the easier river route from Narayanganj to Chittagong.

77. David Ludden and Iftekhar Iqbal have made important arguments about the colonial state's territorial and economic motivations in the partition of Bengal that question the focus on partition as a cynical divide-and-rule policy. See David Ludden, "Spatial Inequity and National Territory: Remapping 1905 in Bengal and Assam," *Modern Asian Studies*, 46(3), 2012, pp. 483–525, and Iftekhar Iqbal, "The Space between Nation and Empire: The Making and Unmaking of Eastern Bengal and Assam Province, 1905–1911," *Journal of Asian Studies*, 74(1), 2015, pp. 69–84.

78. The petitioners' attitudes toward Assam are telling of Bengali cultural chauvinism. As Rajanikanta Ray from Iswargunge wrote in a petition dated January 14, 1904, "being associated with the Assamese, who are savages . . . we shall be subjected to endless miseries by their evil company." Petition from the residents of certain districts of Eastern Bengal protesting against the proposed partition of Bengal, Home Public, 193/215 part B, April, 1904.

79. Petitioners from Noakhali, n.d., ibid.

80. Mahim Chadra Bhaumik, Gayhata, Mymensingh, January 17, 1904, ibid.

81. "Report on the Agitation against the Partition of Bengal," 17th December, 1903, in *State of Affairs in Eastern Bengal and Assam and Bengal in connection with the partition and the swadeshi movement*, Home, Public, Part A, Nos. 169–186, June 1906, NAI.

82. Petition from the residents of certain districts of Eastern Bengal protesting against the proposed partition of Bengal, Home Public, 193/215 part B, April 1904, NAI.

83. From the IJMA to the BCC, January 29th, 1904, Representation from the Bengal Chamber of Commerce and the European and Ango-Indian Defence Association regarding

the jurisdiction of the High Court, Calcutta over the new Province of Eastern Bengal and Assam, Home, Public, Part A, Nos. 19–23, October 1905, NAI.

84. From the BCC to the Judicial Dept, GoB, March 19th, 1904, in Representation from the Bengal Chamber of Commerce and the European and Ango-Indian Defence Association regarding the jurisdiction of the High Court, Calcutta over the new Province of Eastern Bengal and Assam, Home, Public, Part A, Nos. 19–23, October 1905, NAI.

85. From the BCC to the Judicial Dept, GoB, March 19th, 1904, ibid.

86. "Report on the Agitation against the Partition of Bengal," February 8, 1906, in *State of Affairs in Eastern Bengal and Assam and Bengal in connection with the partition and the swadeshi movement*, Home, Public, Part A, Nos. 169–186, June 1906.

87. During the Non-Cooperation/Khilafat movement, Gandhi undertook much more extensive whistlestop tours on railways across the length and breadth of India, firmly establishing the space of the mofussil as a meeting point of metropolitan anticolonial nationalism and peasant politics. See Shahid Amin, "Gandhi as Mahatma: Gorakhpur District, Eastern UP, 1921–22," *Subaltern Studies III*, Delhi: Oxford University Press, 1984, pp. 1–61.

88. Nolini Kanta Gupta, *Smritir Pata*, cited in Rishabchand, *Sri Aurobindo: His Life Unique*, Pondicherry: Sri Aurobindo Ashram, 1981, p. 328.

89. Statement of the Inspector General of Police, January 12, 1905, in *State of Affairs in Eastern Bengal and Assam and Bengal in connection with the partition and the swadeshi movement*, Home, Public, Part A, Nos. 169–186, June 1906, emphasis added.

90. Tour Diary of Mr. L. C. Clarke, Magistrate Collector of Mymensingh, April-May 1907, in *Hindu-Muhammadan Riots in Mymensingh District in Eastern Bengal and Assam*, Proc-A, Home Dept, Political, Nos. 6–16, July 1907, NAI.

91. Statement of the Inspector General of Police, January 12, 1905, in *State of Affairs in Eastern Bengal and Assam and Bengal in connection with the partition and the swadeshi movement*, Home, Public, Part A, Nos. 169–186, June 1906.

92. Copy of Mr. B. C. Allen's diary, dated 21st April, 1907, in *Hindu-Muhammadan Riots in Mymensingh District in Eastern Bengal and Assam*, Proc-A, Home Dept, Political, Nos. 6–16, July 1907, NAI.

93. *Census of India*, 1901, vol. 6, part 1, p. 71.

94. R. Nathan, Collector of Dacca, 24th April, 1907, in *Hindu-Muhammadan Riots in Mymensingh District in Eastern Bengal and Assam*, Proc-A, Home Dept, Political, Nos. 6–16, July 1907, NAI.

95. M. A. Luffman, Officiating Superintendent of Police, to District Magistrate, Mymensingh, 2nd May 1907, in *Hindu-Muhammadan Riots in Mymensingh District in Eastern Bengal and Assam*, Proc-A, Home Dept, Political, Nos. 6–16, July 1907, NAI.

96. R. Nathan, Commissioner, Dacca Division, to LeMesurier, Chief Secy, GoEB, 2nd May, 1907, in *Hindu-Muhammadan Riots in Mymensingh District in Eastern Bengal and Assam*, Proc-A, Home Dept, Political, Nos. 6–16, July 1907, NAI.

97. "Mr. Garlick's report, Mymensingh, April 29th," in *Hindu-Muhammadan Riots in Mymensingh District in Eastern Bengal and Assam*, Proc-A, Home Dept, Political, Nos. 6–16, July 1907, NAI.

98. Ibid., p. 44.

99. *Karmayogin*, no. 27, January 8, 1910.

Chapter 4

1. "Adha mora kore chhara lengti obotar / pete bhat mile na lengti tena osthhi chormo shar," Nagendrakumar De, *Bogra'r Kahini*, Bogra, 1927, p. 3.

2. A. C. Hartley, *Final Report of the Rangpur Survey and Settlement Operations, 1931–1938*, Calcutta: Bengal Government Press, 1940, p. 4, emphasis added.

3. F. A. Sachse, *Final Report on the Survey and Settlement Operations in the District of Mymensingh, 1910–1919*, Calcutta: Bengal Secretariat Book Depot, 1920 p. 25.

4. D. MacPherson, *Final Report on the Survey and Settlement Operations in the Districts of Pabna and Bogra, 1920 to 1929*, Calcutta: Bengal Secretariat Book Depot, 1930, p. 35.

5. BLC, vol. I, no. 2, 1920, p. 188.

6. MacPherson, Pabna and Bogra SSR, p. 35.

7. MacPherson, Pabna and Bogra SSR, p. 38.

8. Tarit Bhushan Roy stated in the Legislative Council that "the prevailing prices of *balam* and *dakshini* rice [local varieties beyond the reach of poor peasants] are universally higher than what they were at season time in the last 12 years." BLC vol. I, no. 1, 1920, p. 29.

9. BLC, vol. I, no. 2, 1920, p. 184.

10. BLC, vol. I, no. 2, 1920, p. 206.

11. BPBEC, vol. II, part I, p. 346.

12. BPBEC, vol. II, part I, p. 210.

13. BPBEC, vol. II, part I, p. 396.

14. BPBEC, vol. II, part I, p. 398.

15. Iftekhar Iqbal, *The Bengal Delta: Ecology, State, and Social Change*, Basingstoke: Palgrave Macmillan, 2010.

16. W. M. Thompson, *Final Report on the Survey and Settlement Operations in the District of Tippera, 1915 to 1919*, Calcutta: Bengal Secretariat Book Depot, p. 37.

17. Tippera SSR, p. 7.

18. Ihtesham Kazi, *A Historical Study of Malaria in Bengal, 1860–1920*, Dhaka: Pip International Publications, 2004, pp. 154–57.

19. Annual Report of the Sanitary Commissioner for Bengal for the Year 1922, Calcutta, 1923, p. 61, cited in Ihtesham Kazi, *A Historical Study of Malaria in Bengal, 1860–1920*, Dhaka: Pip International Publications, 2004, p. 132.

20. BLC, vol. X, 1922, p. 51.

21. BLC, vol. XX, 1926, p. 211.

22. BLC, vol. XXXIV, Calcutta, 1930, p. 192.

23. BPBEC, vol. I, pp. 73–74. This is an important statement because of a widely held opinion that indebtedness was due to peasant profligacy rather than the broader structure of the agrarian economy that was rigged against marginal peasant producers.

24. Report of the Royal Commission on Indian Agriculture, 1926, vol. IV, p. 558.

25. BPBEC, vol. II, part I, p. 217.

26. BPBEC, vol. II, part I, Evidence of Bhabesh Chandra Roy, SDO, Naogaon, p. 187; Evidence of Umesh Chandra Chakladar, Vice-Chairman, Mymensingh District Board, p. 282.

27. "Kono kono mahajan shujog bujhia / shudder harta adhik diye chhebariya. . . . Desher je shomost oachhe mahajan / Krishaker rokto shob korichhe shoshon." Md. Khayer Ali, *Bonya Kahini*, Calcutta, 1922.

28. BPBEC, vol. II, p. 237.

29. BPBEC, vol. II, p. 534.

30. Omkar Goswami, *Industry, Trade and Peasant Society: The Jute Economy of Eastern Bengal*, New Delhi: Oxford University Press, 1991, pp. 153–54.

31. *Season and Crop Report of Bengal for the Year 1930–31*, Calcutta: Bengal Secretariat Book Depot, 1931, p. 3.

32. Omkar, Goswami, "Agriculture in Slump: The Peasant Economy of East and North Bengal in the 1930s," *Indian Economic and Social History Review*, 21, 1984, p. 351.

33. A. C. Hartley, *Final Report of the Rangpur Survey and Settlement Operations, 1931–1938*, Calcutta: Bengal Government Press, 1940, pp. 20–22.

34. Final Report on the relief operations in the Brahmanbaria Subdivision of the district of Tippera, File No. L.R. 11-R-25(1), Nos. 1–2, Revenue Department Proceedings, 1931, IOR/P/11949, IOR.

35. *Proceedings of the Bengal Legislative Council*, vol. XXXIV, no. 2, Calcutta, 1930, p. 67. The Government's response was intended to justify not declaring the floods a famine, thus preventing any expenditure on famine relief in the district.

36. Final Report on the Floods and Distress in the District of Bogra, File No. L.R. 11-R-35(1), Nos. 12–13, Revenue Department Proceedings, 1931, IOR/P/11949.

37. Sugata Bose, "The Roots of 'Communal' Violence in Rural Bengal: A Study of the Kishoreganj Riots, 1930," *Modern Asian Studies*, 16(3), 1982, pp. 463–91.

38. Quoted in Goswami, "Agriculture in Slump," p. 353; see particularly table 9.

39. Famine Inquiry Commission, *Report on Bengal*, New Delhi: Government of India, 1945, pp. 28 and 40.

40. Amartya Sen puts the figure at 2.7 to 3 million and Paul Greenough at between 3.2 and 3.8 million.

41. Paul Greenough has argued that peasant households sometimes chose to let women and the elderly in their household die, with the idea that the surviving younger male members of the household would lead the post-famine recovery.

42. P. C. Mahalanobis, "A Sample Survey of After-Effects of the Bengal Famine of 1943," *Sankhya: The Indian Journal of Statistics*, 7(4), 1946, p. 339.

Chapter 5

1. *Karmayogin*, no. 27, January 8, 1910.

2. Rajat Ray details the course of peasant action during the movement, identifying the moment the movement goes out of the control of Congress political elites, in "Masses in Politics: The Non-Cooperation Movement in Bengal, 1920–2," *Indian Economic and Social History Review*, 11(4), 1974, pp. 343–410. Ranajit Guha provides an analytical model to think about political elites' concerns about undisciplined peasant politics in *Dominance without Hegemony: History and Power in Colonial India*, Cambridge, MA: Harvard University Press, 1997, particularly chap. 2.

3. During 1920 and 1921, the terms of trade between jute and rice had doubled in favor of rice in comparison with prewar levels. With 1914 prices as a base, the terms of trade between jute and rice fell to 0.63 in 1920 and to 0.58 in 1921 and then rose in 1922 to 0.88. It must be emphasized that the improvement in 1922 did not restore the ratio of prices to prewar levels.

4. P. C. Bamford, *Histories of the Non-Co-Operation and Khilafat Movements*, Delhi: Government of India Press, pp. 59–60.

5. Shahid Amin's careful study of peasant perceptions of Gandhi as Mahatma in Gorakhpur in northern India effectively fills in Bamford's notion of a hollow economic determinism. Amin shows how peasants in the United Provinces' sugar tracts translated Gandhi into a deity envisioned as endowed with super powers relevant to an agrarian society. Gandhi's promise of swaraj was also important among the delta's mostly Muslim jute cultivators, though they did not necessarily perceive Gandhi as a powerful deity. Shahid Amin, "Gandhi as Mahatma: Gorakhpur District, Eastern UP, 1921–22," *Subaltern Studies III*, Delhi: Oxford University Press, 1984, pp. 1–61.

6. Abul Mansur Ahmed, *Amar Dekha Rajnitir Panchash Bochhor*, Dhaka: Srijan, 1989, p. 23.

7. Nirad C. Chaudhuri, *Thy Hand Great Anarch!, India 1921–1952*, Reading, MA: Addison-Wesley, 1987, p. 37.

8. Tamizuddin Khan, *Test of Time: My Life and Days*, Dhaka: University Press, p. 75.

9. Khan, *Test of Time*, p. 97.

10. Quoted in Ray, "Masses in Politics," p. 363.

11. Khan, *Test of Time*, p. 101.

12. H. E. Spry, *Report on the Work of the Reforms Office*, Calcutta: Bengal Secretariat Press, 1921, p. 9.

13. The government noted, "The boycott of foreign goods was given a temporary impulse and there were some bonfires of foreign cloth, but it was not popular." Government of Bengal, *Report on the Administration of Bengal, 1920/1*, p. iii. Viceroy's weekly telegram from December 1921, during the height of Khilafat, stated: "Boycott of foreign cloth has lost much of its original attraction." Viceroy, Home Department to Secretary of State for India, December 6, 1921, IOR/L/PJ/6/1789, File 727: Feb 1922–Feb 1923, IOR.

14. Ray, "Masses in Politics," p. 371.

15. Khan, *Test of Time*, pp. 107–19.

16. Ray, "Masses in Politics," p. 382.

17. Ray, "Masses in Politics," p. 371.

18. Assault on Mr. McPherson, ICS, Assistant Settlement Officer, Pabna-Bogra, 1st November 1921, 17th November 1921, IOR/L/PJ/6/1775, File 6943: Nov 1921–Jan 1922, IOR.

19. Ray, "Masses in Politics," pp. 400–401, IOR/L/PJ/6/1803, File 2393: Apr–May 1922, IOR.

20. File 147—Report of an attack on the police at Nilphamari, Rungpur District, Bengal, IOR/L/PJ/6/1786, File 147: Jan 1922, IOR.

21. Government of Bengal, *Report on the Administration of Bengal*, Calcutta, 1921–22.

22. Gandhi brought a halt to the movement after a group of peasants in Chauri Chaura in northern India set fire to a police station and burned to death the twenty-one policemen trapped inside. In a move typical to Gandhian nationalism, control over subaltern protests was more important than the ability to shut down colonial power. See Shahid Amin, *Event,*

Metaphor, Memory: Chauri Chaura, 1922–1992, Berkeley: University of California Press, 1995, and Guha, *Dominance without Hegemony*.

23. Ray, "Masses in Politics," p. 404.

24. Abul Mansur Ahmed, *Amar Dekha Rajnitir Panchash Bochhor*, pp. 28–29.

25. The first quote refers to resistance to survey and settlement officers in Bogra in November 1921. MacPherson, Pabna and Bogra SSR, pp. 93–94. The second quote is from the viceroy's confidential updates on the movement to the secretary of state for India in London, on February 10, 1922, IOR/L/PJ/6/1789, File 727: Feb 1922–Feb 1923, IOR, BL.

26. MacPherson, Pabna and Bogra SSR, p. 93.

27. Ibid., p. 24.

28. This is Nirad Chaudhuri's translation. The original was: "Ke phukichhe singa, / Kon tunga sringe, / Emana marma bhediye." *Thy Hand Great Anarch*, p. 12.

29. A collection of Ruhani's Khilafat and Non-Cooperation poems, *Ruhani Shongit Mala*, was published in 1924 in Dhaka.

30. In urban areas in north Bengal, which includes among others, Rangpur, Bogra, and Pabna, there were 579 Hindus per square mile and 367 Muslims. In urban areas of Dacca Divison, which includes the larger city of Dacca, and the smaller towns such as Mymensingh, Jamalpur, Kishoreganj, Faridpur, and Madaripur, there were 562 Hindus versus 427 Muslims per square mile. And in Chittagong Division, including Noakhali, Comilla, Chandpur, and Brahmanbaria as well as the secondary port city of Chittagong, there were 502 versus 459 Muslims per square mile. Additionally, the towns of Comilla, Kishoreganj, Jamalpur, and Sherpur had Muslim majorities. *Census of India*, 1921, vol. 6, *Bengal*, p. 117.

31. The Census Report of 1921 noted "the difficulties of obtaining accommodation in towns especially by Muhammadans, for the landlords are commonly Hindus who object to a Muhammadan tenant." *Census of India*, 1921, vol. 6, p. 113.

32. The Census report of 1921 stated: "The number of men who are able to find employment in towns whether professionally in the law, in medicine, and in the lower grades of administrative service, or as shopkeepers and servants, has increased. The male population of the average country town has increased, but an increasing proportion leaves its women-folk behind in the country. . . . Town life is not the normal life of any section of Bengalis. They dislike it and do not seem to get over their dislike. The pleader, the clerk, the schoolmaster and the shopkeeper whose work is in the town each has a house of his own or belonging to his family somewhere in the country. There his family can live far more cheaply than in the town and the practice of keeping up two establishments seems to be on the increase." *Census of India*, 1921, vol. 6, p. 113.

33. The catalogues of the Vernacular Tracts Collection at the British Library lists thirty-two books published in Noakhali during the 1920s. The Noakhali presses were the Noakhali Press and the Noakhali Mill Press, the latter of which was owned by a businessman who owned an oil-pressing mill. These presses produced the following newspapers: the *Desher-Bani* (circulation of 500), the *Noakhali Sammilani* (circulation of 200), and the *Tanzeem* (circulation of 300). The two Faridpur presses, the Ambica and Kamala presses, produced three newspapers—the *Kangal* (circulation 750), *Krishi Katha* (circulation 700), and the *Chikandi Hitaishini* (circulation 200). Among the small towns of eastern Bengal, more books were published in Mymensingh during the 1920s than anywhere else—the Vernacular Tracts Collection catalogue lists over 70 original texts published in Mymensingh in this period. The

main Mymensingh newspaper, the *CharuMihir*, is the only *mofussil* paper with a circulation of over 1,000. *Statement of Newspapers and Periodicals Published in Bengal, revised up to 31st December, 1926*, IOR/L/PJ/6/1762, File 4929, IOR.

34. Ashrafuddin Ahmed, *Moslem Bani*, Tipperah, 1927, p. 1.

35. *Statement of Newspapers and Periodicals Published in Bengal, revised up to 31st December, 1926*, IOR/L/PJ/6/1762, File 4929, IOR.

36. Government of Bengal, *Report on the Working of the Reformed Constitution in Bengal, 1921–27*, part I, Calcutta: Bengal Secretariat Book Depot, 1929, p. 8.

37. Shah Abdul Hamid, *Krishak Bilap*, Mymensingh, 1922.

38. Abul Hossain, *Banglar Bolshi*, Dacca, 1926. At the time of publication of this pamphlet, Abul Hussain was a lecturer at Dacca University but the essays in the book were written in the early 1920s when he was still a student. Fazlul Karim was a landlord in Dacca, who had purchased the estate of Haturia—sixty miles from Dacca city—in 1919.

39. "Shuno bhai Mussalman ek hakikat / Mussalmaner shob kam ebadat. / Babsha, banijya, adi karbar / Ebadat bina kichhu nahi aar." Abdul Aziz, *Najat*, Noakhali, 1922, p. 2.

40. My emphasis on the production and circulation of printed agrarian Islamic texts is indebted to Nile Green's analytical model of a "religious economy" in the western Indian Ocean world. Nile Green, *Bombay Islam: The Religious Economy of the West Indian Ocean, 1840–1915*, Cambridge: Cambridge University Press, 2011.

41. Hamid, *Krishak Bilap*, p. ii.

42. Hai, *Adarsho Krishak*, p. 33.

43. Hai, *Adarsha Krishak*, p. 46.

44. "Mussalman goney aaj dekhiya / Hai Hai bukta jai fatiya," Aziz, *Najat*, p. 1.

45. "Kobita shuru kori paye dhori kandi koi / Bangali hoiya mora koto dukkho shoi." Hafez Ashrafuddin Ahmed, *Muslim Bani*, Comilla, 1927–28, p. 1.

46. "Ei jomanar loker astha dekhiya / Osthir hoinu dil gelo ghabriya / Khaite na pay mana bostro na gay / Dinek dui din onahare jay." Md. Akram Ali, *Keno Lok Gorib Hoy*, Comilla, 1917–18, p. 1

47. Abdur Rahim, *Nur-ul-Islam*, Dhaka, 1924 (2nd ed.), p. 2.

48. Pradip Datta, *Carving Blocs: Communal Ideology in Early Twentieth Century Bengal*, Delhi: Oxford University Press, 1999 and Asim Roy, *The Islamic Syncretistic Tradition in Bengal*, Princeton, NJ: Princeton University Press, 1983.

49. "Behuda khoroch jeba korilo / Shoitaner bhai shei hoilo," Aziz, *Najat*, p. 13.

50. Ashrafuddin Ahmed, *Muslim Bani*, p. 11.

51. "Mathhay Albat rakha kemon baka mali'r chhat / Albatey toilo dite toilor porlo bat / Deshey napiter kachhay nahi boshey aar / Shohore dui anna diye chhatay baha bahar." Ashrafuddin Ahmed, *Muslim Bani*, p. 7.

52. "Hindu ukil babu pailey babu pondo mari debo koshi / Nijer chhela murkho shala naila niray boshi." Ibid., p. 8.

53. "Je jati babsha banijyo chharilo / Duniya akherey tara dubilo." Aziz, *Najat*, p. 21.

54. "Korite nahok lojja halal kam / Jei kore ghrina shei beiman." Ibid., p. 21.

55. "Dekho bhinno jati babosha koriya / Amaderi taka nei lutiya / Ei baboshar jorey tahara / Holo probhu, deen honu amra." Aziz, *Najat*, p. 20.

56. Lakshmi is the Hindu goddess of wealth. Muslim texts in the Bengal delta often referred to Hindu gods, goddesses, and festivals, evidence against Asim Roy's and Pradip Datta's

arguments that Bengali Muslim thought in the 1920s and 1930s was about purifying Islam and removing the taint of syncretism. The original lines in transliterated Bengali are below:

"Bilat hoite dekho shetango shokol / Baboshar jorey korey Bharat dokhol / Aar dekho Bikaneri Marwari eshey / Banglar dhon rotno shob loy chushey / Pohela loiya ashey dhuti o kombol / Tarpor korey koto bishal shombol / Babshar jal petey Marwarigon / Rokto mangsho shushe loy nashiya jibon / Rokto shosha kaj shudhu ihaderi bhai / Obojh Bangali mora dishe nahi pai / Takar karoney mora kaka bole daki / Babu bole salam kori mathha niche rakhi / Tader nikote thaki jor hatey mora / Bujhe dekho kishe mora hoi Lakshmi chhara." Asghar Hussain, *Hok Kotha*, Sirajganj, 1933, p. 9.

57. "Koshtar majhete bhai shudhu dekhi churi / Kheyal koriya bujho joto noro nari." Asghar Hussain, *Hok Kotha*, p. 19.

58. "Shokol chizer dor prokashiya bole / Paat becha kaley haat kaporer toley / Paat becha shesh holey dey torey roka / Bichar koriya dekho tumi koto boka." Asghar Hussain, *Hok Kotha*, p. 50.

59. "Prithibitey hoy beshi murgi aar hash / Ei dui cheez kore dhormo-kormo nash." Asghar Hussain, *Hok Kotha*, p. 24.

60. "Iaha shuney dokandar shemanatey boshey / Tarpor aorotera dim liya ashey / Eshe tara dekho bhai kiba kam korey / Char poyshar dimey chay der poysha dam / Dokandar taha shuney poyshay dui koy / Nari lokey boley tobey na dibo tomay / Akherey she dokandar hoye gelo raji / Dim guney dey tarey joto nari paji." Asghar Hussain, *Hok Kotha*, p. 25.

61. "Daladali chacha o bhatija koto kore maramari / Mamu o bhaginar koto hobe foujdari." Abdur Rahim, *Nur-ul-Islam*, p. 12.

Chapter 6

1. Figures for the number of people on the voter rolls are from H. E. Spry, *Report on the Work of the Reforms Office*, Calcutta: Bengal Secretariat Press, 1921. In order to calculate proportions, I have taken population figures from the *Census of India*, 1921, p. 29.

2. Hamid contested and lost the 1923 elections from the Mymensingh East (Muhammadan) Rural constituency. He contested elections again in 1929 when he won. In 1937 Hamid was the Krishak Praja Party's candidate in Kishoreganj East, a newly created constituency under the Government of India Act of 1935, when he won by a thumping margin, gaining 44.5 percent of the vote against the 17.4 percent of his nearest rival.

3. I have discussed an earlier pamphlet *Krishak Bilap* (Peasant Lament) in chapters 1 and 5.

4. Shah Abdul Hamid, *Shashon Shongskarey Gramyo Mussalman*, Mymensingh, 1921, pp. 32–33.

5. This important phrase, the implicit and explicit assumption that Muslims and peasants were interchangeable, is written in Bengali as follows: "Karon gramik mussalman bolitey shadaronoto amra gramyo mussalman krishak shomprodaykei bujhi." Hamid, *Shashon Shongskarey*, p. 25.

6. Hamid, *Shashon Shongskarey*, p. 25.

7. Hamid, *Shashon Shongskarey*, p. 28.

8. Hamid, *Shashon Shongskarey*, p. 3, emphasis added.

9. Hamid, *Shashon Shongskarey*, p. 10.

10. "Thhak amader mota bhat / Ail badha khet / Thhak amader haler lathi / Chai na chikon bet / Thhak amader mara mach / Puran beeler koi / Thhak amaader haaler goru / Bokna gaiyer doi / Thhak amader shada tohbond / Mathhay shada tupi / Chai na mora hat-coat-boot / Khash bilater V.P. / Chai na mora chalak hotey / Chaiko shorol mon / Jani bhondarmir shob chhai bhoshmo / Iman porom dhon." Hamid, *Shashon Shongskarey*, p. 11.

11. S. N. Roy, *Report on the General Election of 1923 in Bengal*, Calcutta: Bengal Government Press, 1925.

12. Khan, *Test of Time*, p. 74.

13. Khan polled 73 percent of the 7,900 votes cast in the Faridpur North (Muhammadan) Rural constituency. O. M. Martin, *Report on the General Elections of 1926 in Bengal*, Calcutta: Bengal Government Press, 1927.

14. BLC, vol. XXV, no. 2, 1927, p. 72.

15. BLC, vol. I, no. 1, 1920, p. 117.

16. Ibid., p. 121.

17. Ibid., p. 122.

18. Ibid., p. 126.

19. Partha Chatterjee, "Agrarian Relations and Politics in Bengal: Some Considerations on the Making of the Tenancy Act Amendment 1928," Occasional Paper 30, Centre for Studies in Social Sciences, Calcutta, 1980.

20. BLC, vol. XVIII, no. 2, 1928. Abul Mansur Ahmed wrote in his autobiography that the tenancy debates of 1926 proved, once and for all, that rural Muslims could not depend on the Hindu-dominated Congress Party for pro-peasant economic reforms.

21. Addresses presented to his Excellency at Faridpur and his Excellency's reply to them, File No. L. 4-A-1(1), Bengal Proceedings, Local Self-Government, Local Boards, 1923, IOR/P/11303.

22. "Resolution on the Working of District Boards During 1925–26," File No. L. 1-R-6(1), in Bengal Proceedings: Local Self-Government, Local Boards, 1927 IOR/P/11637.

23. Frank Bell, *Record of Life in the Indian Civil Service*, unpublished memoir, p. 21, in MSS/EUR D. 733/21, IOR.

24. "Review showing the progress made in the creation of union boards," File No. L. 2-U-44(1), Bengal Proceedings, Local Self-Government, Local Boards, 1923, IOR/P/11303.

25. Babu Daksina Charan Sen and others, rate-payers of the Brahmanbaria Municipality, to the Secretary, Local Self-Government, through the District Magistrate, Tippera, March 3, 1925, Bengal Proceedings, Local Self-Government, Local Boards, 1925, IOR/P/11499.

26. Division of the Jamalpur Municipality into Wards and Reallotment of the Elected Seats to Different Wards, File No. M. 1-M-7(1), December 1925, Bengal Proceedings, Local Self-Government, Local Boards, 1925, IOR/P/11499.

27. From District Magistrate Mymensingh to Commissioner, Rajshahi, 25th September 1922, in Bengal Proceedings, Local Self-Government, Local Boards, 1925 IOR/P/11499.

28. Partha Chatterjee, "Agrarian Relations and Communalism in Bengal, 1926–1935," in *Subaltern Studies: Writings on South Asian History and Society*, ed. Ranajit Guha, vol. 1, Delhi, Oxford University Press, 1982, pp. 9–38.

29. Wasimuddin Ahmed received two hundred votes less than the winner Abdul Ghafur, or 46 percent of the vote as against Ghafur's 52 percent. S. N. Roy, *Report on the General Election of 1923 in Bengal*, Calcutta: Bengal Government Press, 1924.

30. "Election of the Chairman of the Pabna District Board," Bengal Proceedings, Local Self-Government, Local Boards, 1926, IOR/P/11569.

31. "Judgment: Lalon C. Sarkar versus Basir Shaikh, Mojir Shaikh, Nasim Khan alias Lachman Khan," IOR/L/PJ/6/1925, File 2116, IOR.

32. "Judgment: Lalon C. Sarkar versus Basir Shaikh, Mojir Shaikh, Nasim Khan alias Lachman Khan," IOR/L/PJ/6/1925, File 2116, IOR.

33. "The Judgment on Emperor versus Jaynal Abedin and 21 others," IOR/L/PJ/6/1925, File 2116, IOR.

34. "Judgment: Binode Gobinda Sutradhar versus Patu Khan and Meser Molla," IOR/L/PJ/6/1925, File 2116, IOR.

35. Nasiruddin Ahmed, *Report on the Pabna Disturbances*, Calcutta: Government of Bengal Press, 1926, p. 9, emphasis added.

36. The judgment delivered at the Pabna Sessions Judge Court, overturning Judge S. N. Guha's decision, criticized the judgment. IOR/L/PJ/6/1925, File 2116, IOR.

37. In memoranda to the Simon Commission, mofussil and metropolitan Bengali Muslim politicians used the example of biased Hindu judges during the Pabna trials to ask for "constitutional safeguards"—that is, greater communal representation. A memorandum supported by the various district-level Anjuman-e-Islamias in the delta criticized the Pabna sessions judge for an "extraordinary judgment" and S. C. Ghosh, a Calcutta District Court judge, because he "treated the Hindus with a consideration not usually shown to any accused." S. C. Ghosh was removed from hearing the appeal on the trial of Lahiry and others for the violence against Khalifapatti mosque. Nurul Haq, Memorandum, in IOR/Q/13/1/2: Indian Statutory Commission, Memoranda, Bengal 16–615.

38. Sugata Bose, "The Roots of 'Communal' Violence in Rural Bengal: A Study of the Kishoreganj Riots, 1930," *Modern Asian Studies*, 16(3), 1982, pp. 463–91.

39. Maulana Bhashani would go on to assume considerable significance as a peasant populist leader in postcolonial East Pakistan, where his socialist ideology earned him the title of the Red Maulana. Frank O. Bell recalls attending a praja conference presided over by Maulana Bhashani when he was the subdivisional officer at Tangail. He said that "he was not aware of anything untoward being said" at the meeting and that "opposition to payment of abwabs or extras on the rent was perfectly legal for such charges were themselves illegal and their payment should be discountenanced by the SDO." However, Bell's superiors admonished him and asked him to be wary, as Abdul Hamid Khan had the "ability to raise subscriptions." Bell, *Record of Life in the Indian Civil Service*, unpublished memoir, p. 22, in MSS/EUR D, 733/21, IOR.

40. Humaira Momen, *Muslim Politics in Bengal: A Study of the Krishak Praja Party and the Elections of 1937*, Dacca: Sunny House, 1972, p. 41.

41. Bengal Local Government's Fortnightly Report, First Half of March, 1932. The Fortnightly Report for the second half of May reported on local colonial bureaucrats' attempts to maintain control over local krishak samitis. IOR: L/PJ/12/686.

42. Momen, *Muslim Politics in Bengal*, p. 42.

43. Cited in Momen, *Muslim Politics in Bengal*, p. 50.

44. Cited in Momen, *Muslim Politics in Bengal*, p. 58.

45. *Calcutta Gazette*, Extraordinary, January 22, 1938, p. 14. Habibur Rahman filed a petition against Faroqui alleging various electoral irregularities: using government staff in his campaign,

forging A. K. Fazlul Haq's signature on a statement that Habibur Rahman was not a Krishak Praja candidate, and—on the basis of the pamphlet quoted above—"exercising undue spiritual influence." Rahman's petition was upheld, and Faroqui's victory in the election overturned.

46. R. N. Gilchrist, *Report of the Reforms Office, Bengal, 1932–1937*, Alipore: Bengal Government Press, 1938, p. 23.

47. Ibid., p. 23.

48. Humayun Kabir was perhaps the most urbane and Calcutta-centric KPP candidate, whereas Tamizuddin Khan had strong roots in his constituency and in social background resembled KPP candidates in other constituencies.

49. Council Debates, BLC, Sitting of both Chambers of the Legislature, vol. II, 1937, p. 184.

50. See Bose, *Agrarian Bengal*, chaps. 4 and 5.

51. Council Debates, BLC, Sitting of both Chambers of the Legislature, vol. II, 1937, p. 184.

52. Quoted in Donald Stewart, *Jute and Empire: Calcutta Jutewallahs and the Landscapes of Empire*, Manchester: Manchester University Press, 1998, p. 120. Donald Stewart also argued that certain ministers in the coalition held shares in the jute industry and bent over backward to assist the metropolitan jute industry. The primary villains in Stewart's account were Nalini Ranjan Sarkar, the finance minister, who held "substantial shares" and H. S. Suhrawardy, the commerce and labor minister, who took IJMA funds to support pro-employee unions "against the activities of the 'red' unions." Stewart, pp. 119–20.

53. The government's effort to raise prices through propaganda was reported with great concern by a colonial jute trading firm, M. David & Co, to Calcutta's jute mills. This report was included in the correspondence of Thomas, Duff & Co. See Thomas, Duff & Co, Calcutta, to Mr. Mason, Thomas Duff & Co, August 22, 1939, DUA, Dundee.

54. Letter from Suhrawardy to P. S. MacDonald, Secy, IJMA, 3rd November, 1939. Enclosed in Thomas, Duff & Co, Calcutta, to Mr. Mason, Thomas Duff & Co, November 7, 1939, DUA, Dundee.

55. BLA, vol. XLV, no. 3, 1939, Calcutta, pp. 314–15.

56. Thomas, Duff & Co, Calcutta, to Thomas Duff & Co, December 26, 1939, DUA, Dundee.

57. Thomas, Duff & Co, Calcutta, to Mr. Mason, Thomas Duff & Co, February 6, 1940, DUA, Dundee.

58. Mr. Burder, Messrs Barry & Co, to Mr. Walker, Chairman, IJMA, June 3, 1940, enclosed in Thomas, Duff & Co, Calcutta, to Thomas Duff & Co, June 11, 1940, DUA, Dundee.

59. BLA, vol. LVII, no. 3, 1940, Calcutta, p. 237.

60. Enclosed in Thomas, Duff & Co, Calcutta, to Thomas Duff & Co., September 16, 1941, MS/86/V/7/10, DUA, Dundee.

61. Thomas, Duff & Co, Calcutta, to Thomas Duff & Co, May 19, 1942, MS/86/V/7/11, DUA, Dundee.

62. BLA, vol. LXII, no. 3, 1942, Calcutta, p. 41.

63. In a letter from Andrew Yule & Co, to G.M. Garrie, Acting Adviser on Jute Supplies to the Government of India, Yule & Co stated that they could make profits at prices ranging from Rs. 14 to Rs. 19 per maund for raw jute, "at current prices they make a loss of Rs. 8 per ton, and current costs of jute are rising." Enclosed in Private Official from Calcutta to Dundee, 22nd June 1943, MS/86/V/7/11, DUA.

64. Private Official from Calcutta to Mr. MacDonald, Dundee, 21st September, 1943, Thomas Duff & Company, Private Official Letters from Calcutta, 4th May 1943 to 24th October 1944, MS/86/V/7/11, DUA.

65. An exasperated Nalikshya Sanyal, the party whip of the opposition Congress, blurted out, "This is just like you!," BLA, vol. LVI, no. 2, 1940, Calcutta, p. 187.

66. BLA, vol. LX, no. 4, 1941, Calcutta, p. 73.

67. BLA, vol. LXV, no. 2, 1943, Calcutta, pp. 45–46.

Chapter 7

1. Ayesha Jalal has argued that the idea of Pakistan was left vague to allow M. A. Jinnah room to negotiate for his true goal: greater power for South Asia's Muslims within a united India. Ayesha Jalal, *The Sole Spokesman: Jinnah, the Muslim League, and the Demand for Pakistan*, Cambridge: Cambridge University Press, 1985. There is considerable scholarship focused on variation in ideas of Pakistan. David Gilmartin argues that ideas of Pakistan in the Punjab were fully fleshed out during the 1946 elections—similar to the argument I am making here with respect to Bengal.

2. Abul Mansur Ahmed, *Amar Dekha Rajnitir Panchash Bochhor*, Dhaka: Srijan, 1989, p. 248.

3. Abul Mansur Ahmed, "Banglay Muslim Rajnitir Potobhumi o Porichoy," *Millat*, 1946.

4. The utopian poetry of Pakistan was printed in Muslim Calcutta's literary magazines, particularly *Mohammadi* and the *Bulbul*, especially between 1944 and 1947. Some of these poems have been reprinted in Sardar Fazlul Karim, ed., *Pakistan Andolon O Muslim Sahitya*, Dhaka: Bangla Akademi, 1968. Neilesh Bose discusses the formation of these Muslim literary spaces and analyzes some of this poetry in "Purba Pakistan Zindabad: Bengali Visions of Pakistan, 1940–1947," *Modern Asian Studies*, 48(1), 2014, pp. 1–36. Ahmed Kamal's characterization of Pakistan as the "land of eternal Eid" draws on a popular poem of the 1940s and a much wider range of sources to demonstrate how Pakistan was characterized in terms of an agrarian Islamic morality. Ahmed Kamal, "A Land of Eternal Eid—Independence, People, and Politics in East Bengal," *Dhaka University Studies*, Part A, 46(1), June 1989. The end of the description is a translation of a poem by Golam Mostafa, titled "Pakistaner Bhatiyali Shongeet," published in the *Mohammadi* in February 1946 and reprinted in Sardar Fazlul Karim, *Pakistan Andolon o Muslim Sahitya*, pp. 162–63. The original lines in Bengali are: "Pakistaner roj bihaney / Ajan dey bulbul / Him-shishirey oju korey / Namaj porey shob phul."

5. "Record of an interview between Jinnah and Mountbatten, 26 April, 1947," in *Transfer of Power*, vol. 10, *The Mountbatten Viceroyalty, formation of a plan, 22 March–30 May 1947*, ed. Nicholas Mansergh, pp. 451–54 (London: Her Majesty's Stationary Office, 1982).

6. For an account of how Pakistan emerged from partition with a disproportionately small share of undivided India's state institutions, paraphernalia, and resources and how this affected postcolonial projects of state formation, see Ayesha Jalal, *The State of Martial Rule: Origins of Pakistan's Political Economy of Defense*, Cambridge: Cambridge University Press, 2008, particularly chap. 2.

7. Ahmed Kamal, *State against the Nation: The Decline of the Muslim League in Pre-Independence Bangladesh, 1947–54*, Dhaka: University Press, 2009.

8. Ataur Rahman Khan, *Shairacharer Dash Bachar*, Dhaka, 1974, quoted in Kamal, *State against the Nation*, p. 27.

9. In a very important article, Bose demonstrates how Bengali Muslim literary and cultural institutions and aspirations informed their ideas of Pakistan. Neilesh Bose, "Purba Pakistan Zindabad: Bengali Visions of Pakistan, 1940–1947," *Modern Asian Studies*, 48(1), January 2014, pp. 1–36.

10. Mujibur Rehman Khan, *Eastern Pakistan: Its Population, Delimitation, and Economics*, Calcutta: East Pakistan Renaissance Society, 1942. His concerns were not with a division on majority and minority provinces but on securing a territory that would provide for a viable and prosperous nation-state. I discuss his pamphlet and other territorial imaginings of Pakistan later in the chapter.

11. A. K. Fazlul Haq had moved the Lahore resolution in 1940. Notably, the resolution did not use the word Pakistan though its anniversary was celebrated as "Pakistan Day." Jinnah would later claim that the word Pakistan had been "fathered" upon them by the Congress and the Hindu nationalist press.

12. Secret Report on the Political Situation in Bengal for the second half of March 1945 the first half of April, 1945, in IOR/L/PJ/5/152, IOR, BL.

13. Confidential Report on the Political Situation in Bengal for the first half of March 1945, in IOR/L/PJ/5/152, IOR, BL.

14. The Dacca nawab family's residence, the Ahsan Manzil, was an unofficial second office in Dacca.

15. The only parts of Bengal he did not visit were Bankura in western Bengal and the offshore islands of Sandwip and Hatiya in the Meghna estuary in Noakhali. Abul Hashim, *In Retrospection*, Dhaka: Subarna, 1974, p. 52.

16. Hashim also visited local offices of the Communist Party and even spent an evening watching folk performance with Comrade Moni Singh, the leader of a sharecropper rebellion in Mymensingh. Hashim, *In Retrospection*, p. 59.

17. Abul Mansur Ahmed provides a firsthand account of the 1946 election campaign in his autobiography, *Amar Dekha Rajnitir Panchash Bochhor*, p. 248.

18. Quoted in Haron-or Rashid, *The Foreshadowing of Bangladesh: Bengali Muslim League and Muslim Politics, 1936–1947*, Dhaka: Asiatic Society of Bangladesh, 1987, p. 206.

19. Ahmed Kamal, *State against the Nation*, pp. 28 and 35.

20. Kazi Abul Hossain, *Jinnah Nama*, Dhaka, 1961, p. 90, quoted in Kamal, *State against the Nation*, p. 29.

21. Abul Hashim persuaded a reluctant Jinnah to sanction *Millat* in November 1945. As election fever heightened, the paper's circulation reached 35,000. Hashim claims that Jinnah argued that the Karachi-based English-language *Dawn* was the sole mouthpiece of the Muslim League. Hashim, *In Retrospection*, p. 99.

22. "Prachyer gola-ghor Bangla—othhocho ekhane na khaiya manush morey," *Millat*, October 2, 1946, p. 3.

23. "Jamidari Pratha'r Bilupti," *Millat*, July 4, 1946, p. 2.

24. Abul Mansur Ahmed, "Banglay Muslim Rajnitir Potobhumi o Porichoy," *Millat*, October 2, 1946.

25. Ahmed, "Banglay Muslim Rajnitir Potobhumi o Porichoy."

26. Ahmed, "Banglay Muslim Rajnitir Potobhumi o Porichoy."

27. Note on Riots in East Bengal, MSS EUR/F158/551, IOR.

28. Fazlul Karim, in keeping with the League's dominance, received 82.7 percent of the vote. Golam Sarwar, who stood as an independent, was his closest rival and received 15.8 percent of the vote. The Krishak Praja candidate, in keeping with the party's dismal performance, received only 88 votes, or 0.003 percent of the total vote.

29. "Matlabajerai Bongo-Bhonger Awaj Tulechhey," *Millat*, May 16, 1947, p. 1.

30. "Pongu Pakistan," *Millat*, June 6, 1947, p. 2.

31. "British porikolpona keno grihito hoilo," *Millat*, June 13, 1947, p. 1.

32. Mujibur Rehman Khan, *Eastern Pakistan: Its Population, Delimitation, and Economics*, p. 8.

33. "Ninth Miscellaneous Meeting," in Mansergh, *Transfer of Power*, vol. 10, pp. 261–64.

34. O.H.K. Spate, "Geographical Aspects of Pakistan Considered," *Geographical Journal*, 102(3), September 1943, p. 129.

35. "Record of an interview between Jinnah and Mountbatten, 26 April, 1947," in Mansergh, *Transfer of Power*, vol. 10, pp. 451–54.

36. Ahmed Kamal, *State against the Nation*, pp. 11–14, provides an account of the celebrations with which the new state was inaugurated.

37. Provash Chandra Lahiry, *India Partitioned and Minorities in Pakistan*, Calcutta: Writers Forum, 1964, p. 1.

38. O.H.K. Spate, "The Partition of India and the Prospects of Pakistan," *Geographical Review*, 38(1), January 1948, p. 29.

39. Fazlur Rahman, *Industrial Development in Pakistan*, Karachi, October 1948, p. 8.

40. Aslam Hayat, *The Golden Fibre*, Karachi: Department of Advertising, Films and Publications, Government of Pakistan, 1950, p. 9.

41. Government of East Bengal, *The First Complete Jute Year (1948–1949), during the Existence of Pakistan as an Independent and Sovereign State*, Issued by the Directorate of Jute Prices, East Bengal, Narayanganj, 1949, p. 7.

42. The value of Pakistan's exports in 1950–51 was $406 million as opposed to $171 million in 1949–50. Ian Talbot, *Pakistan: A Modern History*, London: C. Hurst, 2009, p. 137.

43. *Just a Peep at Pakistan*, New York: Consulate General of Pakistan, 1953, p. 20.

44. "Jute Bargaining Factor with Bharat: Rahman on Steps Taken to Sell More," *Dawn*, August 28, 1952, in MSS Eur F158/580A, IOR, BL.

45. "Aide-Memoire," from High Commissioner of Pakistan in India to Finance Minister, GoI, October 13, 1947, in Ministry of External Affairs, OSV Branch, File No. 9–5/47-OSV, NAI.

46. "Aide-Memoire," from Secy, Ministry of Finance, GoI, to High Commissioner of Pakistan in India, October 20, 1947, in Ministry of External Affairs, OSV Branch, File No. 9–5/47-OSV, NAI.

47. "Aide-Memoire," from Secy, Ministry of Finance, GoI, to High Commissioner of Pakistan in India, October 20, 1947, in Ministry of External Affairs, OSV Branch, File No. 9–5/47-OSV, NAI.

48. "Report on Trade," Ministry of Commerce and Industry, Jute Branch, 28-Pak(15)/52, NAI.

49. Summary of meeting between Ghulam Ahmed, Finance Minister Pakistan and Commerce Minister, India, April 8, 1949, in Cabinet Secretariat [Economic Wing]/Economic Committee of the Cabinet, 15, 27, ECC(49), NAI.

50. Walton, Calcutta to Kidd, Dundee, April 4, 1952, in Correspondence of Directors while visiting mills in India, 6 July 1946 to 4 August 1952, MS 86/V/7/35, DUA.

51. Fittingly, the Adamjee Jute Mills was also the center of labor unrest in the newly industrialized region. The Adamjee mill riots of 1954—which took the form of clashes between Bengali and Bihari laborers in the factory—resulted in about three hundred deaths. Richard Park and Richard Wheeler, "East Bengal under Governor's Rule," *Far Eastern Survey*, 23(9), September 1954, pp. 129–34, provides a sketchy and pro-government account of the riots.

52. "Estimates of Abolition of Control," in Cabinet Secretariat [Economic Wing] /Economic Committee of the Cabinet, File No. 6/1/ECC/50, NAI.

53. "Note for the Economic Committee of the Cabinet—Indo Pakistan Trade Agreement," July 23, 1952, in Ministry of Com & Ind, Jute Branch, 28-Pak (15)/52.

54. "Editorial: Jute Prices," *Dawn*, July 6, 1949, in MSS Eur F158/580A, BL.

55. "Meeting of the Economic Committee of the Cabinet," November 6, 1949, in Cabinet Secretariat [Economic Wing]/ Economic Committee of Cabinet, 6(II) ECC/50, NAI.

56. "Meeting of the Economic Committee of the Cabinet," November 6, 1949, in Cabinet Secretariat [Economic Wing]/ Economic Committee of Cabinet, 6(II) ECC/50, NAI.

57. The Pakistan Jute Association, Annual Report for the Year 1953–54, Narayanganj, 1954, p. 10.

58. The Pakistan Jute Association, Annual Report for the Year 1956–57, Narayanganj, 1957, p. 7.

59. The Pakistan Jute Association, Annual Report for the Year 1953–54, Narayanganj, 1954, p. 13.

60. The Pakistan Jute Association, Annual Report for the Year, 1954–55, Narayanganj, 1955, p. 55.

61. "Note by Mr. H. A. Luke, Chairman, Calcutta Jute Brokers & Dealers Association," in Ministry of Commerce and Industry, Jute (Pakistan) Section, File No. 28-Jute/55Pak, NAI.

62. "Note by Mr. H. A. Luke, Chairman, Calcutta Jute Brokers & Dealers Association," in Ministry of Commerce and Industry, Jute (Pakistan) Section, File No. 28-Jute/55Pak, NAI.

63. EBLA, vol. III, no. 4, 1949, Dacca, 1950, p. 219.

64. "The Economic Situation in Pakistan: Anxiety over Jute and Cotton," February 15, 1950, in MSS Eur F158/580A, BL.

65. P. Das Gupta, Asst Indian Govt, Trade Commissioner in Eastern Pak, Dacca to C.C. Desai, Secy, GoI, Commerce Ministry, December 14, 1949, Cabinet Secretariat [Economic Wing]/ECC, 15(108)-P/49, NAI.

66. P. Das Gupta, Asst Indian Govt, Trade Commissioner in Eastern Pak, Dacca to C. C. Desai, Secy, GoI, Commerce Ministry, December 14, 1949, Cabinet Secretariat [Economic Wing]/ECC, 15(108)-P/49, NAI.

67. "Twelfth Meeting of the Committee Appointed to Review Indo-Eastern Pakistan Trade," December 8, 1949, in Cabinet Secretariat [Economic Wing]/ECC, 15(108)-P/49, NAI.

68. "Sixth Meeting of the Committee Appointed to Review Indo-Eastern Pakistan Trade," October 27, 1949, in Cabinet Secretariat [Economic Wing]/ECC, 15(108)-P/49, NAI.

69. "Tenth Meeting of the Committee Appointed to Review Indo-Eastern Pakistan Trade," November 24, 1949, in Cabinet Secretariat [Economic Wing]/ECC, 15(108)-P/49, NAI.

70. "Eighth Meeting of the Committee Appointed to Review Indo-Eastern Pakistan Trade," November 10, 1949, in Cabinet Secretariat [Economic Wing]/ECC, 15(108)-P/49, NAI.

71. P. Das Gupta, Asst Indian Gov Trade Comm in Eastern Pak, Dacca to C. C. Desai, Secy, GoI, Commerce Ministry, 14 December, 1949, in Cabinet Secretariat [Economic Wing]/ECC, 15(108)-P/49, NAI.

72. "Thirteenth Meeting of the Committee Appointed to Review Indo-Eastern Pakistan Trade," December 15, 1949, in Cabinet Secretariat [Economic Wing]/ECC, 15(108)-P/49, NAI.

73. "Fifth Meeting of the Committee Appointed to Review Indo-Eastern Pakistan Trade," October 20, 1949, in Cabinet Secretariat [Economic Wing]/ECC, 15(108)-P/49, NAI. See also "Measures to move raw jute from Tipperah State," in Com & Ind/Jute/12(24)-FTE/49, September 1950, NAI.

74. For instance, the East Bengal provincial government's expenditures during the 1950–51 fiscal year were "characterized by a policy of economy while making general administration and police, *especially the border police force*, effective and efficient." "East Bengal Budget for 1950–1," *Weekly Pakistan News*, Office of the High Commissioner for Pakistan, London, 18th March 1950.

75. Ministry of External Affairs, BL Branch, File No. R/52/19319/202, NAI.

76. From S. N. Chatterjee, Dept Secy, Govt of West Bengal to Depy Secy, Home (Political) Dept, Govt of East Bengal, 27th August, 1950, in Min of Com & Ind, Tariff (B) Branch, GoI, File No. 52(16)TB/53, NAI.

77. EBLA, vol. X, no. 1, 1952, Dacca, 1953, p. 225.

78. EBLA, vol. IX, no. 1, 1952, Dacca, 1954, p. 45.

79. "Jute Bargaining Factor with Bharat: Rahman on Steps Taken to Sell More," *Dawn*, August 28, 1952, in MSS Eur F158/580A, BL.

80. IPBA, "Confidential Report on Pakistan, August, 1952," in MSS Eur F158/580A, BL.

81. Ataur Rahman Khan, EPLA, vol. XVIII, no. 2, 17–19 March, 1958, p. 51.

82. Monoranjan Dhar, EPLA, vol. XVIII, no. 1, 13–15 March, 1958, p. 20.

83. Memorandum—Finance Department, in Jute Regulation Dept, Bundle 1, NAB.

84. "Excerpt from the Minutes of Proceedings of the Meeting of the Council of Ministers, 15th January 1948," in Jute Regulation Department, Bundle 1, NAB.

85. "The Dacca Gazette, East Bengal Jute Regulation Amendment Ordinance, 1948," in Jute Regulation Department, Bundle 1, NAB.

86. EBLA, vol. IV, no. 5, 1949, Dacca, 1949, p. 48.

87. EBLA, vol. IV, no. 5, 1949, Dacca, 1949, p. 48.

88. S. Abdullah, Director of Agriculture, to Joint Secy, Dept of Agri & Co-op, GoEB, January 20, 1949, in Jute Regulation Department, Bundle 1, NAB.

89. "Collection of Jute License Fees—Telegram from Chairman Goalmari Jute Committee, September 1949, Jute Regulation Dept, Bundle 1, NAB.

90. S. Hedayatullah, Director of Agriculture, to Joint Secy, Dept of Agri & Co-op, GoEB, April 9, 1949, in Jute Regulation Dept, Bundle 1, NAB.

91. "Joruri Ghoshona," Jute Regulation Dept, Bundle 1, NAB.

92. Note by Malik, August 20, 1949, Jute Regulation Dept, Bundle 1, NAB.

93. M. A. Majid, Joint Secretary, Agriculture Department, to Director, Agriculture, Jute Regulation Dept, August 2, 1949, Bundle 1, NAB.

94. S. Hedayatullah, Director of Agriculture, to Secy, Dept of Agri, Coop, Relief, August 11, 1948, Jute Regulation Dept, Bundle 1, NAB.

95. Director of Agriculture to Secy, Agri, Coop, Relief Dept, GoEB, September 17, 1949, Jute Regulation Dept, Bundle 1, NAB.

96. Kamal's argument is an important corrective to the dominant narrative of Bangladeshi nationalism, demonstrating that the movement was not solely urban and middle-class but had subaltern roots, particularly in the widespread political and economic discontent among East Bengal's peasantry.

97. The ruling Muslim League was routed in the 1954 election, another sign of the powerful anti-incumbency forces in elections in the jute tracts. The United Front, a coalition of opposition parties, won 228 out of 304 seats, while the League managed only seven. The League's electoral devastation of 1954 mirrored the KPP's electoral defeat of 1946.

Conclusion

1. Whereas the delta used to produce about 80 percent of the world's jute, it now produces about 30 percent. The Indian states of West Bengal, Bihar, Orissa, and Assam produce more jute than the Bengal delta.

2. In the four years between 2010–11 and 2013–14, jute acreage was 8.9 percent of the net cropped area and 4.7 percent of the gross cropped area. Net cropped area is the total farmland in the delta, while gross cropped area double and triple counts land that is sown with multiple crops in a year. During the 1900s, jute occupied 17 percent of the delta's farmlands.

3. The introduction of groundwater irrigation, high-yielding rice varieties, and chemical fertilizers and insecticides has increased rice production substantially. Winter rice, or boro, which was an insignificant rice crop in 1900, now accounts for 42 percent of the land sown with rice and 32 percent of the gross cropped area. The three varieties of rice—aus, aman, and boro—account for 77 percent of the delta's cropland, compared to under 60 percent during the 1900s.

4. The acreage of rabi crops like oilseeds, potatoes, maize, pulses, spices, and vegetables is today three times the acreage of jute, while during the 1900s, the acreage of rabi crops was only marginally greater than that of fiber (about 20 percent of the total cropland was rabi versus 17 percent jute).

5. Agriculture today constitutes about 20 percent of the delta's GDP, down from around 80 percent during the colonial and Pakistan periods. However, while agriculture's share of GDP has declined, it remains an important source of livelihood for much of the delta's population—though a far smaller proportion than previously. According to the 2010 census, about half of the official labor force is engaged in agriculture, forestry, and fisheries—that is, a total of 25.7 million people. The garments sector, on the other hand, employs 4 million people. Between 2005 and 2010, about 3 million Bangladeshis migrated abroad to work, primarily in the Middle East and Gulf states.

6. There are many examples of such headlines, but I will cite the following three as instances: "Revival of Golden Fibre," *New Age*, March 11, 2012; "Lost Glory of Jute Needs to Be Revived," *New Age*, February 29, 2012; "Jute Will Regain Its Lost Glory," *Daily Star*, March 15, 2011.

7. Anu Muhammad, "Closure of Adamjee Jute Mills: Ominous Sign," *Economic and Political Weekly*, 37(38), September 21–27, 2002, p. 3896.

8. "Padma Bridge with Own Funds," *Daily Star*, July 9, 2012.

INDEX

Abdullah, S., 190

Abedin, Zainul, 165

Abercrombie, A., 82

Adamjee family, 181

Adamjee Jute Mills, 181; closure of (2002), 196; and the mill riots of 1954, 229n51

Adarsha Krishak (Ideal Peasant) (Hai), 121, 124, 133; dedication of the second edition of, 121; financing of the first edition of, 121; financing of the second edition of, 121; Shah Abdul Hamid on the Bengal peasant's buker dhon (heart-wealth), 125; twenty-one-point program for mukti (freedom) in, 126; vignettes of "ideal peasant life" in, 125–26, 130

Adas, Michael, 6

agrarian leagues, 43, 44

Agricultural Department, 68, 92; founding of (1885), 68; jute agricultural program of, 84–85; jute forecasts of, 82, 83–84; primary purposes of, 82; rice forecasts of, 83

Ahmed, Abul Mansur, 111, 113, 116, 117, 147, 169, 174, 223n20, 227n17; on Pakistan as a space of "cultural autonomy" (tamadduni azadi), 171

Ahmed, Ashrafuddin, *Muslim Bani* (Muslim Declaration), 121, 127, 129–30

Ahmed, Asimuddin, 147

Ahmed, Emaduddin, 101

Ahmed, Kasiruddin, 147

Ahmed, Nazimuddin, 158

Ahmed, Sheikh Bashiruddin, 122

Ahmed, Wasimuddin, 150–51, 153, 223n29

Akhaura, 68, 73, 78; as the railway junction town of Tipperah district, 73; as a union, 213n38

Ali, Akram, *Keno Lok Gorib Hoy* (Why People Become Poor), 127

Ali, M. W., 201n4, 204n1

Ali, Mir Ahmed, 184–85

Ali, Mohammad, 111

Ali, Mohammed Khayer, *Bonya Kahini* (Events of a Flood), 101

Ali, Munshi Keramat, 121

Ali, Nausher, 147

Ali, Shawkat, 111

Ali, Tofazzal, 189

Allen, B. C., 48, 49, 52, 209n35

All-India Kisan Sabha, 172

American Trade Consul in India, 214n53

Amin, Shahid, 219n5

Andrew Yule & Co, 225n63

antirent movement, 42, 43–44, 208n20

Austin, Gareth, 203n18

Aziz, Abdul, *Dunia o Akherat Dojahaner Najat* (Salvation in This World and the Next), 123–24, 124, 127, 128, 133

babugiri, 129–30, 144; and litigiousness, 130

Bamford, P. C., 110, 219n5

Bangladesh, 194; abandonment of nationalization as its economic model, 196; crony capitalism in, 196; the garment industry in, 196–97, 198; neoliberalism in, 196. *See also* jute, in Bangladesh

Islam, Nurul, 134
Islam, rise of in the Bengal delta, 15; and
    Mughal incentives for land clearance,
    15; and Sufi saints from Arabia, 15; and
    syncretic Islamic practices, 15
Islam, Sirajul, 204n30
Ismail, Muhammad, 147
Ispahani family, 181, 187

Jack, J. C., 9, 25, 31, 40, 50, 52, 54–55, 209n34,
    209n55
jagirdaris, 14, 18, 119
Jalal, Ayesha, 226n1, 226n6
Jamalpur, 40, 59, 61–62, 63, 66, 67, 90–91,
    149, 150
Java, and the "Culture System," 6
Jinnah, M. A., 163, 170, 177, 226n1, 227n21
jotedars, 140
Just a Peek at Pakistan, 178
jute: cultivation of in India, 181; decline of
    the importance of in the twenty-first
    century, 194, 231nn1–2; the reference to
    having to eat jute as a popular trope in
    folk literature, 206n33. *See also* jute, in
    Bangladesh; jute, in the Bengal delta from
    the mid-nineteenth to the mid-twentieth
    century; jute, in East Pakistan
jute, in Bangladesh: closure of the Adamjee
    Jute Mills, 196; jute cultivation, 195–196,
    201n2; jute nostalgia, 194–98, 231n6
jute, in the Bengal delta from the mid-
    nineteenth to the mid-twentieth century,
    9, 17, 21–36 *passim*, 195; acreage devoted
    to, 2, 17, 21, 23 (table); beneficiaries of high
    prices of, 98; Calcutta's export of jute, 2;
    collapse of the jute market, 32–36; compe-
    tition of jute cultivation with rice cultiva-
    tion, 17, 24, 29–32; and double-cropping,
    30; effect of the depression decade (1930s)
    on, 102; effect of railway embankments
    and the invasive water hyacinth on, 98–99,
    103; effect of World War I on, 34, 64; effect
    of World War II on, 88, 159–66; emergence
    of jute as a global commodity, 1; European

jute-baling firms in Bengal, 74; expansion
    of jute cultivation during the late nineteen-
    th century, 16; failure of attempts to trans-
    fer jute cultivation to other parts of the
    world, 24; harvesting and retting of jute
    fibers, 27; jute cultivation in neighboring
    regions of the Bengal delta, 201n2; jute
    fabrics as the premier packaging material
    in world trade, 1; jute manufacturing
    industries, 1, 201n3; jute mills, 1; the KPP's
    failure to assert control over jute prices, 19,
    159–66, 166–67; and kutcha baling presses,
    68, 74; and labor intensification, 36; lack
    of colonial oversight over jute cultivation,
    21–22; Marwari jute-baling firms, 74;
    monopoly of in global packaging, 1; and
    peasant choice to cultivate jute, 22, 36; and
    peasant indebtedness, 30; the practice of
    watering jute to increase its weight, 92;
    replacement of jute with rice in the early
    1920s, 113; and risks, 36; and the soil of
    the Bengal delta, 24; tassa jute (*Corchorus
    olitorius*), 26; tending of jute crops, 26–28;
    three booms in jute cultivation, 22–24;
    transportation of jute to Calcutta, 70–72,
    71 (table); the unreliability of colonial
    statistics on, 201n4; white jute (*Corchorus
    capsularis*), 26
jute, in East Pakistan, 17, 170–71; jute smug-
    gling, 19–20, 185–88; jute taxation, 189–91;
    state regulation of the jute industry (*see
    also* Jute Dealers Registration Act [1949]),
    170–71, 176–85, 197
Jute Dealers Registration Act (1949), 182–83,
    184
Jute Song (G. Das), 31, 52
*Jute-Growing Districts and Markets of India,
    The* (Burnett), 76

Kabir, Humayun, 160, 225n48
Kailbartas, 203n25
Kalamal Haq ba Hok Katha (True Words)
    (A. Hossain), 124, 130–31, 133; condemna-
    tion against poultry and eggs in, 133

HISTORIES OF ECONOMIC LIFE

Jeremy Adelman, Sunil Amrith, and Emma Rothschild, Series Editors

A NOTE ON THE TYPE

This book has been composed in Arno, an Old-style serif typeface in the
classic Venetian tradition, designed by Robert Slimbach at Adobe.